GW00392204

Studies in Comparative Politics

POLITICAL OPPOSITION
IN ONE-PARTY STATES

STUDIES IN COMPARATIVE POLITICS
published in association with
the Journal of Comparative Politics
GOVERNMENT AND OPPOSITION

A quarterly journal of comparative politics, published by Government and Opposition, London School of Economics and Political Science, Houghton Street, London, WC2A 2AE

POLITICAL OPPOSITION IN ONE-PARTY STATES

edited by

LEONARD SCHAPIRO

Professor of Political Science with special reference to Russian Studies
London School of Economics and Political Science

Assistant Editor
ELLEN DE KADT

MACMILLAN

First published 1972 by
THE MACMILLAN PRESS LTD
London and Basingstoke
Associated companies in New York Toronto
Dublin Melbourne Johannesburg and Madras

SBN 333 13174 6

Printed in Great Britain by
WESTERN PRINTING SERVICES LTD
Bristol

Contents

Leonard Schapiro

Introduction

THE PAGES WHICH FOLLOW CONSTITUTE AN ANTHOLOGY
of articles and review articles concerned with Russia and the
other Communist countries of Europe which have appeared in
Government and Opposition since its inception in October 1965.
It is the common fate of editors of anthologies to be blamed for
omission or for inclusion, and usually for both. But I am in a
somewhat more fortunate position, since, with the exception of
two categories of articles, this anthology contains everything
that was published in the journal on the countries concerned.
The first group of omissions consists of several articles on
historical themes. I omitted them with great regret. But considerations of space made it impossible to include everything;
and it seemed more logical and harmonious to make the anthology as representative as possible of the study of the
contemporary scene which has taken place in the pages of the
journal. The second group of important articles was omitted
for reasons which are beyond my control: they either have
been or are due to be published in book form elsewhere, or to
become, with revisions, part of a forthcoming book, and were
therefore not available to me for inclusion.

In so far as there is a central theme running through the
articles collected together in this volume, it is the theme of the
strains, the divisions, the tensions, the various forms of 'opposition' to established rule and doctrine which are always and
have always been discernible in the states of the communist
world quaintly called 'monolithic'. That this 'opposition' is as
important an object of study in the communist as it is in other
societies was one of the assumptions on which the journal
based its claim to contribute a new element to the comparative
study of politics. Events in the communist world since 1965
have certainly not made this particular assumption any less

valid. Six years is not, it is true, a very long period to provide
a basis for generalisations. But the scholarly (as distinct from
the merely enthusiastic) study of communist governments goes
back at least some twenty-five years. We know enough about
them at any rate not to be taken in by the nonsense which
their apologists put about, and probably a good deal more. It
therefore seems an appropriate occasion to try to look at the
whole question of government and opposition in communist
regimes in perspective.

The first question is one of terminology. The word 'opposition', in its English usage, is, so far as politics are concerned,
of 18th-century origin, with a peculiarly English connota-
tion. It belongs to the period when, in the aftermath of the
Revolution and of the doctrine of Locke, the idea took root
that the 'party' of opposition stood 'opposed' to the administration of the day, the 'party' of government, ready and anxious
to take its place. In this manner changes in administration
could occur peaceably without the whole fabric of society being
convulsed in a revolution. As Professor Dahl has shown in his
study of political opposition in the leading liberal democracies,[1]
the notion of two parties competing for office is virtually confined to England; and the whole idea of peaceable competition
for government power recent, and, in the long history of
politics, exceptional. Nevertheless, as the studies edited by
Dahl show, the idea has been successfully adapted in a number
of democracies with very different party systems from that of
England. Now plainly in this sense 'opposition' as a political
term is ill-adapted to communist regimes in which rival
political parties are not tolerated, where the fiction of unanimity is maintained if need be by force, and where changes
of administration are normally the result of, or accompanied
by, dramatic power struggles among the top leaders. The
misuse of the term in communist language dates from Lenin,
in 1920–1, when he chose it to designate critics of his policy
whom he intended to silence. Yet these critics in no sense
formed an 'opposition' who wished to replace his administration by one of their own. All they claimed was the right
freely to criticise what they believed to be the faults of his
administration; and the right to advocate changes of policy

[1] Robert A. Dahl (editor), *Political Oppositions in Western Democracies*, New Haven
and London, 1966.

which they believed to be desirable. Their action should more properly be described as 'dissent' – a term which implies a claim to criticise and disagree with the policy of the government, but without any intention or plan of replacing that government by one composed of its critics.

Lenin's use of the term 'opposition' was no doubt intended to smear, and certainly had the effect of smearing, his critics with a taint of disloyalty, even treason, and it has retained this pejorative meaning in communist usage ever since. Lenin's action in virtually stifling 'opposition', in other words all overt criticism, was in part dictated by fear – the fear of a small, embattled minority, clinging to power without the support of anything like the majority of the population. But it also reflected his conviction that there could only be one theoretically correct course of action at any moment, and he claimed the right to know best what that correct theory was. These two reasons – fear, and the intellectual hubris of the leader in power – have remained sufficiently relevant both in the Soviet Union and in the other communist countries to ensure the perpetuation of Lenin's pattern of rule for fifty years. In the study of the divisions, strains and contests inside present-day communist regimes, the use of the term 'opposition' as a generic description (though convenient) tends to be misleading. It retains a useful meaning only when it is contrasted with 'dissent', thus drawing a distinction between those who wish to replace a communist regime by some other regime; and those who merely wish to assert the right freely to criticise the existing regime, to recall it to its duty, and to advocate alternative policies for it to pursue. However, as the essay by Gordon Skilling reprinted later shows, this single dichotomy is inadequate to deal with all the varieties of dissenting political activity which goes on inside communist societies. Yet in the light of further evidence which has accumulated since he wrote, his (fourfold) division also seems in some respects inadequate, and a somewhat different one will therefore be attempted in the paragraphs which follow.

It would seem that disagreement with or pressure on the existing administration in a communist country can take one of the following five forms – always subject to the overall proviso that the boundaries between the different categories are not necessarily permanent or clearly distinct, in the sense that one form of such political activity can easily pass into another, or in the sense that several forms of the activities described can be pursued at the same time by the same individual or group of individuals. The first form to be found is that of all-out rejection of the whole communist system of rule, coupled with a desire to set up some alternative form of rule, whether clearly defined or not. This form of political activity, which necessarily has to be secret and conspiratorial, and pursued at great risk, is the counterpart of that of the 19th- and 20th-century Russian revolutionaries who rejected all hope of compromise with, or improvement of, the imperial regime, and devoted themselves to its overthrow. It seems best to retain the same term, 'revolution', for the modern counterpart, where it exists. (Skilling's term 'integral opposition' lacks clarity: 'counter-revolution' is an emotionally and ideologically loaded term.) But revolutionary activity is very rare in communist societies – no doubt by reason of the excellence of the security forces which all such states regard as their very first priority. The 'counter-revolutionary' plots publicised under Stalin were for the most part invented in order to justify the elimination of those who were, or were suspected of being, critical of Stalin's rule. The Hungarian revolution of 1956 was a revolt against Soviet domination and Soviet nominees as much as a revolt against communism as such, and the same is largely true of the developments in Czechoslovakia in 1967 and 1968. In each case Soviet repression was portrayed by the Soviet leaders as defence of proletarian or socialist internationalism against counter-revolution: but rhetoric must not be allowed to disguise the fact that each of these events was at least as much a national revolt as a revolution. Naturally, all communists, Soviet or Soviet-sponsored, have a strong interest to subdue any form of revolt against their own rule. It is also notable (as the experience in Poland and elsewhere has shown) that communist regimes are much more tolerant of popular revolts motivated by dissatisfaction with material conditions than they are of any kind of politically motivated revolt.

The second form of political activity which falls into the general category now being considered is that commonly known as the 'power-struggle'. This takes the form of one leader, either at the highest national level or at the highest local or regional level, successfully ousting another. These operations, which are very frequent in communist regimes, take place in conditions of intrigue and secrecy, but their frequency has made it possible for a general pattern to be discovered from the overt signs by which they are accompanied. Thus, a power struggle will almost invariably be associated with some fundamental question of ideology or policy – even if it has been true in some cases that the issue of policy has been used artificially as an excuse or a device. This becomes apparent subsequently when the new leader virtually adopts the policy of the displaced leader. (This political device is not, incidentally, peculiar to communists.) The second main feature of the power struggle is the way in which the displacement of one leader by another is succeeded, and usually also preceded, by extensive changes of key personnel which enables the new leader to provide himself with a following of adherents who are likely to support him in power. Indeed, the close study of changes in appointments has proved in practice the only reliable indicator (in the case of the Soviet Union, at any rate) of an impending change at the top. The power struggle is the most important phenomenon in a communist regime, because it is by means of it that political change is accomplished. Since its aim is to replace one adminis- tration by another, and since latterly the change has often been accomplished relatively bloodlessly, it is the closest approxi- mation in communist conditions to 'opposition' in the liberal democratic sense. On the other hand it is usually completely undemocratic in the sense that it results from an intrigue in a closed circle and not from any kind of democratic pressure in the party as a whole – usually, but not invariably, as the re- placement of Novotný by Dubček in Czechoslovakia in 1968 showed. This closed nature of the power struggle is due to two factors. First the political apathy usually prevalent in a com- munist party, whose members are conditioned to act only in response to a signal from above. And secondly by reason of the absence of any independently functioning institutions below the level of the Politburo, or its equivalent.

The third category is that of dissent in the true sense, more exactly, in Russian conditions, a-political dissent. This form of dissent has become particularly evident in recent years in the Soviet Union, and has shown a remarkable capactiy to survive – in spite of severe police repressions, which include the confinement of some dissidents in lunatic asylums by means of

co-operation between the KGB and subservient psychiatrists.[2]
This form of dissent is a-political in the sense that its exponents
do not for the most part (there are exceptions) advocate either
the overthrow of the regime or the replacement of the existing
administration by another. They assert the right, which they
claim derives from Soviet law, to criticise freely illegal government acts and policies with which they disagree on moral
grounds, and to demand the observance of the guarantees of
civil rights which are embodied in the codes of law and in the
Constitution. The significance of this body of a-political dissenters is difficult to assess. On the one hand they have been
able with relative success to disseminate their protests outside
the Soviet Union and have thereby probably forced the Soviet
authorities to exercise greater circumspection in their customary
abuse of legal process. In the past few years for the first time in
many years, dozens, even hundreds, of voices have been raised
in protest against the arbitrary abuse of law, procedure and
civil rights by the Soviet authorities; against policies like the
invasion of Czechoslovakia, or the oppression of national
minorities; and against interference with freedom of speech
and writing which are ostensibly guaranteed by the Constitution. Judges, police and psychiatrists join in solidarity to
ignore, twist or abuse legal procedure in order to secure conviction or confinement in lunatic asylums in cases where even
Soviet law does not permit such action. Nevertheless, the number of those who courageously protest does not diminish;
authentic and full reports of the actions of the authorities are
regularly circulated inside the USSR, and published outside.
It is probably true to say that all this activity is, slowly, beginning to have some effect on the behaviour of the Soviet authorities, who are not entirely indifferent to the image which they
present abroad. The influence of these dissenters has been
enormously strengthened by the adherence of prominent
scientists of international reputation whose services the Soviet
government cannot easily dispense with; and of international
figures like Solzhenitsyn whom it could be embarrassing to
put on trial or certify. On the other hand, the total number of

---

[2] For detailed discussion of one case see the recently published *A Question of
Madness* by Zhores and Roy Medvedev, Macmillan, 1971. For a collection of all
the available evidence on other cases (believed to total around two hundred) see
Kaznimiye sumasshestviyem, Possev, Munich, 1971.

dissenters is small; and it is unlikely that their cause evokes much sympathy in the party or the army, to say nothing of the working class. Nevertheless, to ignore dissent in present-day Soviet politics is to misjudge the whole political scene, if for no other reason than that of the effect which it appears to be having in inhibiting to some degree the arbitrariness of the Soviet authorities who seem unable, or unwilling, to repress it in the way that Stalin did. Certainly, the parallel between Czechoslovakia and the Soviet Union should not be stressed too much: the Soviet government is not an alien import, and there is little if any social-democratic tradition left alive in the USSR. Nevertheless, the role played by dissent in Czechoslovakia in the period of the 'Spring' could conceivably be a pointer to a future trend in the Soviet Union.

The fourth category of political activity to be examined is something which by analogy (even if inaccurate analogy) with liberal democratic politics is called 'interest group' or 'pressure group' activity. This interest group aspect of communist politics has been closely studied in recent years both as regards the non-Soviet European communist states[3] and in the Soviet Union.[4] It is necessary in this context to draw some distinction between an interest and a pressure group. An interest group seeks to exercise pressure on the government in order to promote its own interest. A pressure group on the other hand seeks to promote some policy or aim of a more general nature. (This distinction is only one of many canvassed in the literature of politics, but it must serve for present purposes.) Now, however it may be described, it is plain that all such pressure activity must necessarily be of a very different nature in communist regimes and in liberal democratic states. There are at least five conditions which, in a liberal democratic state, are essential to the effective functioning of a pressure or interest group: all of them (with the qualification noted below) are virtually absent or very much restricted in the communist regimes. These five conditions are: free and unrestricted combination into a group, including the freedom to operate without interference from any government or party authority; a vigorous public opinion on which pressure can be exerted in

[3] G. Ionescu, *The Politics of the European Communist States*, London, 1967.
[4] H. Gordon Skilling and Franklyn Griffiths (editors), *Interest Groups in Soviet Politics*, Princeton University Press, 1970.

order to influence the government; a high standard of professional ethics among lawyers, doctors, academics and other leaders of public opinion, and sufficient independence to resist party and government pressure; some economic independence; and sufficient cohesion to act as an independent group when required.

Nevertheless, when all the necessary qualifications have been made, it is plain that for many years past (even during the period of Stalin's rule) in one form or another this kind of group activity has persisted in the communist regimes. The various components of what Professor Ionescu has called the 'apparat state' – the party, the police, the army, the government bureaucracy – have striven and competed for greater influence on the policy-making elite, and have promoted each its own interest and autonomy. The 'collective leadership', for one thing, which still precariously prevails in the Soviet Politburo, bears witness to the effectiveness of this struggle. The offices of General Secretary of the CPSU and Chairman of the Council of Ministers are still divided and separate, and, in spite of serious encroachments by the party, the government machine still manages to maintain an area of independent action. Another Soviet example is the increased degree of influence which the armed forces have succeeded in winning, albeit in areas of direct concern to themselves rather than in the sphere of general policy. Lawyers, economists, scientists and writers have all left an important mark on the development of Soviet politics, though they have, it is true, done so more as individuals than as groups. These examples could be multiplied well beyond the space available. The important deduction is that no study of communist politics which ignored this process of pressure going on inside the monolithic cooker could conceivably do justice to the subject.

While it is true that the five conditions listed above as essential for the effective operation of political pressure groups are generally absent in the communist regimes, there are two groups in the Soviet Union whose character approximates very closely to them, which may therefore be the harbingers of future changes to come. The first such group is that of the a-political dissenters described above – the 'democrats' as they generally describe themselves. Although not homogeneous (they fall into several ideological divisions) they have certain common characteristics which apply to all or the great majority of them. By reason of the persecution to which they are sub-jected they have become a 'group', in the strict sense of the term, totally independent in their activity from government influence (however much they may be harried). Their courage in disseminating their writings in a manner which ensures their publication outside the Soviet Union has enabled them to exert pressure on public opinion abroad, and, to some extent, since their writings are re-broadcast to the Soviet Union, on opinion at home. They have developed a high ethical standard which is fully resistant to government and party pressure and blandishments – they have the solidarity and cohesion of out-laws. In this respect they are in marked contrast to the officially recognised academic unions or the unions of writers and the like which the party is always able to divide and rule; and where the authorities are never short of means to mobilise the conformist compromising and compromised majority to harry the courageous minority of men of integrity. Paradoxically, the 'democrats' enjoy economic independence: frequently deprived by the government of the means of earning in their normal pro-fession and occupation, they have to eke out a living as best they can, with the result that the more fortunate help the less fortunate. They are a group in every sense of the term; and they act as a group, as a pressure group in the true sense. The second real Soviet group, an interest group in this case, is that of the Soviet Zionist Jews. They have the great advantage over the 'democrats' that they enjoy the much more vigorous sup-port of public opinion, both in Israel, to which they seek to emigrate, and in Jewish communities in Western Europe and the USA – the Crimean Tatars, the Volga Germans or the Baptists, for example, have nothing comparable to lean on in their struggle against the Soviet authorities. In the result Soviet Jews have achieved, at the cost of considerable per-secution, remarkable success (having regard to the extreme reluctance which the Soviet authorities have always shown to permit any citizens to emigrate) in their aim of emigrating.

The last category of what is generically described as 'oppo-sition' in communist states is the least spectacular, and probably the most effective. This can best be described as pragmatic dissent and means the pressure and resistance which is con-stantly exercised by the scientists, technicians and experts of

all kinds in the interest of the greater efficiency which they seek
in the pursuit of their skills, free from party interference and
from doctrinal inhibitions. This quiet revolution of the technological age should not, perhaps, be underestimated. It has
already won Soviet scientists a degree of freedom from party
control which was inconceivable under Stalin – with momentous consequences for Soviet science. In Hungary the economists seem to have achieved a degree of freedom from
dogmatic control which is the envy, and aim, of the Soviet
planners and economists. Pragmatic dissent has the great
advantage that it usually raises no immediate ideological
hackles. It has nothing to say on freedom, legality, civil rights
or other such notions which are anathema to communists –
except when expressed by themselves in the terms of their own
doublespeak. Pragmatic dissent is dissent in the name of
efficiency, material progress and military might. It demands
rationality, not freedom or legality. But rationality by its
nature entails some of the very same conditions which are the
result of freedom and legal order. And so it can come about
that pragmatic dissent, if it is successful, can lead indirectly to
greater legality, less arbitrariness, more predictability, more
freedom of expression, more free exchange of ideas. It is
jealously watched and contained by the communist parties,
fearful of the erosion of their power: the demise of the so-called
'Lieberman' economic reforms in the Soviet Union is eloquent
proof of the fact that the struggle is not easy. It is, however,
arguable that 'history is on the side' of pragmatic dissent; and
that in the end, even in the Soviet Union, it may succeed in
effecting momentous changes.

Such then in outline is the general character of 'opposition'
to communist government as it is to be found today. The
present anthology contains both more detailed studies of some
of the matters discussed, and studies of other matters which
have not been touched on in this Introduction – to say nothing
of a variety of opinions and judgements which differ considerably from those which have been put forward by me. But,
it may be asked, what is the value of studying 'opposition' in
communist regimes when it is at most inchoate, spasmodic and
only rarely effective? The answer is that the student of politics
must study a situation as it is in order to be able to discern the

direction in which it is most likely to move. In many respects the government of the Soviet Union has remained almost static in its essential features – almost as unresponsive so far as its political system is concerned to the social and economic changes which have been taking place in the country as was the Imperial government between 1861 and 1905 – when events proved it was already too late to change. The future of the other communist countries of Europe also depends in large measure on what happens in the USSR: the case of Czecho-slovakia has demonstrated that there are limits to which a communist regime of the Soviet bloc will be permitted to change, but that is not to say that no change at all will be tolerated. The future of the USSR is for other obvious reasons one of the two or three most important problems which the political scene presents for all the inhabitants of this earth. Will the Soviet government remain as obstinately resistant to change and adaptation as did its Imperial predecessor, relying on its superior police forces to avert an explosion similar to the one which swept Nicholas II from power? Or will it in time adapt and modify its contours which were so rigidly fixed by Lenin fifty years ago? Obviously no one would venture a confident answer either way. But close study of the Soviet scene does enable one to discern some of the factors which may operate in favour of adaptation and evolution and against stagnation. The same holds for the study of other communist regimes, notably perhaps the one which has travelled farthest on the road to adaptation, Yugoslavia. But even within the Soviet bloc each country has interesting and individual lessons to offer. When looked at together the comparative study of the slow evolution of communist regimes, which has so far hardly been at-tempted,[5] offers a rich new field to the political scientist. To the student of Soviet politics such comparative study opens up the possibility of interesting parallels, even if these must be used with caution – unlike Ulbricht or Kadar the Soviet com-munist leaders have in the last resort no outside power to look to to rescue them in case of need.

What then, are the main factors revealed by a study of 'opposition' in the Soviet Union, which incline one to the view

[5] However an important series of such studies, undertaken by eight British Universities, sponsored by the Social Science Research Council and under the general direction of Professor Ionescu, can be expected in the not too distant future.

that some kind of evolution and adaptation are not necessarily for all time excluded in the USSR? First among these is the decline of naked terror since the death of Stalin. This is no mere accident of personalities – though no one who has studied the history of the Soviet Union without a fixed and determined bias can fail to discern the extent to which Stalin's personality contributed to the nature of the regime which he erected and sustained. But naked and unrestricted terror requires the dominant hand of one man, unrestrained either by colleagues or by institutional safeguards: there is every indication that it is precisely the re-emergence of such a dominant individual that all Soviet leaders are determined to prevent. This determination is, of course, no guarantee for all time. That it can be expected to last for quite a number of years while memories of the dreadful past, which put everyone without exception, high and low, in jeopardy, are still green. Much can happen during these years. Without terror on the scale that Stalin was able and willing to practise, the other influences, the forms of 'opposition' which have been described above, may well be prevented from reaching anything like explosion point; they cannot be completely put down and exterminated. And so long as they persist the experience of the past years suggests that they are more likely to grow than to remain at the same level. There seems indeed to be no middle way with the 'monolithic' societies: either you exclude every crack of light, as Stalin did; or you allow the occasional beam of truth to penetrate, with the result that for all the more perceptive minds the official structure of lies is destroyed beyond repair. This process was probably already completed in the Soviet Union by Khrushchev: it is difficult to see how it could be reversed, at any rate in the foreseeable future.

I have already suggested some reasons for the view that the most effective 'opposition' is likely to be that described as pragmatic dissent; and this form of dissent seems, in the nature of things, likely to increase rather than diminish so long as the present trend towards an elaborate consumer and highly technological economy continues, since such an economy depends all the more on rationality for its progress. There are also a number of less easily defined factors at work. One such is the influence of the Sino-Soviet rift, even if one may assume that it is likely to diminish in intensity after the death of Mao.

The mere existence of two centres of revolutionary leadership and authority of itself gives greater mobility of action to the communist powers of Europe in their dependence on the USSR. Moreover, Chinese criticism of the Soviet Union, while it may not necessarily win friends for China among these communist powers, is certainly more effective and insidious than any of the strictures that have come from non-communist sources in undermining Soviet authority and infallibility. Another such factor is the growing might and authority of the Soviet Union in the international sphere, notwithstanding, indeed perhaps because of, the fact that the advance of Russia has in such large measures been due to the failures and weaknesses of American and European policy. Lenin's internal system which has persisted for fifty years was in large measure the result of fear and of a sense of insecurity. The greater confidence which grows with success may conceivably, even in the Soviet Union, with all its traditional, irrational fear of the truth, of criticism and of legal order (and this traditional fear goes right back to the pre-revolutionary regime) lead in time to greater relaxation.

Finally there is the question of generations, a problem, which so far as Poland is concerned, is analysed in the following pages. In the Soviet Union it bears an aspect of peculiar importance. No doubt the familiar factors operate as well – the general tendency of the sons to revolt against the fathers; and the fact that the young, with little stake as yet in the hard material side of living, tend to be more impetuous, more idealistic and more irresponsible in the remedies for our ills which they propound. But in the Soviet Union there is the additional fact that, so far as the leading party hierarchy is concerned, the over-fifties (and over-sixties) are firmly entrenched, and the emergence of the younger generation, who form the overwhelming majority of party members, is slow and difficult. None of the evidence suggests that the younger party men, or at any rate those in professional party work, are particularly idealistic – they seem to be very much the same hard-bitten, cynical apparatus-men as their elders. But they have grown up in a different world – the world of technological and military efficiency and the world of Soviet success, and not the world of Stalin, of fear and terror, hatred, death and destruction. They may, when they reach high office, prove little different from their elders. But it is conceivable that they will prove less dogmatic, less obstinately blinkered, and in particular that they may prove more amenable to pressure from those who have been described above as the pragmatic dissenters.

Here, then, are some of the factors which suggest that the study of 'opposition' in the communist countries is of vital importance to the student of change in communist societies. *Government and Opposition* has tried to make its contribution to this study, and will endeavour to continue to do so in the future.

Can the Party Alone Run a One-Party State?*

A discussion

'WHAT ARE THE LIMITS ON THE EXERCISE OF POWER, regardless of the number and type of party – this is the most crucial question in political sociology', concluded Ralf Dahrendorf, summing up at the chairman's request, a four-hour debate on the one-party states held at a meeting of a seminar at the London School of Economics and Political Science on 20 May 1966.[1] 'Was the exercise of power limited by the existing structure of interests – and could these limits be extended? Even Stalin for instance could not do all he wanted to do – what could he *not* do?

With these remarks, Ralf Dahrendorf brought the meeting back to the theme with which Raymond Aron had inaugurated the debate and in which Edward Shils, W. H. Morris Jones, R. Mackenzie, Bernard Crick, Alec Nove, Donald MacRae, Michael Kaser and Leonard Schapiro took part.

ARON: HOW NON-MONOPOLISTIC CAN A MONOPOLISTIC PARTY BE?

Raymond Aron drew attention to the difference which time had made in the approach to this subject. Ten years ago, discussion centred on how monopolistic a monopolistic party could be; today, the emphasis was rather on discovering how non-monopolistic it could be. The expression 'monopolistic' party, which he had coined some ten years ago, was not often

[1] A special meeting of the 1964/66 Seminar on 'The Politics of the East European Peoples' Democracies' under the chairmanship of Ghiţa Ionescu organised on 20 May 1966, to sum up the general theme of the seminar. This is a summary of the spontaneous exchange of views that took place. *Government and Opposition* is grateful to the participants for permission to reproduce this account of the meeting, edited by Isabel de Madariaga.

* Vol. 2, No. 2, January–April 1967.

used in English writing on the subject, and he stressed the necessity to distinguish between a monopolistic party and a monolithic party. In his definition, a monopolistic party claimed to have a monopoly of political activity or political representation. A monolithic party meant something quite different; the adjective referred to the internal structure of the single party, its unity and coherence. A party could be monolithic without being monopolistic, as for instance the French Communist Party, which was monolithic in opposition but had no monopoly of political activity. Or it could be monopolistic without being monolithic. But certainly when a monolithic party came to power it became monopolistic.

Ten years ago Orwell's *1984* incarnated in literature the ideal type of totalitarianism, not only single-party rule, but one-man rule of the single party, and the absorption of society into the state. The tendency now was to go to the other extreme and to find subtle ways of explaining that there was not really so much difference between single-party states or the multi-party competition in multi-party states. This raised the question of how non-monopolistic could a monopolistic party be or, in other words, what was the limit of the possible liberalisation or pluralisation within the one-party regime. Without denying the possibilities of some kinds of liberalisation inside a single-party regime, the claim to a monopoly of political action had profound meaning in terms of ideologies and in reality, and there were thus limits to such a liberalisation.

The single party claimed to be the supreme arbiter of the ideological truth, and to retain supreme control of mass decisions in the life of the community. Such a claim could only be made in a single-party regime, for there was a seeming contradiction in a regime which wanted to be democratic and have at the same time only one party. Both *parti* and *partie* implied that the part was a fragment of the whole; a party which denied the existence of other parties was a part which claimed to be the whole. That this placed communist regimes in a difficult position was proved by the fact that they had produced no justification for single-party rule, they had no theory of single-party rule as a permanent system of politics. They justified themselves with the idea that in a time of class struggle, the working class, through its vanguard, should be in power in order to eliminate its enemies; or they argued that the state becomes the state of the whole nation, or that in a homogeneous and coherent society there could not be a duality of parties. The nazis and the fascists could put forward a theory of one-party rule, but then they did not claim to be democrats. The bolsheviks did not put forward the theory of the one-party state, and the idea of the domination of the vanguard of the working class applied only to a limited period of time.

Quite apart from the official communist view on this problem, Raymond Aron had attempted in private discussion to find out how far people in the Soviet Union accepted that there was a theory of one-party rule. The unofficial view that single-party rule was not the real expression of communist or socialist society was often expressed. The real political life of the future would do without any parties at all. The present single-party rule in the Soviet Union was regarded as a provisional phase in historical evolution, as an instrument for changing society. Thus whereas in the West multi-party rule was justified as an expression of the democratic idea, the single party was not put forward as a justification of the democratic idea in the Soviet Union, but as a necessary historical phase.

If the monopolistic party was a party which claimed the monopoly of ideology and supreme power, this raised the question of the extension of the field of ideology, and equally the extension of the use of political power.

In the Soviet Union there had been a considerable reduction in the extension of ideology, and much artistic, intellectual and scientific activity might drop out of the field of ideology and hence of the monopoly of the party. What had remained untouched was the ideology of the party, and within this ideology the assertion that no other parties had the right to exist. There was thus a limit beyond which the reduction of the extension of ideology could not go, and there were certain key propositions which could not be discussed. The logic of the situation was that precisely those propositions which could not be discussed were the most difficult to justify. One of these propositions was the notion that the party was the working class; if this proposition were questioned, the principle of the legitimacy of the party would be jeopardised, and the right of existence of the single party would be compromised at the same time. Thus the limit of the demonopolisation of the monopolistic party, in the field of ideology, was reached at that point which touched those ideas or principles which were absolutely necessary in order to justify the existence of the single party or the absence of any alternative party. It was a limit, and yet not a limit. For on the one hand it was possible to discuss almost everything; and on the other hand it was difficult to avoid discussing the main principle of the legitimacy of the single party. This feature explained the character of the evolution of ideological life in the Soviet Union, which oscillated between enlarging and shrinking the field of discussion. And of course, as long as there was no alternative government, and no alternative policy, the extent of liberalisation, and the possibility of a return to the past remained in doubt.

But the question was can the party alone in a one-party state run the state? Here, first, the concept of the one-party state, and secondly that of 'running the state', should be defined. One of the main difficulties in the typology of political regimes was that if classification were limited to the political field, there could be political institutions which were more or less the same in completely different societies. In making his classification, Aristotle had assumed that he was dealing with the political structure of the *polis*, the Greek city state. Today it was doubtful if valid classification could be made without discriminating between the political regime on the one side and the social infra-structure on the other. There were all sorts of societies at different stages of evolution towards modernisation or industrialisation on the one side; and on the level of the political superstructure regimes ranged from purely one-party states of communist type, through the single party without ideology, the single party without revolutionary ambition, the military regime without any party, the conservative regime, like the Portuguese, almost without any party, the Spanish regime, with social pluralism without parties, to the perfect democratic state with competition between parties. To classify regimes all sorts of variables would have to be used, because one only, such as single party, or multi-party, was not enough. One could not put the Soviet Union, China, the Congo and Cuba into the same category.

In order to answer the question, Raymond Aron pointed out that (a) there was obviously a certain degree of social pluralisation in all societies existing at present; (b) there were all sorts of regimes between the pure communist type and the full multi-party system of the West; and (c) that a lot depended on what was meant by 'running the state'. The party could not, obviously, as a party, run all the activities of the society. But the subsystem of politics in Soviet society was characterised by the existence of a single party, the single party retained supreme power, and supreme power in any political regime meant (a) imposing a certain functioning on the state; (b) providing the justification for the sort of regime which existed (the principle of legitimacy); and (c) determining the goals of the society and the relations between the political community and the others. Thus the real function was to take the key decisions, to give an orientation to foreign policy.

If the concept 'running the state' were limited to those specific functions, then obviously the single party was running the state, since it retained the necessary amount of supreme power. But to run the state in this sense was not the same as running the administration, as a glance at Western regimes would show. Was the Labour Party running the state in Great Britain? Administration was carried out by the high civil servants, who had an easier life when they did not have to convince governments or politicians. But something was lacking in civil servants. They did not rest on any principle of legitimacy, and they had no power to take fundamental decisions on economics or foreign policy. Yet the difference between civil servants and politicians in the West was not quite the same as the difference between party and non-party men in the Soviet Union. Many who would be civil servants or technical experts in the West were party members in the Soviet Union. In the sense that important people belong to the party one could probably say that the party ran the state. But this did not necessarily mean that the man who was running a factory was running it in the name of the party. The question which then arose, however, if one accepted that the party ran the state, was whether the decisions were taken on an ideological or on a pragmatic basis? And it would be difficult to answer, since many party men might not be ideologically minded, and some technical experts might be ideologically minded.

But if the notion of running the state were limited, as it should be, to the retention of the supreme power of taking the main decisions, then it could be said that the Communist Party did run the state even if it was not necessarily running it in the same way as it did fifteen years ago. There might have been changes, even though not very fundamental ones, in the manner of running the state, but the party still took the main decisions, though it might leave greater freedom of action to directors of enterprises, and to some of the technical experts. What might, however, be growing was what Ghiţa Ionescu had called the 'checks' within the system, and within the single party itself.

The concept of a one-party state: Turning to more abstract questions, Raymond Aron wondered whether the concept of a one-party state was still useful in the classification of political regimes, and warned against the danger of concentrating on one aspect of a regime and omitting others. In speaking of one-party states, for instance, one should not fail to consider the structure of the single party concerned. The structure of the Communist Party itself in the Soviet Union had changed in many ways since the death of Stalin. Moreover, below the single party, there was social pluralism and the nature of this pluralism was an important element in defining the political regime. Thirdly, many social forces might limit the control or check the power of the party.

In spite of these drawbacks, the concept of the one-party state still had a certain value in the abstract classification of political regimes. If modern society brought with it some sort of democratic philosophy, there seemed to be three ways in which this philosophy could be translated into practice in the organisation of society.

One way of translating the democratic idea into institutions was by the competition through elections between many parties. The second way, which did not belong in quite the same category, was the single party, which justified itself by the necessity of accomplishing some historical task. In theory there was a third answer: no party whatsoever. But this seemed to be the sort of regime which could not maintain itself in modern society. Indeed, it would be interesting, if there were time, to pursue the problem of why it was so difficult in modern society to have a planned regime without a party.

One school of thought found grounds for the validity of the concept of the one-party state in the fact that the single party itself felt the need to produce social pluralism and organised group support. Another stressed the fact that in all regimes where there was no free competition between parties, there was always an element of uncertainty attached to any progress or liberalisation. It seemed for instance improbable that the Soviet Union would return to the extreme forms of one-man rule. But the party was prevented from going to the end of its own tendency to liberalisation by the fact that it could not admit free discussion in the field of political organisation. As the people could not be asked the question, the party must for ever remain in doubt whether the people would freely say 'We don't need any other party, the party has become the party of the whole nation.'

Yet another school of thought stressed, especially with reference to one-party states in Africa, that the essence of the single party in the single-party state was the claim to the monopoly of political representation. Raymond Aron referred here to the courageous discussion by Sir Arthur Lewis of the assumption, almost universally accepted in the West, that African states needed a 'single party'. Sir Arthur had shown that although maybe African states could not avoid becoming one-party states, yet such regimes were inefficient both in political and in economic terms. Sir Arthur's thesis was that the claim to a monopoly of political representation meant the exclusion from the state and from political life of a good deal of the population. The so-called virtue of the single party was that it created the nation; but if there was no political representation of groups, the single party ran the risk of making impossible the creation of a unified nation. What Sir Arthur suggested was that though only one party could be in power yet those who had not voted for that party should still feel that they were represented in the state. When, for instance, in Britain the Labour Party was in power, the rest of the community was not excluded from political life, and retained some feeling of inclusion in the political process. But Sir Arthur had shown that this was not the case in the single-party African states.

What lessons could be drawn from this brief introduction? Raymond Aron suggested that since the political processes of Western democracies were also under question, majority voting and proportional representation should be re-examined in terms of 'do people feel represented when a definite party is in power', and indeed by the party which was not in power. And his second point, a modest one, was to draw attention to the difficulty in speaking of these problems of one-party rule in connection with underdeveloped countries. For the alternatives seemed to be either to suggest to them that though multi-party democracy was the best form of government, they would have to wait for it until they became rich enough – an attitude which was slightly insulting to them; or to proclaim that the institutions of the West were their only salvation, and yet it might seem rather parochial to attempt to impose Western institutions on the rest of the world. In the circumstances the lesson to be drawn was to avoid both these attitudes and let other people make their choice.

THE STUDY OF THE FACTS

Edward Shils, W. H. Morris-Jones and Robert Mackenzie, who were pressed for time, made brief contributions to the discussion, taking up some of the points made by Raymond Aron. All three drew attention to the danger of reading into one-party states, or some of them, our own definitions and classifications at the risk sometimes of overlooking the factual realities. Edward Shils's first point was that a single party had run the state sometimes but only in certain conditions. Such an operation required continuous vigilance, a considerable degree of ruthlessness and a capacity for combining and manipulating people. It also required great intelligence and coherence and an ideology which was both believed in and believed to be necessary by quite a large number of people. However, the pressing demand for education might in the long run render such an operation more difficult. Educated people acquired a different attitude towards themselves, their self esteem grew, they became more dissatisfied and more demanding, and this in itself was disturbing in a one-party regime. The second point, which Edward Shils believed should be stressed, was that there were single parties which were single parties only in name merely because they used the terminology, imprisoned their opponents, and were called thus by the friends abroad. What struck him about some of these regimes, however, was that they were almost as weak as the oppositions which they imprisoned or otherwise persecuted. The condition which enabled the single party to continue to appear to rule for so long in parts of Africa was the political apathy or ignorance of most of the population, and this situation would not continue for long unchanged. Rulers were bound to fall as people became more politicized, and began to demand that their rulers should derive their legitimacy from the people. It seemed to him that some of the single-party states which had emerged were not at all effective in terms of ruling. They had sometimes been replaced by no-party regimes, but these too were unstable.

W. H. Morris-Jones, commenting on the distinction drawn by Aron between monopolistic and monolithic parties, suggested that our analyses of that end of the political spectrum often seemed to be based on an over-simplified and unrealistically exacting notion of the opposite, 'competitive' politics end. The latter was seen as manifested only in the form of two or more parties alternating in office. But did free politics *require* such alternation? It might be useful if some more attention could be given to the cases of 'dominant' parties: perhaps these would throw light on the extremes at both ends.[2]

What was important was the degree to which dissent could be expressed in the political system – and this might be more easily measured than the degree to which there was a 'sense of participation'. Dominant party systems themselves covered quite a range of different cases, but they all combined in some proportion features of 'single-party' as well as 'perfect competition' regimes. Finding these opposite features side by side in one system could be such a striking phenomenon that its analysis would bring to light characteristics of both extremes which escaped the notice of those who specialised in the study of one or other extreme. 'East' and 'West' could be illumined by the Third World.

Study of dominant parties (i.e. parties continuously in power but not in exclusive possession of political influence) should focus on three aspects: their internal structure – how much scope was there for real debate, how much 'federalism' in the party's working, how much influence lower organs had on the leadership, etc.; second, the interaction between the dominant party and the other 'surrounding' political organisations in the system; third, the place occupied by the party in society as a whole – i.e. its role in the processes of interest aggregation and social mobilisation.

[2] See notably W. H. Morris-Jones, 'Dominance and Dissent', in *Government and Opposition*, Vol. I, No. 4, 1966, pp. 451–66.

Robert Mackenzie thought that the Westminster and Washington patterns of party politics had proved difficult to adapt in the developing world partly because in these two systems the losing party was excluded to an extraordinary degree from any sense of participation in the formulation of policy. Participation in Senate committees did exist in the American model, but in the Westminster model the losing party was excluded from everything except parliamentary debate, and this model was therefore not likely to work successfully where the losing side might represent an ethnic or religious minority of great importance. He had, however, been struck by the failure of the developing countries to evolve any institutionalisation of dissent even within the broad consensus of the revolutions which had occurred in most of these areas. He had on the occasion of recent conversations with President Nasser, found the President only too aware of the difficulties of institutionalising dissent, within his own established revolution, quite apart from the problem of whether to permit dissent about the revolution itself – and very familiar with the literature on the subject. This led Mackenzie to the conclusion that evolutions had taken place in one-party states of which the consequences were unclear. In Mexico, for instance, the problem of the transfer of power every six years had been solved in a one-party state in a way which seemed to work. The most important development seemed to him to be the growth of the interest group system within the one-party state, since such a system was far and away the most important continuing vehicle by which demands and ideas from the whole community could be transmitted to the rulers of that community in the single party. This could go some way to promoting the institutionalisation of dissent. In the transition stage between single-party and multi-party politics, one could hope to see freedom for the presentation of demands. Interest groups should not be stooge organisations, but genuine bodies representing genuine demands. A legitimate input of demands to the system must be achieved as a stage in the liberalisation of one-party regimes.

BERNARD CRICK – THE BASIC INCOMPATIBILITIES

Bernard Crick, while expressing his general agreement with Raymond Aron, wondered nevertheless whether the party itself – the central theme of the debate – was always as important as was sometimes thought in the typological problems of government. We were so obsessed with the necessity of party to economically progressive governments that we might give it more priority than common sense required. It had become a key factor in classifying systems of government, in the sense of systems related to social structure. In studying typical systems that had some claim to stability, some singled out the electoral structure, some selected types of participation, others noted institutions as systematised habits, others still looked to the doctrine of efficiency, others to social structure. Morris-Jones had spoken of degrees of domination, others of degrees of criticism. All these were relevant in different circumstances.

Party was only one way of tackling the problem, and in some cases, notably in the Ghanaian, it seemed to have become merely a method by which a regime which was basically personal and dictatorial sought to give itself legitimacy. Then there were so many varieties of systems, that it was sometimes indifferent whether they were called one-party or non-party systems. Was England between the death of Queen Anne and the American War a non-party state or a one-party state?

What is more, Bernard Crick rather doubted whether one-party government was uniquely attached to new states and territories; autocracy was their obvious feature, with a bureaucracy trying to dress itself up as a party. Indeed he doubted whether these were 'new categories' of government in the sense implied, for instance, by Ernest Gellner in some of his writings. In so far as these were new forms of government they were certainly very unstable, approaching the condition described by Aristotle as *stasis* more than that thrust upon them by Western intellectuals of being a new type of 'revolutionary government'.

Perhaps one of the reasons for their instability was their intolerance of criticism, and he raised this point not in terms of human rights or models of democracy, but as one of the straightforward weaknesses of any tyranny: the difficulty of knowing the truth about anything. Such regimes were at a disadvantage as compared with republican or multi-party regimes where there was open criticism of the government. Whether they resorted to complete suppression, or merely to selective censorship, they were in a difficulty about knowing the truth. And yet total planning must involve total truth.

He saw no contradiction between the most advanced socialism and the freest kind of society precisely on this ground. The more planning, the more necessary the feedback in criticism.

Were the reasons given for the creation of a number of one-party states in recent years likely to be valid for long? There was much confusion in contemporary social science over the justification which successful holders of power give for their actions. American historians still based their interpretation of the American Revolution on what the Founding Fathers said they were trying to do. A large number of Soviet accounts and nationalist accounts were also accepted at face value. Yet the ideology of nationalism, as distinct from totalitarian ideologies, set no goals; it was an end in itself. If one-party regimes in nationalist states were justified, in the sense that one could attribute some chance of stability to them, then a more precise quality of the realisation of national goals must be found. One-party, nationalist states were not likely to form a new sort of government. They would probably pluralise and Tanganyika might be the pattern of the future.

ALEC NOVE – INTEREST GROUPS IN ONE-PARTY STATES

Alec Nove put forward the proposition that one reason for the existence of the autocratic or totalitarian state was that many people, both the rulers and the ruled, thought that it was needed. This would explain the success of Ivan the Terrible, since both he, and the people he oppressed, believed absolute rule to be necessary. Unless such a belief existed – whether we believed in it or not – the morale of the rulers and their legitimacy would suffer considerably. Communist ideology was not exclusively, but very largely, a formulation of the reasons why those who ruled should rule, and why this should be accepted as right.

Belief in economic development, in a country where traditional forms were breaking down, might bring into power as a result of revolutions a dynamic regime with utopian aims perhaps, in the name of imposing order on chaos. Of course it might not be efficient, but the question of efficiency seemed to him beside the point. Even if inefficient, it might still be preferable to civil war and anarchy.

Even under Stalin, enough people believed that stern, ruthless, one-party government was essential to make it work. Such a belief was now in process of erosion; what would happen if the power to enforce absolute government, and the faith on which that power rested, disintegrated? There was no doubt that a long period of the monopoly of power created very powerful vested interests in its continuance. People clung to power, even when they were unable to find very convincing reasons for doing so.

The reverse of the problem was that long years of autocratic rule, and the suppression of all vestiges of free institutions had created something of a vacuum, and even liberal reformers clung to the one-party system as better than anarchy. This view was reflected in such stories as the Russian, asked whether there should not be two parties, who replied 'Two? Isn't one enough!'; or the Yugoslav, asked if an opposition party would not be a good thing, and who replied: 'If we had an opposition party everyone would join it, and again we would have one party.'

At present there was more scope for discussion on practical issues, and for pressure groups to operate within the party, to some extent even publicly. Economic issues were argued. To this extent dissent within the consensus had become possible. The point at issue now was the relationship between party control and social and economic evolution. There were two kinds of decisions: those which genuinely changed the situation, and those taken by people in authority which reflected the situation, and were conditioned by circumstances. An increasing number of the decisions taken in the Soviet Union were of this latter type and the choice was more restricted by social and political restraints and technical requirements. The social gap between the party commissar and the educated manager was disappearing, the people they supervised were mainly party members, and a gradual merging of party control and state control of broad economic and technical areas seemed likely. It

was a question of trying to define where politics ended and where
technology began. There were vested interests with a potent
influence in determining how much criticism should be allowed;
change in the direction of political pluralisation would be
rather slow.

DONALD MACRAE – STAGNATION OF THE ONE-PARTY STATES

Donald MacRae doubted the implicit assumption which he
thought had been made, that monolithism was evolutionary.
In his view it became static. Arising from the nature of the
subject, all sociology of a serious and general nature must concern itself with the political, and normally politics was stronger
than society. The principal instrument of politics (not the only
one of course) was the party, and the natural history of parties
should depend on rather simple principles of which he would
suggest only three.

The idea of competition had been constantly referred to but
he suggested that it might be confusing in that it suggested a
kind of market model, an economic model with a political aura.
This made it difficult to deal with a situation in which there
was little political competition and no persecution. He thought
there were two sorts of political parties and systems: those which
tolerated the existence of others, and those which destroyed the
institutional being of rival parties.

The fundamental issue was the difference in kind between
parties in the use of power. One-party systems of the kind
discussed were systems where the dominant party was intolerant
and used its power to destroy the institutional being of the others.
Moreover, cutting across this point, there were certain kinds of
parties which came into being to institute one single kind of
change. What were the problems of such associations, when they
had attained power, achieved their single aim and their occupation was gone? In his view, many of the intolerant parties in
existence at present contained stronger indications than their
members realised of being parties of this kind. They were concerned to attain power, much more than with what to do with it.
This explained the situation in many parts of the world, particularly those under communist rule. They got on with the business of administration, and people got used to them; but this

hardly generated enthusiasm. It was indeed a deterrent to successful recruitment and successful mobilisation in critical circumstances. Most human beings were seldom political for very long. As the authors of the Enlightenment had already pointed out, the despotic society was not necessarily the one in which despotism was constantly exercised in the fullest sense; what made despotism was that every individual and group was unprotected from state power. In this sense modern one-party states were despotic.

Even modern mass-communications could bring in diminishing returns – an example of this could be found in the fall of Nkrumah in Ghana, where communications were good. Thus we had intolerant parties, uncertain of their long-term purpose, faced with problems of mobilisation and recruitment and with diminishing returns from their hold over communications and society. However despotic, such societies had got into an *impasse*. The importance of ideology could lie in the creation of a law which shaped the regime in power and helped to maintain it in power. But however permissive, ideology was bound to constrain the behaviour and the political actions even of those with political power, and it prevented the circulation of ideas connected with problems, and hindered mobilisation and recruitment – another aspect of the *impasse*. One might expect a slackening of tension, a kind of thaw, but he did not think this should be regarded as an evolution towards a different destiny or the production of a new species. The *impasse* might be a pleasanter place to be in than some phases of the past but it was not a permanent place for societies, and the way out for one-party states seemed to be extremely difficult. For a long time they would be stuck and we would be stuck with them.

The Westminster model had been mentioned in passing, and he would like to add that, in his view, none of the new states had attempted to set up the particular British model of the party system. He believed that as a model it was more adaptable than it was now the fashion to think.

Michael Kaser thought the problem was not whether the party ran the state efficiently, but whether it ran it. In his view, the party in the Soviet Union was the final arbiter of policy in the field of macro-economics and the regulator of economic activity. It chose the officials, imposed discipline, provided the criteria by which to measure achievements, and served as

the trouble-shooter if the plan did not work. Thus, though the
party did not exercise overall control it did run the one-party
state at the margin of choice. In this sense the Soviet Union
differed from the single-party states in Asia and Africa, where
the administration was too small and the number of decisions
too large for the parties to carry them.

LEONARD SCHAPIRO – SOCIAL GROUPS AND POLITICAL REALITIES

Leonard Schapiro raised what seemed to him the difficulty of
generalising about 'one-party states', when in fact so many
different models existed. The idea that the party 'ran' the state
was certainly fallacious in the case of the Soviet Union. In fact,
it was a body which existed to make it possible for the leader of
the moment to see to it that the state was run in a particular
way. In this sense, Mussolini's definition of the Fascist Party
fitted the Soviet Communist Party: 'a civic militia at the service
of the Duce'. Yet, plainly, there were enormous differences
between Fascist Italy and the Soviet Union. Throughout
Soviet history the dualism between the party and the state had
created problems which so far had proved insuperable. Mac-
Rae's emphasis on the impossibility of evolution in the so-called
one-party states seemed to him to be right. The party leaders
did not allow groups to form, and only sought opinions from
those who were allowed to hold opinions. Moreover, the supposedly growing expertise of the party professional from which
Nove derived comfort, seemed to him of little benefit to the
regime. It only increased the friction by bringing about collision between the man who knew just a smattering of a technical
subject, and the expert who knew all about it. This perennial
friction had never been solved in spite of all kinds of attempts.
Stalin's method was the most successful, but then Stalin had
evolved a personal despotism of which the party had been only
one of several instruments of rule. He disagreed with Aron that
under Stalin the party had been monopolistic. It was true to say
that the party was 'monopolistic' under Khrushchev, or at all
events nearly so – the failure by Khrushchev in this respect was
one of the reasons for his fall, since the planners and technicians
were not prepared to accept this monopoly. Now once again
attempts had been made to draw lines of demarcation between

the party apparatus and the state machine, and once again there were friction and inefficiency. It was difficult to see any solution so long as the party successfully asserted its vested interest in privilege and interference.

RALF DAHRENDORF – THE LIMITS OF THE EXERCISE OF POWER

Ralf Dahrendorf, who had been asked by the chairman to sum up the meeting, attempted to formulate a few of the questions which had emerged, and which seemed to him worth further exploration. In his talk, Raymond Aron had raised the question of the no-party state. Could there be such a thing? If one excluded the military and conservative states, was the notion of a no-party state the equivalent of a stagnant society? Or of a society in which conflicts failed to be translated into political initiatives? What of the concept of 'pillarisation' which had been applied to the Dutch political system; could parties become institutionalised to such an extent as to cease to be parties? Was it possible to analyse the political process successfully without reference to political parties? Attempts had been made but where such societies were not of the straightforward conservative type, did they not turn out to be states of equilibrium, which therefore failed to allow for any movement or dynamism?

Turning to the analysis of the one-party state, Dahrendorf suggested that most political processes were present even in them, namely the recruitment of leaders (based on ambition); the mobilisation of initiative (where opinion entered the picture) and the organisation of dissent (for all government was bound to offend some people some of the time). Unless political sociology was all wrong, these three features were all socially structured interests in all countries. If this assumption was true, then several general questions arose; could recruitment, initiative and dissent be organised for these three processes by one single party? Under which conditions did societies try to accomplish these three tasks by one or many parties? What were the limits of monopolisation if these three tasks were monopolised by one party? How monopolistic could a monopolistic party be? Was there not the possibility that the more monopolistic it became, the *less* monolithic? What were the limits of competition in Western societies? How many parties could there be?

Was contemporary Germany a one-party state because the opposition did not oppose?

Further, what were the differences in societies which led them to develop these different types of party organisations? Which were the more desirable, in terms of efficency, or morally? Was this desirability conditioned by any regional differences if parties were considered as expressions of the structuring of interests?

Turning to the methodological question raised by Schapiro, Dahrendorf suggested that there were two approaches: one could formulate general statements about one-party states, or one could look in great detail at the history of one particular country. Was it possible to extrapolate and draw general conclusions, or should the student confine himself to historical analysis? This problem remained undecided, and he thought most of the speakers would disagree on the subject; he himself hoped that a general explanation could be developed though he was aware that political sociologists might fall short of the legitimate desires of historians.

Leonard Schapiro

'Putting the Lid on Leninism'*

Opposition and dissent in the communist one-party states

IT WILL SOON BE FORTY YEARS SINCE LENIN DECIDED
to 'put the lid on opposition', as he expressed it himself at the
dramatic Tenth Congress of his party in March 1921. Much
has happened since then, both in the Soviet Union and in the
countries which have by imitation adopted the same pattern of
one-party government. It is therefore worth reflecting on the
reasons which led Lenin to adopt this drastic policy; and to
pause to enquire into the results which have flowed from his
action – whether he intended them or not.

The bolsheviks took power in 1917 without having (as on so
many other vital questions) formulated any precise theory about
their future policy towards those who disagreed with them.
There was a general acceptance of the need to deal sternly with
'enemies' – indeed no revolutionary government could hope to
survive for long if it did not do something of the kind. But who
were to be considered as enemies? Lenin never clearly stated
bolshevik intentions on the subject before he came to power. He
had, it is true, shortly before the October *coup d'état,* made some
detailed promises about the purpose of the bolsheviks to allow
representatives of every shade of opinion who could muster a
sufficient number the freedom to express themselves in a newspaper, with the guarantee of the necessary newsprint and facilities. But no one except the more naïve party members could
have taken this exercise in demagogy very seriously. Theory
apart, Lenin's practice after 1903 as leader of the bolsheviks
did not augur well for tolerance of any kind, either of differences
of opinion inside his own party, or of criticism from the socialist
parties. As against this, the Bolshevik Party had grown tenfold

* Vol. 2, No. 2, January–April 1967.

in size between February and October 1917, and the problems
of discipline had grown with it. Besides, all the evidence of the
early elections to the Soviets and to the Constituent Assembly,
in the few months before the bolsheviks had been able to rig
them effectively, showed that the socialist parties enjoyed considerably more support in the country as a whole than the
bolsheviks.

As was to be expected, therefore, bolshevik policy in this
matter, as in so many others, was decided on the basis of ex-
pediency. Members of political parties from the *Kadets* right-
wards, the Church, the bourgeoisie generally, and for a time
officers, were broadly regarded as enemies, who would be prepared to overthrow the new regime if they could. Rough and
ready violence and restraint were therefore applied by the
bolsheviks to all individuals whom they saw no hope of persuading to cooperate, and of course to many more as well. In so far
as this form of revolutionary terror should be given a theoretical
basis, it could be described as suppression of opposition – using
'opposition' in its strict sense of an organised political group, or
groups, of which the aim is to oust the government in power
and to replace it by one of its own choosing. It was not to be
expected that the bolsheviks would tolerate opposition in this
sense. Indeed, tolerance of organised political opposition is, as
Dahl has reminded us,[1] recent, novel and not always easy to
achieve with success. For a political party like the bolsheviks,
who believed not only in the rightness of their cause, and of their
cause alone, but also in the sanction of history for their title to
rule in the name of the proletariat, willingness to co-exist with
an organised opposition would have been inconceivable and
that is what anti-bolshevik parties and movements after 1917
amounted to from the bolshevik point of view. But if suppression of the opposition was taken for granted by all bolsheviks,
so, curiously enough, in view of Lenin's ruthless intolerance
during his years as leader of the underground party, was the
freedom of dissent within the ranks of the Bolshevik Party. No
bolshevik, certainly not Lenin, would have seriously contended
before March 1921 that party members had no right to disagree among themselves. For the first three and a half years
after 1917, at any rate, debate inside the party remained free

---

[1] In his Preface to *Political Oppositions in Western Democracies*, New Haven, Conn.,
1966, of which he is the Editor.

and often furious. If it was true that Lenin's view nearly always
prevailed, it was also true that this result was achieved by Lenin
and his supporters not through fraud or force, but by their
greater authority and cogency of argument.

I have called this form of disagreement 'dissent', not 'opposition' – and indeed the latter term would have been quite
inapplicable to disagreements within the party, and was not
applied to them before March 1921. For dissent, as distinct
from opposition, is not organised, or at all events not organised
for political action; and it does not seek to replace the existing
regime, or to challenge the right of existing rulers to exercise
political authority: it merely seeks to criticise, to exhort, to
persuade, and to be listened to. For dissent tolerance is enough:
opposition, in the sense of a legal opposition, requires organisation and other facilities in order to enable it to achieve political
power by displacing the present incumbents from their offices.
Or, as Burke put it, 'Dissent not satisfied with toleration is not
conscience but ambition.'

THE BANNING OF OPPOSITION

But in Russia between opposition and dissent lay a no man's
land of socialism, in which the bolsheviks for the first few years
trod very warily. Their attitude to the two main socialist parties,
the mensheviks and the socialist revolutionaries, was, until 1921,
to say the least ambivalent. The socialists were regarded as
enemies in one sense, because they criticised the bolshevik
seizure of power; at the same time, few bolsheviks would have
been prepared to treat them in the same wasy as the real 'class
enemy', the monarchists or the bourgeoisie, because they were
after all spokesmen for the workers and peasants. So the bolsheviks pursued, not for the first or last time, a dual policy
towards the two socialist parties. Except for a short period
during 1918, they were not outlawed. Some of their candidates
got themselves elected to the Soviets, and, in spite of all difficulties, the party spokesmen were able, until 1921, by the exercise of courage and ingenuity, to make their views known. On
the other hand, every conceivable kind of fraud and violence
was used by the bolsheviks against them to make the exercise of
their nominal rights impossible. The position was perhaps best
expressed by Lenin in July 1918 in a private communication to

the local bolsheviks at Elets: 'It is a pity you have not arrested
them (i.e. the left socialist revolutionaries of Elets) as is being
done everywhere. It is essential to oust all Socialist Revolutionaries from responsible posts. . . . We cannot of course give you
written authorisation to arrest Socialist Revolutionaries, but if
you drive them out of Soviet organs, if you arrest them and
expose them before the workers and peasants . . . you will be
doing good revolutionary work, and we in the centre . . . will
only praise you for it.' [2]

Strictly speaking, neither party was ever declared illegal by
any express enactment. But by the beginning of 1921, if not
before, mensheviks and socialist revolutionaries were being
arrested, imprisoned or exiled to labour camps (in some few
cases they were allowed to emigrate) and by 1922 a trial of
socialist revolutionary leaders was staged. After that time any
activity in one of the independent socialist parties could easily
be caught under the wide umbrella of 'counter-revolution'.
Ostensibly this development was justified by the supposed
participation of the two parties in armed revolt against the
communist regime, and especially in the Kronstadt Rising of
March 1921, and in the peasant risings which by 1922 amounted
to a virtual guerrilla war. The charge that the socialist parties
were implicated in a policy of violent opposition to the regime
was palpably false so far as the mensheviks were concerned, and
at most true of some of their number so far as the socialist
revolutionaries were concerned. It was of course the case that
their vigorous criticism of communist policy [3] helped to increase
worker and peasant dissatisfaction, and made the government's
slender hold over the country even more precarious. But was
their policy opposition or dissent? On the one hand neither
party pursued any express policy of ousting the communists
from power: both had aimed at the very most at achieving
participation of socialists in the Soviets and in the government,
on a proper representative basis, which the communists had
violated. Both parties accepted the October Revolution as
irreversible; and thousands of members of both parties had fully
supported the communist side in the Civil War – the fact that

[2] Reprinted in Volume XXIII of the *Collected Works of Lenin*, Second-Third
Russian Edition, p. 558.
[3] The bolsheviks renamed their party the All-Russian Communist Party
(Bolsheviks) at their Seventh Congress in March 1918.

the socialists were, if only barely, tolerated while the war was raging, and destroyed only after the war had been won, is proof enough of this. But on the other hand, it is arguable that, had the socialists been allowed full freedom of action during the tense and precarious years of 1921–2, the communist government would have been ousted by the force of popular discontent in favour of a socialist government – with, or more probably without, participation of the, by then, almost universally detested communists. As the self-appointed agents of the forces of history, the communists could hardly have been expected to face such a prospect with equanimity.

THE BANNING OF DISSENT

A quite different and novel issue arose at the Tenth Party Congress in March 1921 – the banning of dissent, as distinct from opposition, even though characteristically, the dissent was branded as 'opposition' by Lenin. It is essential to note at the outset that the Congress met in an atmosphere of panic and uncertainty. The Kronstadt Rising was in full swing while the Congress met, and some two hundred delegates were dispatched for political work in connection with its suppression. The peasants were literally up in arms throughout the country, the toll of devastation, collapse and hunger during the civil war had left general morale at a very low ebb, now that the incentive of an enemy at the gate was gone. Support for the communists had sunk to its very lowest level since 1917, even among the proletariat. The Congress members were prepared for drastic action against dissenters, including perhaps even those members who were themselves prone to criticise government policy. The mood was well expressed by Karl Radek at the end of the Congress, when the drastic curtailment of all freedom of speech for party members had been voted: 'In voting for this resolution, I felt that it could be used against us too, but, in spite of that I stand for it. . . . Let the Central Committee in a moment of danger take the severest measures against the best comrades, if it thinks it necessary.'[4] Evidently Radek, like many others,

---

[4] The verbatim account of this Congress has only been published in Russian. A new edition was printed in Moscow in 1963, and this is the edition which I have used for this article. The quotation from Radek is on p. 534. The intelligent

thought, as indeed Lenin implied, that the measures were to be
temporary only. We shall return to this question. But first it is
necessary to look at the background to the Congress and the
circumstances which led to the banning of dissent, under the
guise of 'putting the lid on opposition'.

For some time before the Congress several critical trends had
been discernible inside the party. Common to all was dissatisfaction with what spokemen of these trends alleged were violations of party democracy – suppression of criticism, dictatorial
methods on the part of the leaders, forcible mobilisation of
party members for duty, 'bureaucratisation', alienation of party
leaders from the workers, and the like. Much of the criticism
was, no doubt, well founded. Much of it was certainly a libertarian hankering after the idealism of the early days which had
been superseded by the grim reality of a small, unpopular
clique of commissars, clinging to power in the face of overwhelming unpopularity. What few of the critics fully realised
was that the power which they, as communists, did not hesitate
to enforce against anyone and everyone outside their own party
could only be preserved by pretty drastic discipline inside that
party. Two types of critics could be particularly distinguished,
to whom the names 'Workers' Opposition' and 'Democratic
Centralists' were to become attached. The former were to be
found mainly within the trade union movement and argued that
the trade unions should take over the management of industry.
It need hardly be said that by 'trade unions' the supporters
of the Workers' Opposition meant the existing communist-
dominated unions, from which mensheviks and other non-
communists were excluded by force, and by rigged elections.
The Democratic Centralists were mainly supporters of what they
called soviet democracy, by which, again, they meant the com-
munist-dominated Soviets, none of which had been freely
elected since 1917. Neither group of critics was in any sense
organised for action, neither had its own press, neither had its
own officers or programme. No one, not even Lenin or Zinoviev, the prime movers in destroying them, ever suggested that
either the Workers' Opposition or the Democratic Centralists
was planning to oust the existing government from power and

anticipation by the two worker delegates, which far surpassed the political judgement of all the intellectuals present at the Congress, and which is referred to later,
will be found on p. 525 (Kamensky) and p. 527 (Medvedev).

to replace it with one of their own choice, let alone that either of them was opposed to the Soviet regime. So far, therefore, these groups of critics would have seemed to fall into the category of dissenters, certainly claiming the right to voice their criticism freely, but not intent on setting themselves up as alternative sources of political authority.

However, by the end of 1920 serious differences of opinion on the policy to be adopted towards the trade unions appeared within the Central Committee of the party. It should be emphasised that there was no question of any support for they Workers' Opposition among members of the Central Committee – indeed the dissident trade union communists were voicing an essentially rank and file point of view, which no party 'general' of Central Committee rank would have dreamt for endorsing. The division in fact centred on the degree of force which ought to be applied to the unions – with Trotsky on the side of greater force, and Lenin on the side of more compromise, and with various shades of opinion in between. According to party tradition such a difference of opinion can only be resolved by a full-scale debate (this is indeed still provided for in the party rules currently in force) and a debate was accordingly ordered. The matter was further complicated by two factors. First, the intention of Lenin's principal adjutant at that time, Zinoviev, to settle personal scores with Trotsky by striking at him through the secretaries of the Central Committee, who happened to be Trotsky's supporters. And secondly, the desire of all the party leaders, including Lenin, to find some way of dealing with the growing criticism inside the party which they were all beginning to find very irksome.

Accordingly, in pursuance of these objects and in preparation for the great debate on the trade union question, every opinion group within the party, however vague, was ordered to prepare its 'platform' on the trade union issue, and the party was thus artificially split into supporters of the majority Lenin platform, of the Trotsky platform, of several other minor platforms, and of the platforms of the Workers' Opposition and of the Democratic Centralists. Long before the Congress met, it became clear that the Lenin platform would have little difficulty in securing a majority in the party. Nevertheless, as a result of Zinoviev's manoeuvre, elections of delegates to the Congress were ordered to be held by platforms, with the result that

Workers' Opposition and Democratic Centralist sympathisers
found themselves labelled with the name of their 'fraction' at the
Congress. At the same time, in preparation for the Congress,
and in the course of the great party debate, a violent attack was
launched on the allegedly dictatorial and undemocratic
methods used by the secretaries of the Central Committee,
Krestinsky, Serebryakov and Preobrazhensky. This assault was
designed by Zinoviev, who ran the campaign for party democracy, to discredit Trotsky. Several results were thus achieved
by the party managers who sponsored these steps. First, the
extent of dissent inside the party was revealed in the course of
both the official debate, and of a great deal of local debate
which took place at the same time. Secondly, some superficial
semblance of truth was lent to what was to become at the Congress the main charge against the 'opposition' groups – that
they had organised themselves as separate and distinct 'fractions'
inside the party. And thirdly, as a special bonus for the private
ambitions of Zinoviev, Trotsky was, at any rate temporarily,
discredited; and the three Central Committee secretaries were
removed in favour of a new team, headed by Molotov, who, as
it turned out, was to keep the seat warm for Stalin. The combined effect of all this rather distasteful political chicanery and
of the shock of the Kronstadt Rising on the party ranks is not
difficult to imagine. Frightened, bewildered, weary, disap-
pointed and baffled, they proved to be very malleable material
in the hands of Lenin who, still at the height of his vigour,
stage-managed the Congress from start to finish.

The main event of the Congress was perhaps the announcement of the New Economic Policy which, although it aroused
some misgivings among the left-wing extremists, was widely
welcomed as promising some very necessary relief from an
economic situation which was catastrophic. (The mensheviks
had for some time been advocating a similar policy.) We are,
however, concerned with the political results of the Congress.
At a fairly early stage of the Congress a resolution on party
organisation was debated and adopted which appeared to go a
long way towards conciliating the many critics who were disturbed by the decline of democratic practices and by the alienation of the masses from their leaders. This resolution provided
for the fullest freedom of discussion, for ample participation of
rank and file members in decisions at all levels and for detailed

responsibility of leaders at all levels to their party electors. However, at the very end of the Congress, when all the scheduled business, including the election of a new Central Committee and secretaries, had been completed, two surprise resolutions of a very different nature were introduced by Lenin, and adopted against the votes of the Workers' Opposition delegates. Since, however, at least a quarter of all Congress delegates had already left, including many Workers' Opposition supporters, the opposing vote fell far short of the total number of delegates who were known to be critical of the policy of the Central Committee. The first resolution, on 'Party Unity', with scant regard for the facts, noted signs in the party of the formation of groups determined 'to a certain extent to become self-contained and to create their own group discipline', and hinted that this had given encouragement to enemies of the revolution (meaning the Kronstadt insurgents). Henceforward all public criticism must be conducted with the situation of the party in the midst of its enemies in mind. All groups were to be immediately dissolved, on pain of expulsion from the party. The second last-minute resolution condemned the views of the Workers' Opposition as an 'anarcho-syndicalist deviation'. [5]

THE DISSENT IN THE PARTY

Several points about this story of the Tenth Party Congress must be noted for the purpose of our study of dissent and opposition. In the first place what were ostensibly condemned were 'fractional' activities and ideological deviation from orthodoxy. Both of these, had the accusations been well founded, could be regarded as transcending the bounds of dissent. It is, however, very doubtful if either of the accusations was based on any real facts: there had been no 'fractional' activity except in so far as it had been artificially called into existence by Zinoviev's machination; and the Workers' Opposition doctrine, if such it can be called, was in fact based on the party programme which had been adopted in 1919. Lenin repeatedly emphasised, as did the resolution on party organisation, that criticism and discus-

---

[5] I have dealt in detail with the whole story here summarised in my *The Origin of the Communist Autocracy. Political Opposition in the Soviet State. First Phase: 1917–1922.* London, Harvard, 1955. The curious reader is referred especially to Chapters VII to XVII.

sion were the inalienable rights of all party members. It was
true that the resolution on party unity imposed a serious limitation on criticism – as two worker delegates pointed out, if the
party authorities were given the right to decide what criticism
gave encouragement to the enemies of the revolution, and what
did not, nothing much would be left in practice of the supposed
freedom of party members to criticise. (Events were almost immediately to show how right these two workers were.) But here
the majority of the delegates were probably able to derive
comfort by persuading themselves that the restriction was only
temporary, and would not outlast the present situation of
danger.

Lenin never actually said that the restriction was to be temporary, but he may well, by his repeated stress on the danger in
which the revolution was placed and on the fact that public
debate in the party at such a time was an impermissible 'luxury',
although as a matter of principle the right of party members to
criticise was sacrosanct, have conveyed that impression. If he did,
it would be difficult to say on the evidence that this was necessarily dishonesty on his part. His management of the Congress,
which was a political *tour de force*, was certainly far from
scrupulous. But bolshevik tradition had always regarded political method as of very subordinate importance when compared
with the result which it was considered desirable, in the interests
of the revolution, to achieve. True, immediately after the Congress there began a systematic repression of criticism and the persecution of party critics. But even so, for so long as Lenin retained
his health (it deteriorated sufficiently in the course of 1921 for
him to cease regular work in December) it can fairly be said
that the dangerous situation of the party had not yet abated.
There are some, not very conclusive, indications that during
1922 Lenin may have had some second thoughts on the way in
which the party was being run. But if so it was already too late. [6]

Whatever may have been Lenin's intentions in March 1921
with regard to the toleration of dissent in the party, there is no
doubt about the use to which his successors put the measures
which he then introduced. Control over dissent had in practice
been vested in the party secretariat – by May 1922 Stalin had
taken charge of this vital organ. The course of events since that
date is too familiar to require any detailed recounting. Between

[6] Ibid., pp. 339–42.

1923 and 1936, in his slow rise to absolute despotic power, Stalin, by his manipulation of the party machine, was able first to control then to stifle all legitimate dissent. Denied the tolerance which would have enabled them to express their criticism of policy, without seeking to replace the existing political authority, the critics turned to opposition – which had precisely this aim. Opposition was then treated as treason – as well it might be, since by the time of the holocaust of 1936–8 Stalin had made himself into so much of a personal autocrat that no change could even be contemplated that did not start with his removal. The course of opposition in the Soviet Union between 1923 and 1939 tells an interesting story of the way in which the suppression of all dissent must of itself necessarily create violent opposition, even among those ideologically committed party members who are traditionally most opposed to it. Trotsky was a case in point. An obviously possible, and indeed natural rival for power as against Stalin, he made no move of any kind to further his own advancement, indeed failed to make many obvious moves in order to protect himself. Whether his conduct was due to devotion to 'the party' or to fear of bringing the whole regime down about his ears, if once Stalin's grip were loosened, is not here material. Nevertheless if he carefully avoided (as long as he could) opposition (in the strict sense) he valiantly asserted his right to dissent. But Stalin was not content until he had driven or provoked him into opposition – into futile acts of open revolt in the streets, so that he could the better destroy him politically.

This was still the early stage – the equation of *opposition* with treason. The case of Bukharin and of the 'right' opposition carried the process a stage further – the equation of *dissent* with treason. In Bukharin's case there was no question of rivalry for power, only a desire to challenge Stalin's reasons for making the sudden change in economic policy after 1928. But the days of rational discussion in the party were long over – since 1921, in fact. It took Stalin seven years, from 1929 to 1936, until he was strong enough to unleash the final stage of the purge and the show trials. Those seven years remain the most obscure period of Soviet history in our present state of knowledge. It would seem that the dissenters, denied the elementary right of making their voice heard, with the whole future of their country at stake, made a desperate effort to replace Stalin by Kirov. Thwarted

by Stalin, who had Kirov murdered, but still found it necessary
to temporise with the 'right' (even to the extent of tolerating the
constitutional façade of 1936, of which Bukharin was the main
author), the leading members of the Central Committee cast
about for some way to remove the maniac who was at the helm.[7]
We know the result. The lesson of the *Ezhovshchina*, as the years
of horror were named, has not yet been forgotten in the Soviet
Union, or in other communist countries, even though the
situation has changed: to dissent from the leader was only a
short step away from the executioner's bullet. We shall have
occasion to return to this.

AFTER LENIN'S DECISION

We may never learn, unless further evidence emerges, what
Lenin's ultimate intentions were when he put an end to dissent
in March 1921 – even if he called it opposition. What is quite
certain is that he could never have contemplated that he was
making possible the national lunacy which was to be associated
with Stalin. Lenin's immediate motives in 1921, as repeatedly
emphasised in his speeches to the Congress, were clear enough:
fear that criticism could help the enemies of revolution, as
symbolised by Kronstadt; and a desire to strengthen the unity
of the party for decisive action. The abstention from criticism
in time of national danger is, as a short-term measure, perhaps
justifiable, if it is accepted as a self-limitation, voluntarily submitted to in the interests of all. A necessary condition for such
voluntary submission is some kind of safeguard to ensure that
full freedom to dissent will be tolerated once again the moment
the emergency if over. The situation becomes quite different
when the clamp of silence is imposed for all time, as it was by
Stalin. It was probably true that so long as he was strong enough
to suppress dissent, not only in his own country, but in all communist parties throughout the world, Stalin forged an inter-

[7] The main source of this story is Bukharin's account as given to the late B. I.
Nicolaevsky in 1936, and printed by the latter in disguised form in the exiled social
democrat journal, *Sotsialisticheskiy vestnik*, under the title *Letter of an Old Bolshevik*.
A translation of this document together with Nicolaevsky's account in 1964 of his
talks with Bukharin will be found in Boris I. Nicolaevsky, *Power and the Soviet Elite*,
New York, 1966. For a short summary of the supporting evidence of Soviet sources
(including the speech by Khrushchev in secret session in 1956) and of memoirs, see
my *The Communist Party of the Soviet Union*, London, New York, 1960, pp. 394–417.

national communist machine which was well able to stand up to its enemies, and even to carry with success the assault into the enemy camp. Yet one may well ask whether the effect has not in the long run proved of greater help than hindrance to the enemies of communism.

After the death of Stalin, and the inevitable collapse of his system of rule (since it depended on his personality) the disintegration of communism, both as a world movement and in individual countries, has proceeded more rapidly than anyone could possibly have anticipated. The seeming perfection of the system of the organised lie devised by Stalin proved to be the undoing of communism. When once the lie had been exposed, the credit of communist leaders everywhere was so far undermined that they have since then often found it hard to secure credence, even when they are telling the truth. Would the damage to the communist movement in the long run have been anything like as severe, one wonders, if Soviet policy had been hammered out, in fierce public debate, out of which the right course of action was allowed to emerge from the clash of opposing opinions?

Lenin's second motive, the desire for greater unity, is perhaps the one which remains most relevant to the communist one-party states today. The search for the strength which unity provides is as old as politics itself. The problem of reconciling unity of action with man's need to dissent, with the genuine variety of opinion which is natural in human society, is as old as mankind. This problem has of late revived with new vigour in all communist one-party states, including the Soviet Union, and is still far from resolved. It should be emphasised that we are concerned with dissent alone. The tolerance of opposition which seeks to replace one type of government by another, which organises itself as a political party in opposition to the ruling communist party, is inconsistent with the ideology and tradition of communist states – they are by definition as it were 'non-opposition' states. But dissent does not seek to challenge this ideology or tradition, so long as it remains dissent, and a number of the communist one-party states are searching for the way in which difference of opinion can be tolerated, indeed welcomed as a valuable adjunct to sound government, without at the same time undermining the dominant position of the communist party, and of the form of social order for which it

stands. The experience of the Soviet Union, since the death of
Stalin, illustrates the difficulties which have been created by a
system of one-party government which succeeded for so many
years in eliminating all dissent. These difficulties, which the
Soviet party has not yet found any way of overcoming, can be
summarised under four heads.

EFFECTS ON POLICY DECISIONS

The first effect of 'putting the lid on opposition' was to destroy
all rational basis for policy decisions. If dissent cannot be freely
voiced, for fear of disturbing the outward unity of party policy
which is traditionally considered necessary, then in the end one
man will decide, and will decide arbitrarily. During the period
when Khrushchev was at the helm, the view was often expressed
that policy was now being decided more by rational discussion
and less by one-man command, that the Central Committee
had become a real debating chamber, that party organs were
displaying real initiative, and so forth. Since his fall in October
1964 it has become evident that this was only true at the time to
a very limited extent. It now appears that some of his policies,
which, to put it mildly, seemed somewhat eccentric when he
proposed them, although outwardly fully endorsed by the
Central Committee at the time, were in fact just one man's
brain children about which many of his colleagues had serious
misgivings. Such was the virgin lands scheme, such the policy
of widespread maize growing, of the destruction of grasslands,
of the splitting of the party organisations into agricultural and
industrial components, and many more. Why, one asks oneself,
if it was not due to a tradition which inhibits dissent and stifles
genuine discussion, did these colleagues on the Central Committee who had misgivings, as they now say, vote unanimously
at the time for the First Secretary's proposals?

This problem of the unreality of much of the activity of Soviet
party organs is one which is now often discussed in the Soviet
party press, though such discussion is by convention, it would
seem, always carefully restricted to what goes on at the lower
levels. In a recent article in *Pravda* a fairly senior central party
apparatus official, F. Petrenko, has argued the case for greater
initiative and responsibility of party members, and for greater

freedom of dissent.[8] Mr Petrenko's central theme is that 'collective' decisions should form the basis of all policy-making in all party organs – 'from the bureau of a primary party organisation up to the Central Committee'. He tells us nothing about the Central Committee, but is eloquent on practice in primary party organisations – not in the past, but today. 'If there are dozens, if not hundreds, of persons sitting in the hall, who have been summoned to discuss from every angle and then to decide some question on the agenda, and if one does all the talking, or at most several, and if those who talk are the same people who have prepared the meeting, and who have drafted both the report and the resolution, and who guide the discussion along a previously determined channel, then collective decision is evidently weakened.' Evidently. But it will require rather more than exhortations in the party press to evoke the kind of collective free discussion, leading to a genuine majority decision, which Mr Petrenko now considers desirable. Such discussion can be the product of many years, if not generations, of responsible, free and independent thought and speech in the party, of the kind which have been dead for at least forty-five years.

EFFECTS ON SUCCESSION

The second consequence of the suppression of dissent in the Soviet Union has been to complicate the problem of legitimate succession to the leadership of the dominant party. Free elections in party organs, at any rate at the higher levels, are, of course, something which has long ceased to exist. There can be no question of any legally recognised groupings of leaders who freely voice their opinions, and whose views are therefore known to their electors. All is intrigue, manipulation and adjustment at the highest level of the party, conducted under the cloak of perfect unanimity, which no longer convinces even Mr Petrenko. For, as he remarks, 'differences of opinion among communists are inevitable, since there exist differences of experience, of knowledge, of levels of culture, of capabilities and of psychology among all people'. Yet, if these natural differences of opinion cannot be openly expressed, owing to habit and convention, then how are party members to judge one leader as against another? And why, when one leader replaces another, and

[8] F. Petrenko, 'Kollektivnost' i otvetstvennost'', *Pravda*, 20 July 1966.

proceeds to criticise his predecessor and make new promises, should they believe him, when they have heard him in the past, with equal emphasis, support the policy of the fallen and now rejected leader?

The consequence is that the party leaders lack both legitimacy and moral authority, and are treated with apathy and indifference by those whom they are supposed to lead. The recent succession of Messrs Breshnev and Kosygin is a case in point. There is much to be said in favour of the new leaders. They certainly have a strong case against their predecessor in office, Khrushchev. There is a good deal to be said for their present policy of attempting to disentangle the confusion of party and government functions, and to restrict party interference in the technical sphere of administration which is of such vital importance in a modern, planned industrial state. Yet, since neither of them ever voiced any open criticism while Khrushchev was in power, but on the contrary fully supported him in public, they derive little benefit from the justice of their present claim to rule. Their assumption of power must necessarily appear to all in the party as an intrigue, with the aid of the security forces, to overthrow and oust a leader who once raised each of them to his position of power. And indeed such an intrigue it was. In Soviet conditions, where dissent is not tolerated, there is no other way in which a change of leadership can be effected.

EFFECTS ON THE PARTY'S VITALITY

The third result of trying to run a country without any tolerated dissent is that the institutions of the party or of government become debased, and atrophy. If a party committee is regularly manipulated over the years by its secretary in order to produce the predetermined unanimous result required by higher authority, then it is not going to retain much political muscle if the time comes when there is a genuine desire for change, and according to the Soviet party press such a time has now come. Then, naturally enough, it is very difficult to change a long-established habit. 'They say', laments Mr Petrenko, 'that the preparation of reports (*scilicet* at party organ meetings) in accordance with a predetermined pattern is "the usual practice". But one may well ask: by whom has this "usual practice" been established?' The answer is quite simple, though Mr

Petrenko does not supply it: by the generations of Petrenkos who by their conformity, their sycophancy and their continuing pretence that dissent does not exist in the party have reduced party meetings to the kind of farce which Mr Petrenko himself now deplores. There is no reason to doubt the genuineness of the present wish of the party authorities to see the development of more independent-minded, more self-reliant, in a word, more free party organs. But their desire cannot be achieved by ordering, exhorting or cajoling party members to behave less like automata and more like human beings. It will only come about as a result of conditions in which party members, and for that matter those outside the party too, feel free to voice their opinions without fear of reprisals, and without the suspicion that if they fall foul of the party secretary or other authority to whom they are subordinate, the consequences will be very unhealthy.

At present there are, in the jargon of the Soviet party, two forms of criticism: one is 'constructive, healthy criticism', which is ostensibly encouraged; the other is 'demagogy', which can entail serious consequences for a party member. The trouble is that there is no certain way of knowing which is which, at any particular moment, since not only are terms of so subjective a nature incapable of definition, but, as every party member knows from experience, their interpretation varies from time to time. If a party member should get into trouble with the authorities in his own party organisation, he can of course appeal up the scale to higher organisations, but he can never carry his appeal to any independent, judicial authority, which can be relied on to decide impartially, and not on the basis of party policy, since none such exists. If he should be expelled from the party, the effects on his career are bound to be disastrous. Nor can he with any degree of confidence expect to get justice outside the party in the courts of law, since the judges too are bound by party policy and are in practice very unlikely to challenge the party's ruling. Is it to be wondered at that the great majority of ordinary party members prefer, as Mr Petrenko points out, to remain prudently silent, and leave the running to the experienced party apparatus professionals who have a better chance of keeping out or trouble?

As should already have become evident from the foregoing paragraphs, there is yet a fourth consequence of the banning of

dissent and it is the worst: the difficulty which it has put in the
way of reform. This has been particularly evident in the Soviet
Union where the dead hand of Leninism, has proved a continuing obstacle to the development of conditions in which free
expression of opinion becomes the rule rather than the exception. Of course no one would deny that enormous changes
relating to freedom of expression have taken place – in literature,
in technical matters such as economic theory, in science, even
in party matters, though only at the lower levels. But the element
of uncertainty always remains as a limiting factor: the not
infrequent outbursts of arbitrary repression of opinion and
victimisation of individual critics act as a constant reminder that
to voice dissent still means to take one's fate into one's hands.
At the root of the whole Soviet system there lies the stubborn
fact that the party, and its executive organ the security police,
can, when need be, operate outside the law. This is every bit as
true of the other communist one-party states as of the Soviet
Union.

But in one country, Yugoslavia, the problem of the tolerance
of dissent has at any rate been discussed with greater freedom
and incisiveness than in any other. Indeed the whole role of the
party, as the sole authority for the enunciation of the truth, has
been questioned. As Professor Djordjević writes elsewhere in
this issue: 'The Communist League has not abdicated its right
and its responsibility to seek and eventually to proclaim the
truth. But from now on it publicly declares that truth is not a
matter to be enunciated *a priori*: the party has no particular
truth of its own. On the contrary, truth is born and takes shape
in the workers' councils, in men's deeds and creative activity,
in science, in free discussion and in critical analysis based on
practice.' Plainly such a view of the party entails recognition of
the right, indeed of the duty, to voice dissent, in the sense in
which it has been used throughout this essay in contrast to
opposition. The limits of permissible dissent are laid down in the
Yugoslav constitution adopted in 1963; and have recently been
further discussed by so eminent an authority as Mr Edvard
Kardelj.[9]

[9] Edvard Kardelj, 'Notes on Social Criticism in Yugoslavia', *Socialist Thought and
Practice*, No. 20, Belgrade, October–December 1965, pp. 3–61.

MR KARDELJ AND THE CONSTITUTION

The Yugoslav constitution of 1963 deals in some detail with the rights of citizens to express themselves freely in words or in print. These rights are 'guaranteed' under Article 40. But certain limitations on the rights are also imposed by this article: they may not be used 'to overthrow the foundations of the socialist democratic order determined by the Constitution, to endanger the peace, international cooperation on terms of equality, or the independence of the country, to disseminate national, racial or religious hatred or intolerance, or to incite to crime, or in any manner that offends public decency'. The scope of these quite extensive limitations 'shall be determined by federal law'. However, the constitution requires that all federal law should be consistent with the constitution; and Article 70 forbids the restriction 'by any act' of the rights and freedoms guaranteed by the constitution. This Article also requires that these rights and freedoms 'shall be provided judicial protection'. The overall protection of constitutionality is vested in constitutional courts (Article 74). The constitutional courts have the power to adjudicate on the question of the conformity of other laws with the constitution in order to ensure that the latter prevails. Moreover the constitutional courts are charged with the duty of safeguarding the basic rights and freedoms guaranteed by the constitution in cases when the other courts have failed to do so (Article 150). This would seem to open the constitutional courts to individuals who feel aggrieved by the failure of the ordinary courts to protect their constitutional rights. Fairly detailed provisions are laid down, so far as the Federal Supreme Court is concerned, to ensure the independence of its judges (Article 243). Of course the importance of constitution does not lie in what they say, but in the effect which they have on shaping the functioning of institutions and on government practice. The new Yugoslav constitution has not been in force for long enough for any fair assessment to be made of its overall practical effects. But a good constitution is always better than a bad one, and, when compared with the relevant provisions relating to freedom of expression are immeasurably more effective. Article 125 of the Soviet constitution provides that citizens are 'guaranteed by law' freedom of speech and press, 'in conformity with the interests of the working people, and in order to strengthen the socialist system'. It also states that these rights are 'ensured' by placing at the disposal 'of the working people and their organisations' the material requisites for the exercise of these rights. There is no provision for judicial enforcement of these rights and no effective limitation on the passing of laws inconsistent with these rights. There is no system of judicial review of any kind. The result has been that during the thirty years that have passed since the constitution was adopted there has been no known instance where the constitution has had any effect whatever in safeguarding freedom of expression; and no known case where the Soviet authorities have been inhibited by the constitution from infringing or controlling freedom of expression whenever they have thought it necessary.

The restrictions on the expression of dissent contained in Article 40 of the Yugoslav constitution are certainly in some respects extensive, but they are beyond question capable of objective judicial interpretation and definition. In some of their aspects (inciting to crime or offending against public decency) the limitations on freedom of speech are in substance no different from those which are to be found in some countries where there is a long tradition of civil freedom. On paper, at any rate, there is all the difference in the world between the Soviet limitation 'in conformity with the interests of the working people and in order to strengthen the socialist system', which leaves the door open, in the absence of any kind of judicial interpretation, to the most arbitrary and subjective interpretation by the party; and the Yugoslav Article 40. The words used in Article 40 – 'overthrow', 'endanger', 'disseminate', 'incite' – all suggest something rather more than the mere voicing of opinion. An English lawyer is immediately reminded of the difference, say, between an article on the merits of pacifism, which could never constitute a criminal offence; and 'inciting' a soldier not to fight, or to desert, which almost certainly would. Thus, in Yugoslavia, one can expect that the constitutional courts will in the fullness of time delimit the boundary between permissible voicing of balanced opinion, including, one must hope, dissenting opinion; and, say, the unrestrained and violent expression of criticism in circumstances which are likely to cause disloyalty or unrest. The words 'overthrow', 'endanger', or 'incite' are certainly not so wide in their meaning as to be capable (without

abuse of language) of applying to any kind of dissent from official
practice or government view of policy; and are moreover
precise enough to make it possible for the judges to give them a
limited and specific meaning – so long as the judges are independent, and so long as the citizen is allowed free access to the
courts. Only time can show whether the constitutional courts
will be fully allowed to perform their interpretative function.
The experience of the United States, for example, has shown that
the full translation of a written constitution into practice can be
a long and laborious process. Yugoslavia faces special problems
as a federal and multi-racial state. But she also has to consider
the tolerance of dissent in the light of two special circumstances
which arise from her history and from the ideology which
underlies the revolution which brought the present regime to
power: the need for time before any revolutionary regime can
feel that it has fully consolidated itself; and the fact that the
whole system of government is designed to secure a particular
type of social order, the virtues of which are regarded as
axiomatic.

These two matters figure very largely in Mr Kardelj's discussion of what he calls 'social criticism', a term which differs
little from what in the pages of this essay has been entitled
'dissent'. Mr Kardelj starts by rejecting the proposition that all
criticism should be tolerated. Society is not a debating club.
Although he does not say so in terms, Mr Kardelj would clearly
not accept the view of J. S. Mill that it is only out of the clash
of freely expressed opinions that the minimum of error in conduct is likely to result. For him, as a Marxist, society is founded
on a previously accepted pattern. Therefore criticism must be
adjudged good and permissible, or bad and repressible, by 'its
influence on the disposition and strength of those social factors
on which the progress of socialist relations hinges . . .' (p. 6).
This is in effect a restatement in other words of the essence of
Article 40 of the constitution. As examples of impermissible
criticism he gives the cases of those who advocate a return to the
Stalinist type of political system, or who oppose worker management and self-government and 'stress that the intelligentsia is
the "critical conscience of society" ' (p. 12). Yet a further example which he gives is the argument of those who, in criticising
bureaucracy, try to prove that 'bureaucracy is a subjective
human trait, and, on the basis of this conclusion, seek solutions

in formalism, in the replacement of individuals, in subjectivistic preaching etc.'. Such criticism, he says, 'actually disarms the social forces actively engaged in the struggle for socialism' because it prevents them from learning the truth. Mr Kardelj by way of a parallel, contrasts revolutionary criticism of capitalism, designed to destroy it, with Keynesian criticism, which is designed to preserve it (pp. 42–3). (He does not incidentally point out that capitalism in many countries has for some time quite successfully withstood every kind of criticism.) The translation of Mr Kardelj's article is not always very clear, and I may have misunderstood the force of his examples. But they would seem to go a good deal further in their restrictiveness than the language of Article 40 of the constitution warrants. Mr Kardelj draws no distinction between say, the critic who tries by his arguments to dissuade the workers from activity in workers' councils; and the academic critic who calmly and objectively discusses the question of the value of the councils. Nor does he appear to explain why any particular form of criticism of 'bureaucracy' should 'disarm' the social forces, provided that all other points of view are given similar right of expression. If, as Professor Djordjević says, there is no longer any *a priori* truth, how is truth to emerge, except through the conflict of arguments, in which the soundest argument prevails?

But whatever criteria one may seek to apply to dissent, the main question will always be: who decides what is and what is not permitted? On this question Mr Kardelj seems to be far from precise. He recognises that there can be no 'infallible arbiter' in such a matter, and praises the new constitution for its aim of 'consolidating a political order in which the possibility of subjective interpretation of the limits of democratic rights and freedoms is reduced to a minimum' (p. 56). What is more, he fully recognises the boundary between dissent and opposition, and suggests that it is only the latter which is destructive: 'Once social criticism ceases to represent the struggle for power, it becomes *only a form of the struggle of opinion among equals* (original emphasis). In that capacity, criticism will be constructive, persuasive, humane and democratic, although it will at the same time be unsparing and radical' (p. 45). Mr Kardelj also sees restriction on criticism as something which should become less severe as the regime becomes more consolidated: 'Yesterday,

when "to be or not to be" was still an undecided question for
our revolution, socialist forces had to use different weapons in
their struggle from those they use today, when the socialist
system has become incomparably more stabilised. In the future
again, with the growing stability of socialist and democratic
relations, this problem will become less and less severe, until
such social relations are established that it will be possible, as
Lenin put it symbolically, to have a speaker's rostrum on every
street corner' (pp. 54–5). The constitution of 1963 exists, presumably, for the purpose, among others, of defining the stage
which had been reached at that date in respect of the degree of
dissent which can now be tolerated. Now one would expect Mr
Kardelj to follow the provisions of the constitution, and leave
it to the judges to decide what is and what is not 'destructive'
criticism – or in other words, as Article 40 provides, criticism
which is used to 'overthrow' the social order.

'ADMINISTRATIVE MEASURES'

It comes as a shock to discover in a thoughtful and responsible
article such as this that its author seems to believe that dissent
should still be controlled by administrative and not by judicial
measures. The relevant passage contains such alarming under-
tones that it must be quoted at length: '. . . on the other hand,
criticism which is the expression of superseded relations and
backward social-political tendencies, or such criticism which
borrows methods from the arsenal of the class society, methods
which have the same character as administrative measures,
must in present conditions provoke the opposite reaction and
even the inevitability of administrative measures. In order that
criticism should become more and more free it is, therefore,
indispensable that it should become more and more responsible
towards truth and towards its socialist roots, especially where
the fundamental question of the existence and advancement of
socialist society are concerned. Blind, destructive criticism is no
less dangerous for socialist society than administrative intervention in the struggle of opinion' (p. 48). Now, if this passage
means what it appears to say (and the translation, as already
stated, is not always clear), it contains three assertions that seem
to be very far removed from the provisions of the constitution.
First that the mere expression of such things as 'backward political

tendencies' is not permissible; secondly that in some circumstances at any rate, the repression of criticism, or of the critics,
should be left to administrative measures; and thirdly, that
critics must, as it were, work their passage by becoming more
responsible towards 'truth and its socialist roots'. The effect of
all this would be very unfortunate in practice: it would substitute for the objective criteria laid down in the constitution
('destroy', 'incite', endanger') purely subjective criteria ('socialist roots', 'backward social political tendencies'); and would
entrust the decision as to the degree and kind of dissent that will
be tolerated to administrative organs and not to the judges. It
is very much to be hoped that Mr Kardelj does not really intend
this, and that the passage does not mean what on the face of it
it appears to mean.

It is of course always a temptation for all governments to
suppress the critics, as an alternative to modifying their own
conduct in response to criticism, where this proves to be well
founded. But so long as any government seeks to do so it will
have to maintain strict control over opinion in the form of a
security police – organs endowed with arbitrary powers, and
not subject to public control. Now it is an elementary fact that
to endow any body of men with secret, arbitrary powers which
are not subject to public control, whose actions are not exposed
to the light of day, is to ensure that they will abuse them. This
has nothing to do with Marxism, capitalism, liberalism, socialism or any other doctrine: it is a plain observable fact of political
life at all periods, and in all societies. Since Mr Kardelj's article
appeared, some alarming disclosures have been made in Yugoslavia of the activities of the secret security police in recent years.
The placing of microphones in the President's bedroom was
perhaps the most startling of their activities; but the undiscov-
ered and unpunished doing to death of some eight people by
them was by far the most shocking. This is what 'administrative
measures' mean in practice. It would indeed seem difficult in
the face of such evidence, to agree with Mr Kardelj that any
forms of unbridled criticism can be 'no less dangerous' than
administrative measures.

Except possibly for Yugoslavia, the communist one-party
states have still not broken out of the self-defeating system for the
arbitrary suppression of all dissenting opinions and criticism
which was imposed by Lenin on Russia in 1921. The Yugoslav

constitution of 1963, if it is in practice implemented, will be the first attempt to integrate dissent into the policy of a communist one-party state, while at the same time protecting society against those whose object is to overthrow the existing order. This constitution leaves the decision on the criteria which are to be applied to the judges, and entrusts them with the interpretation of the laws. No judge is infallible, but experience has shown that an independent judge can at least be impartial, just as experience has everywhere shown that the secret police of a ruling single political party will be corrupt, untrustworthy, venal, brutal, arbitrary, and in the end, more of a liability than an asset to those who employ them. If the judges are not independent then the main purpose will be defeated – and 'independent' means free from *all* pressure, direct or indirect, by the party. But given such independence, the judges can interpret Article 40 of the constitution, on the basis of the concrete cases which will arise, and determine clearly the limit between dissent of which the aim is the overthrow of the social order, or one of the other forbidden aims; and dissent which is the only natural and healthy safety valve in every sane society. But this result can only be achieved if public confidence is created that the limits laid down by the judges are not going to be manipulated by the party at will, with impunity, in order to suit its own ephemeral policy; or to pander to some real or imagined contingency on the international scene; or to please the spite or vanity of some top leader. For only then will the ordinary citizen learn that discussion and criticism are not alone a privilege but a duty; and only then will there become evident in a communist one-party state the kind of constructive social criticism which Mr Kardelj seeks to encourage; and not the cautious avoidance of all real participation in public affairs which so shocks Mr Petrenko.

Jovan Djordjević

Political Power in Yugoslavia*

THE INSTITUTIONAL PROCESS IS ESSENTIALLY AN outcome and a reflection of political action. It is therefore understandable that political institutions have always interested not only political thinkers and politicians, but also those nations and groups which are struggling to set up, reorganise or abolish any given political institutions.

Their importance lies, too, in the fact that they reflect fundamental political aspirations and relationships. They are more or less the true image of a political system and of the structure of a society at a given epoch. But when seen in a more general perspective, institutions are merely the framework of power. The complexity of and problems inherent in society, its permanent need for further material, cultural and political development have led to an expansion of the institutional structure of political society. This expansion is brought about by political organisations, especially by political parties, as well as by other organisations, such as trade unions, citizens' associations, pressure groups, etc.

THE PROBLEM OF INSTITUTIONALISATION

Lenin thought that he had at last found in 'the power of the Soviets' and in the 'Republic of Soviets' the formula for the social and direct constitution of political society which would be tantamount to the promotion of the working class to a status of hegemony. But because of deterministic historical causes, which were the inevitable legacy of past centuries, Lenin himself had to start, in his lifetime, yet another institutionalisation. Further-

* These are edited extracts from a paper on 'The Anatomy of Political Institutions in a Society in Transition', presented by Professor Djordjević at the *Futuribles* conference in Paris, 1965. It also appears in *Government and Opposition*, Vol. 2, No. 2, January–April 1967.

more, he consolidated the institutions of the new power by drawing on the technical and institutional heritage of the past. Later, Stalinism represented, in this respect, a total swallowing-up of the political organisation of the state. The state identified itself with the macro-structures, such as the central organs of power and, in particular, with the executive ones and the party, especially with its central ruling apparatus. Since then the development of socialism as a world-wide phenomenon has taken place almost entirely on the political plane and within the general framework established by the macro-political organisations.

The political history of the socialist countries has followed its course – and continues to do so – within an elementary and primitive system of political institutions. From the start, this was shown by the explicit structure of power set out in the various constitutions. The Stalin constitution of 1936, which served as a politico-organisational model for most of the socialist countries, is an elementary one: it is simpler than the constitutions which preceded it (the RSFSR constitution of 1918 and the USSR constitution of 1924). This model is based on the following principles:

(a) explicit concentration of political power in the representative bodies, and in the executive power in theory (but not 'in fact');

(b) centralisation of power, of the material means of action and of the more important decisions, in the organisational mechanism of the federal power;

(c) a concept and structure of power and of the ruling of society by the state that are essentially political, traditional and Jacobin.

This process of streamlining and of politisation of the organisational structure of power and government can be summed up in the Soviet formula of the exercise of power by 'government and party', conceived as the fundamental ruling organs of state and society and exemplifying the theory of the 'dual and unified power'. This is based on the principle of so-called political rule. Khrushchev laid particular stress on this principle in his criticism of Stalin's personal power. Yet the desire to bring about – and the necessity of bringing about – personal rule was one of the causes of Khrushchev's own downfall. In fact, the formula of 'collective rule' is only one of the forms of concentrated political power. It is not a form of democratisation or institutionalisation. Its essential aim is to distribute the various sectors of decision among several individuals, who, however, must neither be too numerous nor allow their power of decision to 'go downwards'. Fundamental political decisions are taken at restricted meetings of the holders of central power or by agreement between them. But this does not exclude the effective exercise of power by one individual. On the contrary, his 'right to arbitrate', or even to take decisive action, is implied from the outset. Collective rule of this type, which in theory tends to prevent or to limit personal power and 'the cult of personality' does not prevent, either organisationally or politically, the increase of the power of one individual on the basis of the 'cult of personality'. A proof of this is the establishment of Stalin's own personal power, although he, too, had begun by observing the forms of collective rule.

Long before the October Revolution, before the appearance of this type of political power, clear-sighted socialist and Marxist writers had perceived the danger. Rosa Luxemburg (and Trotsky) on several occasions between 1905 and 1910 asserted that the general concept of a centralised, monolithic and ruling party would lead inevitably to a total deformation of the dictatorship of the proletariat, Instead, there would be the dictatorship of the party, which would in turn be replaced by the dictatorship of the central committee, until the moment in which power finally fell into the hands of a dictator.[1]

The contradictions in modern society, which is and will always remain political and dominated by power and politics, cannot countenance for long an historical situation of this type. Modern society tends to set up a more complex organisation of power, more decentralised and more stable. This was as true of Stalinist society as it is of any other type. Therefore, practical attempts to de-Stalinise have not only taken the form of 'collective rule', but have also, and above all, implied the recognition of the existence and function of institutions other than the party and the government and, in particular, of parliament, courts of justice, local self-government and other more or less autonomous and self-managed social, economic and cultural institutions.

[1] Rosa Luxemburg: *The Russian Revolution*, 1946.

All this shows that the institutionalisation of political power is, at present, the main and even historical problem of the socialist state and society. It is not confined to admitting the necessity and importance of classical, political institutions – parliament, governments, courts of justice, party organisations, etc. It also embraces the problem of the nature and structure, of the status and activities, of the social functions of these institutions, of their inter-relationships, etc. But the problem of paramount importance is that of the political system, or of what is called in different terminology, the macro-structure of political society. The political system is based not only on its principles; it is based especially on the way in which the 'rules of the game', compulsory for all, are observed by all, regardless of whether or not these rules are defined by the constitution and its laws.

THE PERSONAL POWER

Every power tends, by virtue of its nature, to be effective and active and, at the same time, in each of these organisations of power, one or more centres of monopolisation or of prevalent activity tend to appear (if by 'active power' one means the capacity to initiate and take fundamental decisions and to control the execution of decisions). In the complexities of social reality, no power is capable of being totally active, and this is why power tends to fall back upon itself, to concentrate and 'centralise' itself. From this it follows, sociologically speaking, that every power is 'oligarchic'.

Bureaucracy, administration and the police are the classical conveyors, ever and always present, of an active power of this kind. However, it is in what are generally called the 'organised political systems', more and more rooted in the state economy and planning, in which the state plays the leading role in social activities and political processes, that the political party takes on a quite special significance in the 'anatomy' and 'physiology' of this kind of power. It is the organic fusion between the party organisation and the exercise of power so as to render power more active, which brings about the transformation of contemporary political processes. The domination of political power by the party is one of the characteristic phenomena in the post-revolutionay period, not only in socialist countries, but also in the 'non-aligned' states and in a whole series of older

states, including the parliamentary democracies. This phenomenon acts against the objectivisation and institutionalisation
(democratisation) of power. At the same time, it introduces a
new element into the expansion of power and activation, and
provides new means for the handling of the masses. This leads
ultimately to the personalisation of the centre of supreme
power.

The problem of what is usually called the personalisation of
power is, at present, an essentially new one, corresponding to
the new social structures and to the new phenomenon of 'active
power'. Before the 19th century, and even later in some countries, personal power was to be found in two different forms. The
first, the traditional one, was the power that Max Weber called
charismatic; that is, power founded on the personal position,
the personal magic of an individual, the 'natural' or selected
leader. The second is personal power that has cut itself off from
society and has become independent of society, under the
influence of personal relationships and deficiencies in society.

In the course of analysing the contemporary phenomenon of
the dictator, the 'heaven-sent leader', the 'chief' or 'guide' of
the nation or class, one must first of all adopt a critical attitude
towards the two moral and ideological orientations that are
important in the problem of personal power.

Both these orientations, although opposed from an ideological point of view, are equally the product of abstract rational-
ism. But, whereas one of them is romantically optimistic, the
other is romantically or rather traditionally pessimistic and
fatalistic. The first is founded on the belief in the absolute power
of the industrial revolution, the power of machinery, technique
and science. One can, no doubt, find it set out in the doctrines
of Saint-Simon and Max Weber, but also in the various
theories of technocratic mythology. According to the authors
of these theories, industrialisation and technique will give birth
to a new force that will render politics and politicians superfluous: – the management of social affairs will pass into the hands
of the technicians, the scientists, the 'managers' and other
rulers of a new kind, who will be concerned with the administration of machinery, rather than with the government of men,
with efficiency, administration and 'service', but not with
power.

Bukharin and other 'left-wing communists' asserted in the

years immediately after the 1917 October Revolution, that this era had already dawned, that the administration of things would replace the government of men, and that technique and the science of management would render political science and public and constitutional law [2] obsolete and superfluous. It is not only the true history of his own country, but that of all other social systems and countries, that has given the lie to this naïve analysis. Reality revealed not only the presence, but also the monstrous increase of power (including personal power) of domination and manipulation, of all that makes for 'politics' in the strictest and most negative sense of the word. Contrary to expectation, politics and political institutions have become – and are called upon to become more and more in the future of nations – far more decisive factors than are economics, technique and science. These cannot in fact – and it would, by the way, be dangerous if they could – become independent new hegemonies. Moreover, they tend to become ever more entangled in the web of power and politics.

Thus, one of the most important problems of contemporary society, and more particularly of an evolutionary industrial society lies in seeking the means and force to limit and overcome personal power. More than ever before are the conditions present which make possible the establishment of such power. This is so because of the monopolisation and technicalisation of relationships that allow the forces of domination to conquer immense power, which is capable of becoming an all but limitless force of domination over the individual citizens and the masses.

This problem has been solved in different countries by different, sometimes even antagonistic methods. In fact, it is quite certain that no one has an infallible recipe for solving it, and that choice between different forms of the institutionalisation of political society is, in socialist countries as elsewhere, not only possible, but inevitable.

THE YUGOSLAV 'DE-CENTRALISATION'

The socio-political and constitutional development of Yugoslavia is, from this point of view, characteristic.

In Yugoslavia, after the war of liberation, and up to quite

[2] N. Bukharin, *Le Matérialisme historique*, Paris, 1932.

recently, but decreasingly, the organisation of power has shown the characteristic features of post-revolutionary political systems, as described above. The executive organs (government and central or local administration) concentrated in their hands very considerable power, which also included a very strong party. They then became the executive organs of the party. At the summit, there was 'personal union' between the government and the supreme party forums (Politbureau and Central Committee). In the lower echelons, the local party organisations controlled local power, and in fact also ruled. This political formula of power ran the risk of becoming a system which would bring about the formation of a privileged and alienated ruling group. This political danger was to be seen in Soviet Russia immediately after the revolution. Stalinist policy tended to transform this particular situation into a 'system'. which permanently jeopardised men's freedom and lives. In Yugoslavia, it was detected earlier and more clearly, partly because Stalin had put that country in a situation in which it had to fight for its independence and its own free development. Resistance to external hegemony demanded the modification of internal hegemony since the struggle for one's freedom can never be confined to international relationships alone.

That was why, as early as 1949–50, a process of gradual transformation of 'public power' was begun in Yugoslavia. The initial measure, and the most modest one, consisted in what it has become usual to call decentralisation. This meant in fact the decrease in the functions of power held by the central state organs, as well as the transfer of these functions to the federal (or public) bodies which make up the Yugoslav Federation, and to the local organs of power which simultaneously acquire autonomy or self-government. In this way, 'decentralisation' succeeded in limiting centralism and political and administrative hierarchy, not only in the organisation and functioning of power, but also within the party system and the other social organisations.

Decentralisation, however, cannot alone modify the character of executive power. Another process had the effect of achieving the qualitative transformation of power. This process was *sui generis*: the reduction of the power of the state itself. In addition to the transfer of the functions of power from the higher to the lower organs, which were, nevertheless still state organs, new organs, partly state and partly social, called 'councils' were formed. These councils, at the very beginning of the decentralisation, were organs in which representatives of the various autonomous public institutions participated. In a certain measure, they replaced the state administration in the field of management of the social service, health, social insurance, education, culture, science and so on. But here too what occurred, at the beginning, was merely a kind of horizontal decentralisation: functions which formerly were state functions were transferred to state organs, or to partly state and partly social organs, which in many ways remained under the control of the state mechanism. Very soon, however, decentralisation as an objective process led to the beginning of the transformation of the classical or political state.

THE SOCIAL AND POLITICAL EFFECTS OF SELF-MANAGEMENT

To begin with, what came about was a form of participation. Organs elected and controlled by the workers and the manager, who held a kind of power of attorney from the state, shared in the management. But, very soon, workers' self-management became a unitary whole that included the manager himself, and then became an organ in which the nomination and activities were subordinated to the workers' decision, or to be more exact, to that of the workers' councils.

Since 1950, because workers' self-management was originally only established in economic concerns, workers' self-management has increasingly become social self-management, and is now the characteristic feature as well as one of the social and political driving-forces, of the Yugoslav 'system'. Self-management is the basic principle of the autonomy of labour organisations and of their autonomous power of decision.

Social self-management is, historically speaking, a new institution that is in a sense tantamount to the de-institutionalisation of social relationships. But it is also, as a political institution, an application to politics of the ideas relating to 'industrial democracy' and to 'workers' councils'. The end of personal government in economic and social activities did not mark the beginning of the democratisation of the spheres in which

autocracy and oligarchy had taken refuge: it provided a basis for
the transformation of the macro-institutions, and, consequently,
for the process of reconstruction of power and decision. A new
democracy, at the same time political and socio-economic,
direct and self-managed, could only be created and grow, above
all in a socialist society, on this kind of foundation. In other
words, it was based on the transformation of the fundamental
relationships between men, in the course of the process of production and distribution of the social product.

It is this democratisation which has not yet entirely become a
system, that has characterised the evolution of Yugoslavia since
the adoption of the second constitution, in fact from the application of the first constitutional law of 1953, and up to the passing
of the third, the constitution of the YFSR of 7 April 1963.

At the present stage of Yugoslavia's development, the political
organisation of the country is founded, according to the terms
of the 1963 constitution, upon the three following political
principles, which are relatively new or at least conceived in a
novel way:

(1) social self-management, which is a manifestation of the
     activation and socialisation of sovereignty and the system
     of popular power;
(2) federalism, conceived of not only as a guarantee of the
     equality of rights of the Yugoslav nation within the
     general framework of the common federal state, but also
     as the form taken by a socio-political collectivity consti-
     tuted 'from the bottom upwards' by the integration of
     functional and territorial self-managed wokers' organisa-
     tions, communal and self-governed;
(3) constitutionalism, both in the classical democratic sense,
     as a legal objective which is compulsory for all; and in
     the general sense of the forces by means of which power
     is limited by autonomous centres of decision that should
     provide an effective check both to the 'tyranny of a
     minority', and to the 'tyranny of the majority'.

Such a socio-political system doubtless required the revitalisation of parliament, but it also needed new forms in the organisation of power, from the federal down to local communities. In
conformity with the logic of the system and in order to prevent
alienation, monopolisation and personalisation of power, the

statutes, functions and the very structure of the representative assemblies were modified.

Acting, to start with, upon the principles of 'government assembly', the Yugoslav assemblies appeared as legislative bodies; but they were also fundamental political institutions taking political decisions. The assembly itself nominated its executive power, now undergoing a change in nature, functions and structure. The conception of a government holding both executive and administrative power has therefore long been abandoned in Yugoslavia.

Executive power from now on is divided into what is usually called the executive political function on the one hand, and the administrative function, on the other. The first is entrusted to a permanent political committee of the Federal Assembly, called the Executive Council. This is the executive organ of the Assembly, which also constantly controls the activities of administrative organs and of the administration itself. The Executive Council is elected by the Assembly and its members. The Assembly can revoke its authority completely or in part, before its four-year mandate has expired.

This is the most interesting reorganisation which has taken place in Yugoslavia in the field of political institutions, more especially in those relating to parliament and the executive power. The essential reason for this reorganisation is the attempt to broaden the scope of political participation and to find a more immediate social basis for institutions and political power. Social ownership of the means of production and management, the consciousness of there being no possibility of either progress or socialism without free initiative and without collective and individual freedom, are the general conditions which have favoured the structural changes and made them possible. But behind all this there lies a very clear political motive: the transfer of leadership and decision-making in government and management to the organs closest to the citizens which are not as liable as the executive organs to turn their activities into a permanent monopoly. This goes together with the effort to 'deprofessionalise' power and politics, so that they should become the prerogatives of assemblies of men who only become 'legislators' or 'politicians' because they are engaged in creative and productive work in society.

The stand against political professionalism led in Yugoslavia to the adoption of the principle of rotation of the holders of public office. The representative assemblies are permanent working organs, but are subject to a renewal of half their members every two years. Moreover, no holder of a public office of any importance is elected for more than four years. Re-election, very broadly applied in nearly all the institutions and public offices, is drastically limited to only one new term of office lasting for four years with respect to members of the government and of the executive organs, and applies also to the high dignitaries of the state.

So far as the judiciary is concerned, the constitutional courts (whose members are elected by the Assembly for a period of eight years) have the power to interpret the constitution, to abrogate laws and other regulations, including federal ones, that might jeopardise any constitutional principle or any right or freedom guaranteed by the constitution. Constitutional jurisdiction is one of the factors that ensure the constitutionality of a political system. This is conceived, in Yugoslavia, as a counterbalance to despotism, to any tendency towards absolutism on the part of any holder of power, not excepting the Federal Assembly or the assemblies of the Federal Republics, the supreme organs of power and of administration.

SOCIALISM AND DEMOCRACY

This relatively short and as yet unfinished story of the constitutionalism and political institutionalism that has just been set down in broad outline is more particularly relevant to the political organisation of a society taking the road to socialism.

The organic solidarity that binds together socialism and democracy is, at present, almost a commonplace of the theory and political programme of socialism. But it is also a fact that, because of historical or other circumstances and also, up to a point, because of the dogmatisation of socialism itself, the building of the social and political system of a socialist society began with the use of some of the elements of totalitarianism, so that it later became enmeshed in the web and contradictions of the latter. Totalitarianism (even in the form of the 'dictatorship of the proletariat') is no longer a possible concept for the defence of socialism. It can no longer be tolerated under the pretext that it is 'defending socialism', as it was in the past under Stalin. On the contrary, the fundamental problem of politics at present, and also of socialism in its own capacity, consists in detecting and eliminating the sources of totalitarianism and in discovering the bases and forms suitable for the establishment of a socialist democracy.

A purely political or purely parliamentary regime, containing the inevitable executive power in the capacity of an acting and ruling political institution, could in no case serve as a model for the contemporary political system of socialism. A purely political arrangement, founded on individualistic representative democracy would be simply, in the general condition of present-day socialist countries, a form of the establishment of a bureau-cratised political power. The political validation of the worker and his labour organisations, and those of the productive and working forces of society, are the prerequisites of the political structure of such a society.

THE NECESSARY TRANSFORMATION OF THE PARTY

Moreover – and the Yugoslav example offers abundant proof of this – the political system of a contemporary society, developing in the conditions of socialism, cannot be primitive, as is the liberal, negative state, nor can it be founded on the principles of 'reason and efficiency, pure and simple' as the advocates of the bureaucratic and technocratic plans and doctrines, both inside and outside socialist society, recommend. This system must contain numerous and diversified institutions, sometimes original ones. 'Pure politics' is no longer able to cope with the complexity and dynamism of the economic, social and cultural relationships and tendencies in society and man.

But these new factors of contemporary society cannot be found outside the political process. It follows from this that the problem of the transformation of the party, in particular if political pluralism is to be avoided, remains an open question and, in a sense, a decisive one, for the revitalisation of political institutions and the introduction of new forms of democracy.

The party is no longer subject to fetishes in socialist countries, or at least not so much as it was some ten years ago. It is no longer 'taboo' as a subject for scientific discussion or public debate. The problem of its nature and functions in the new conditions is, in fact, being objectively scrutinised in nearly all socialist countries, even if (apart from the cases of Yugoslavia and the Italian Communist Party) it has not been analysed critically and, what is more important, has not been effectively dealt with. Khrushchev was aware of this problem: he attempted to find a solution for it, primarily by means of limited 'debureaucratisation' and the political deprofessionalisation of the ruling party instances by introducing into them economic experts and elements of some kind of technocracy. But in Yugoslavia, the problem has been tackled for more than a decade. It is gradually being solved by a process of searching for new forms and relationships, and by firmly rejecting old ones; it is being solved by the effort put into the transformation of the party, by turning it from the ruling organisation in society which it has been, into a socio-political organisation that will become part of this same society, and its constitutional system and which will be its internal force, although subordinated to society. By a change in name, by becoming the 'Communist League', this political organ has not entirely ceased to be a political party (nor has it ceased to be a political party with regard to doctrine – that is according to the idea it has of itself, and in certain practical instances in its effective behaviour). But if one considers its standpoint and its policy, one sees that the party is no longer a mediator between the people and the system of power and administration. Without from now on wanting to take part in all social activities, without claiming to know all the answers to all the questions which are pending, it is trying to be a political force of general guidance. It is no longer an instrument of power, but, on the contrary, an expression of conscience. The Communist League has not abdicated its right and its responsibility to seek and eventually to proclaim the truth. But from now on, it publicly declares that truth is not to be enunciated *a priori*: the party has no particular truth of its own; on the contrary, truth is born and takes shape in the workers' councils, in men's deeds and creative activity, in science, in free discussion and in critical analysis based on practice.

But this transformation of the function and of the ideology of political organisation cannot be taken for granted; it is not automatic. It demands not only that the principles and organisation we have just mentioned be applied, but also that the forces of conscience, knowledge, autonomy and democratic action, that are the sole effective carriers of political activity of the socialisation of politics and power, be created and reinforced. At a given stage in the development of material, cultural and spiritual unity, these forces alone are capable of showing that the first dimension of society is the political one and that the mediation of the state or of political organisations should thus alone be taken into consideration.

This brings us to the new complexity of political life in contemporary society, and of the structure of society. Contemporary society is in no way reduced – and should not be reduced – to 'macro-structures'; it must include 'micro-organisms'. It should at the same time contain a complex institutionalisation and *deinstitutionalisation*. It must of course have its historical meaning, but also leave a place for the meaning that man's life will have and, more generally speaking, for what is called everyday life, which is the whole of human relationships. Sociological and psychological research, carried out in Yugoslavia, in Poland, and even in the USSR, shows that at least up to now, socialist society has been essentially constructed, just as were other societies, by means of all-embracing political institutions. In the meantime, man's every day life remained as it had been before, imbued with conservatism and futility and, as it would seem, depolitised, full of apathy and mean egoism and of the fears inevitably bred by isolation and the feeling of being forsaken. It was this division between institutions and everyday life, to be more exact between living practice and the mutual relationships of millions and millions of 'ordinary men', that was at the root of alienation and of the degradation of political institutions themselves.

H. Gordon Skilling

Background to the Study of Opposition in Communist Eastern Europe[*]

TO DISCUSS 'OPPOSITION' IN A ONE-PARTY SYSTEM, and in particular in a communist one, might seem on first thought to involve a contradiction in terms. Communist governments have normally been regarded in the West as systems without opposition except in the form of illegal resistance by sections of the population to the regimes themselves. Yet Leonard Schapiro, in his foreword to the first issue of the journal, *Government and Opposition*, expressed the view that both government and opposition are always and at all times present (or potentially present) in every political order and referred to 'the tentative process of loyal dissent' becoming apparent in one-party states.[1] A striking feature of many of the communist states since the death of Stalin has in fact been the emergence of political tendencies that can only be called 'oppositional', in the form either of resisting policies enacted or offered by the ruling party, or of proposing alternative courses of action. The observation of these tendencies by Western scholars, and the analysis of the experience of non-communist states in Africa and Asia, have led to a re-examination of the nature of one-party states in general, and to the recognition that not only has opposition never been totally absent from communist systems, but that it has assumed more vigorous and varied forms in recent years.[2]

[1] Vol. 1, No. 1, October 1965, pp. 1, 3.
[2] See in particular the special issue, 'The Dead End of the Monolithic Parties', *Government and Opposition*, Vol. 2, No. 2, Jan.–Apr. 1967, pp. 165–80 (pp. 15–32 above) and ensuing articles in the same issue. See also two earlier articles by Jerzy J.

* This article (published in *Government and Opposition*, Vol. 3, No. 3, Summer 1968), written before the latest developments in Czechoslovakia is reprinted here by permission of Yale University Press.

Although the process of opposition may be regarded then as a universal one, characteristic of all political systems, its importance, and the forms which it takes, vary widely from country to country, and from period to period. As Robert Dahl's earlier volume has clearly demonstrated, even in Western democracies, where opposition is an integral and legitimate part of the political system, the patterns differ fundamentally.[3] In their treatment of opposition the contributors to that book concentrated attention almost exclusively on the legal and formal types of opposition manifested primarily in competing political parties and in parliamentary and electoral procedures.[4] Yet as the editor admitted, political opposition of this orderly and peaceful kind is a rare phenomenon in historical experience, and governments have traditionally sought to suppress or contain opposition.[5] Although in Western democracies opposition normally enjoys constitutional sanction and assumes institutional forms, probably in no country is it exclusively institutionalised and based on constitutional foundations. In non-democratic countries, opposition has normally been forced to assume a variety of non-legal or illegal forms and to express itself in other than a formal and institutional manner.

COMMUNIST THEORY AND PRACTICE

Not surprisingly, the nature of opposition and the forms of its expression in Eastern Europe have been profoundly affected by the character of communist politics and have assumed peculiar and unusual forms. The crucial difference between the communist and the democratic regimes has been the absence of an institutionalised opposition expressed and guaranteed in constitutional principles or in political custom.[6] In particular, this is

---

Wiatr and Adam Przeworski, 'Control without Opposition', ibid., Vol. 1, No. 2, January 1966, pp. 227–39, and Ghiţa Ionescu, 'Control and Contestation in some One-Party States', ibid., pp. 240–50. In a fuller study, *The Politics of the European Communist States* (London, 1967), Ghiţa Ionescu modified some of the concepts and definitions quoted here. Cf. D. J. R. Scott, 'Resistance and Opposition', *Survey*, No. 64, July 1967, pp. 34–44.

[3] Robert A. Dahl (ed.), *Political Opposition in Western Democracies*, New Haven and London, 1966, p. 332.

[4] Ibid., passim.   [5] Ibid., pp. xi–xii, xiv.

[6] Ionescu uses the term 'political opposition' to refer to opposition that is 'institutionalised, recognised and legitimate'. In this sense, communist states are, in his view, 'oppositionless'. Nonetheless, there exists 'opposition' in a broader sense,

manifested in the absence of two or more major and competing
parties, and in the limited degree of economic, social, cultural
and political pluralism. The ruling communist party possesses
a monopoly of political activity, and asserts a monolithic unit
within itself. Even in the more relaxed period since Stalin,
opposition to the ruling party as such, either from within or
from outside, has been strictly excluded. The notion of a multi-
party system is rejected, and factions or organised groupings
within the party are banned. There is, therefore, really no opposition in the sense common in Western democracies, i.e. in the
form of opposition parties, and the expression of opposition
policies or platforms. Yet as we shall see, opposition does exist,
although in forms unlike those identified by the students of
democratic systems.

Communist theory and practice have traditionally denied
the legitimacy of any form of opposition. The doctrine of the
proletarian dictatorship, as developed by Lenin and Stalin,
conferred on the so-called party of the working class the exclusive authority to exercise leadership and denied to other parties
the right to share this power or to counteract it. At the same time
the principle of democratic centralism assigned supreme authority to the top party leaders and required disciplined obedience
by all lower officers and members. As interpreted and applied
by Lenin, these theories led to the banning, not only of 'opposition' in the form of organised groups seeking to replace those
in power, but also 'dissent' in the form of criticism of policies
adopted or proposed by these leaders.[7] Carried to its extreme
conclusion by Stalin, this strategy led eventually to the complete
elimination of opposition in almost every form.[8] At the most,
passive resistance or revolutionary conspiracy remained as the
only vestiges of opposition. In Eastern Europe this practice was

---

signifying 'any concerted attitude or action, spontaneous or deliberate, sporadic
or continuous, of anomic or associational groups under any circumstances or by
any means'. (*The Politics of the European Communist States*, pp. 2–3.)

[7] See Leonard Schapiro, ' "Putting the Lid on Leninism", Opposition and Dis-
sent in the Communist One-Party States', pp. 34 ff. above. See the fuller treatment
in his book, *The Origin of the Communist Autocracy. Political Opposition in the Soviet
State. First Phase, 1917–1922*. London, Cambridge, 1955. See also Frederick C.
Barghoorn, 'Soviet Political Doctrine and the Problem of Opposition', *Bucknell
Review*, XII, 2, May 1964, pp. 1–29.

[8] See Robert V. Daniels, *The Conscience of the Revolution, Communist Opposition in
Soviet Russia*, Cambridge, 1960.

introduced in its full form after 1948, when communist power was everywhere fully established and the people's democracies were identified as forms of the proletarian dictatorship. Any opposition, inside or outside the party, was regarded as disloyal and impermissible.

In the fifteen years since Stalin's death there have, however, been striking changes in the role of opposition in Eastern Europe. Paradoxically, in no country of the area has there been any fundamental doctrinal change in the attitude of the regime towards opposition as such. Even in Yugoslavia, where the position and the role of the party have been significantly modified, the idea of a multi-party system, or of an opposition party, has been explicitly rejected.[9] In none of the countries is genuine opposition inside the ruling party permitted.[10] In Yugoslavia the party's internal structure has been amended and widespread debate often occurs, but dissidence on basic issues among party members is not tolerated. Not surprisingly, revolutionary or conspiratorial opposition of any kind is everywhere strictly curbed by law and by force. Even peaceful advocacy of basic opposition to the regime and its policies is, however, not tolerated and can express itself usually only through subterranean channels. Despite these restrictions, dissent has been expressed in diverse forms and, in varying degrees, has been encouraged or tolerated by the regimes.

TYPES OF OPPOSITION

We may distinguish four types of opposition which are characteristic of, although not necessarily peculiar to, the communist systems of Eastern Europe. In the first place, there may be opposition to the system itself, what we may call 'integral opposition'.[11] This will involve overt or covert disloyalty, and if

[9] M. Mihajlov, lecturer at the University of Split, was imprisoned in 1966 and again in 1967 for criticising the one-party system and seeking to establish an opposition journal. Cf. the rejection of the idea of an opposition party by a Czech theorist, V. Mejstřik, 'The Concept and Practice of Party Democracy', *Nová mysl*, XX, 8, 19 April 1966, pp. 29–31.

[10] In Hungary, for instance, the existence of 'separate platforms' or 'factions' within the party was explicitly rejected by the party daily newspaper, *Nepszabadsag*, 16 May 1963. Cf. the views of the Czech leader, J. Hendrych (*Rudé právo*, 10 February 1967), that there can be 'different opinions on different problems', but not 'representatives of different ideologies'.

[11] This is close to what Robert Dahl refers to as revolutionary 'structural opposition'. See *Political Oppositions in Western Democracies*, p. 342. It is not unlike what

expressed in action, may take such forms as revolutionary conspiracies designed to seize power and overthrow the existing regime, or lesser forms of resistance such as underground activity, sabotage, or political emigration. This kind of anti-system opposition will normally be carried on by anti-communist forces, who may owe allegiance to a democratic faith or to conservative or extreme nationalist beliefs, but may in certain cases be the work of dissident communists or even rival communist parties functioning illegally. It may also manifest itself more inchoately in alienation from the established order and in emotional or intellectual resistance to it, as for instance in a-political attitudes of a part of the youth, 'underground' creations of writers or painters, or the hostility of a national or regional sub-culture. In the case of the churches, it may involve not so much active resistance as a passive rejection of communist doctrine and the acceptance or propagation of an alternative faith.

In the second place, there may be opposition to the leaders in power, normally by rivals for the topmost positions, sometimes by partners sharing power with those whom they seek to oust. Paradoxically, the 'opposition' may hold high rank in the power structure, as for instance, a Prime Minister, such as Yugov, in Bulgaria, or a First Secretary, such as Rakosi, in Hungary.[12] This *factional opposition*, as we shall call it, is carried on by individuals or groups within the highest organs of party and government, although support may be sought in broader social and political groupings. Such opposition, although by definition equated with disloyalty to other leaders, does not represent opposition to the communist system as such, and does not always involve even basic differences of view concerning public policies. Normally, however, it will embody a fundamental ideological rift, say, between 'nationalist' and 'prole-

---

Brzezinski and Huntington call 'alienation' or 'unorthodox dissent'. See *Political Power: USA/USSR*, New York, 1964, pp. 114, 105, resp. Barghoorn, in his chapter in this volume, uses the term 'subversive'. Cf. the term 'contestation' employed by Ionescu, 'Control and Contestation', *Government and Opposition*, Vol. 1, No. 2, pp. 240 ff. This was defined as 'the anti-system, basic and permanent postulates of any opposition on the grounds of fundamental dichotomic differences of opinion and ideologies'. In his book, cited above, he has abandoned this term and employs the word 'dissent', which, he argues, is not always against the government or the holders of power (op. cit., pp. 169, 178).

[12] Yugov was described by one of his critics in 1962 as being the only Premier who was in opposition to his own government.

tarian internationalist', 'liberal' and 'conservative', or 'leftist' and 'rightist' viewpoints.

In the third place, there may be opposition to, or severe criticism of, a whole series of the key policies of the regime, based on crucial differences in standards of value, without, however, a rejection of the communist system itself. This kind of *'fundamental opposition'* may be, and often is, linked with the factional antagonisms among the topmost leaders just referred to. It may also, however, take the form of resistance on the part of key interest groups within or outside the party, and may seek not to displace the leaders, but rather to resist, or to influence, the policies pursued by them. As we shall note more fully later, the major occupational groups, e.g. party *apparatchiki*, state bureaucrats and police, or writers, lawyers, and economists, may divide into opinion groups, defending or opposing as the case may be, 'hard' or 'soft', 'conservative' or 'reformist', policies. In some cases a powerful ruling group, such as the state administrators, or even the *apparatchiki*, may be subject to severe criticism by other governing elements. Such opposition may express the discontent of key nationality groups, such as the Slovaks in Czechoslovakia, or the Croats or Slovenes in Yugoslavia, who desire an improved position with the system. Although intra-party opposition of this kind does not necessarily challenge either the system, or its leaders, it may verge on opposition of the integral type if it is intense enough and embraces a wide range of policy questions.

Finally, there may be opposition to specific policies, without a rejection of the regime, or its leaders, or its basic policies in general. Such *'specific opposition'* or 'dissent' may be relatively orthodox in its general attitude, but may be quite unorthodox in its particular recommendations.[13] This opposition is normally

[13] Barghoorn uses the term 'segmental' opposition. This is comparable to Alec Nove's 'dissent within consensus', p. 27 above. Cf. the term 'orthodox dissent', in Brzezinski and Huntington, op. cit., p. 110. Ionescu and Wiatr use the concept of 'control' in this connection. Ionescu defines 'political control' as *non-constitutional* and *non-institutional* direct participation in, and influencing of, the decision-making processes in a non-parliamentary society by forces, groups and agencies indispensable to the running of that society (*Control and Contestation*, p. 240). Wiatr and Przeworski define control in the political sense as 'the possibility of influencing those who hold power in such a way that they take into account the interests of groups exerting this control' (op. cit., p. 231). In his book cited above, Ionescu has abandoned the term 'control' (as well as that of 'contestation') and replaced it with that of 'checks'. He classifies the two major forms of opposition in communist states as (1) 'political' or 'plural checks', exercised on the party by subordinate appara-

conducted by communists, either inside the party, even within the apparatus, or outside the party in officially-approved organisations and associations. If opposition of this kind is extreme enough, it may verge on fundamental opposition, at least in the sense of seeking a radically reformed communism. In some cases, such opposition 'within the system' may be a veiled form of integral opposition, and may in any case be treated by the regime as disloyal. In the main, however, it is a loyal opposition, seeking to change or influence public policy by criticising established policies, offering different measures to those proposed, or suggesting future courses of action. This discussion of policy alternatives is carried on partly in public, and partly in secret. The opposition is sometimes open and explicit, sometimes veiled and subtle. The party, while encouraging this kind of criticism, also seeks to channel and limit it, but it often escapes party control and goes beyond permissible limits. If the differences are serious and the issues basic enough, this may lead to changes of leadership. Specific opposition may thus be linked with factional opposition.

It is not assumed that all of these oppositional tendencies will always be present in communist systems. Indeed, it can hardly be sufficiently emphasised that the types of opposition predominant in the various communist systems differ greatly from each other from one period to another, and in the intensity and the forms of the various kinds of dissent. Moreover, the oppositional tendencies present at any time in a given country cannot be sharply marked off from each other, and may to a considerable extent overlap or be combined. In particular, opposition attitudes and behaviour will alter with changing conditions. Specific dissent may gradually develop into fundamental or even integral opposition, and may merge with factional conflicts among leading groups. Integral opposition may recede with leadership changes and policy shifts, and with increased opportunities for the expression of specific opposition. As will be

---

tuses, such as the state or the trade unions, as well as by broader unorganised social groups, such as the workers and peasants, and certain constitutional bodies, such as the courts, the assemblies, local government organs and the press, and (2) 'dissent', expressed by other groups such as the churches, the students and universities, the cultural reviews, etc. Checks give expression to 'interests' contradictory to those of the party apparat; dissent to 'values' contrary to those officially demanded (op. cit., pp. 2–3, 90–5, and Parts II and III).

discussed below, much will depend on the attitude of the ruling group towards opposition of varying types, since intolerance towards specific opposition may generate fundamental or integral opposition.

A simpler dichotomy between 'orthodox' and 'unorthodox' dissent, 'control' and 'contestation', or 'opposition' and 'dissent',[14] as employed by various students of communism, does not fully bring out the complexity of opposition under communism. If such a dual classification *is* used, it must be understood not as a clearcut demarcation of two sharply opposed forms, but as a continuum stretching between opposition and dissent, control and contestation, orthodoxy and unorthodoxy.[15] The fourfold classification suggested here may reveal more clearly not only this spectrum of degrees of opposition, but also the distinctive forms and methods of the types listed.

PHASES OF OPPOSITION IN EAST EUROPE

Even before 1948, when in some countries such as Czechoslovakia or Hungary, more or less genuine coalitions existed, neither integral nor fundamental opposition was regarded as legitimate, and a kind of consensus was embodied in the National Fronts on which the governments were based. No doubt there was strong dissent on the part of sections of the population in view of the radical disruption of the *status quo* espoused by the communists and implemented in part with the consent of the other coalition parties. Integral opposition by those opposed to the National Front itself was, however, banned, as was fundamental opposition to the Front's policies. There was in certain countries some occasion for competitive electoral struggles and opportunity for the expression of dissent in public discussion. None the less, in the elections there was often a pre-arranged distribution of seats among the National Front partners, and there were limitations on public discussion, sometimes self-

---

[14] Schapiro defines 'opposition' as 'an organised political group, or groups, of which the aim is to oust the government in power and to replace it by one of its own choosing'. 'Dissent', on the other hand, seeks 'merely to criticise, to exhort, to persuade, and to be listened to' (pp. 34–5 above).

[15] Whether an opposition should be regarded as 'orthodox' or 'unorthodox' will depend on the context of their ideas in relation to more traditional versions of communism, and on the views of the incumbents in power who may themselves hold ideologically unorthodox views.

imposed, in other cases reflecting the prevailing atmosphere of conformity. Even within the coalitions themselves there was, however, opposition by non-communist members to policies advocated by their communist partners, and opposition by the communists to actions of their 'allies'. Although this opposition was normally directed against specific policies, it often, implicitly and covertly, or even openly, involved resistance to the system as such and the whole range of policies advocated by the opposite party. In fact there was a scarcely veiled struggle for power between the competing parties, communist and non-communist. Although during these early years, the communists in varying degrees tolerated a certain freedom of discussion and some element of opposition by their coalition partners, their ultimate goal was a complete consensus unmarred by difference of views or opposition to their own ends. By 1948, even the less extreme forms of inter-party competition, expressed in parliamentary debate and in electoral contest, or in criticism of specific policies, were eliminated and the full-blown Leninist doctrine was imposed wherever it had not yet been introduced.[16]

During the period of Stalinism after 1948, the East European states with the exception of Yugoslavia, assumed the monolithic or totalitarian form which had been established in the Soviet Union in the 1930s. Other parties, where they existed, were required to give full and unconditional support to the ruling Communist Party. No opposition parties were permitted to function. Representative assemblies became nothing more than 'rubber stamps', and societal organisations, such as the trade unions, mere 'transmission belts'. Severe coercion was employed to stamp out not only integral, but also fundamental and specific opposition. Although 'criticism' and 'self-criticism' were officially encouraged, this practice in fact allowed little or no room for the open expression of conflicting views or the advancement of alternate policies. Within the party command, as in the Soviet Union in earlier periods, various factional 'oppositions' emerged, but were dealt with severely by purges and by the strictest penalties, including imprisonment and execution. None the less, the nature of the system and the radical policies introduced generated intense oppositional attitudes among some communists as well as non-communists. Coercion did not mean the

[16] For the above see my book, *The Governments of Communist East Europe*, New York, 1966, especially pp. 36–9.

elimination of opposition, but simply deprived it of all means of overt expression and forced it to assume underground and anti-system forms. Indeed, since all forms of lesser opposition in dissent from specific policies were curbed, opposition inevitably took the more radical form of rejection of the system as a whole, and of the leaders and their policies.

In the post-Stalin period, as noted, there has been a significant rise in opposition in Eastern Europe, and a marked shift as between the various types set forth above. Analysis is rendered difficult by the differences in the development of the eight communist countries, with the special circumstances and the peculiar traditions of each affecting the course of events. There is in fact a wide spectrum extending from Albania, where no basic change in the traditional Stalinist system has occurred, and coercion prevents all forms of opposition, to Yugoslavia, where the Stalinist system has been modified since 1948 in fundamental ways, and opposition of certain kinds is permitted and even encouraged. Between these extremes, each of the other countries has evolved a particular variation on the theme of de-Stalinisation, less pronounced in the case of Rumania, East Germany, and Bulgaria, more marked in the case of Poland, Czechoslovakia, and Hungary.[17] The differences are not, however, clearcut, nor are they fixed and changeless, but on the contrary blurred and ever-shifting, so that the analysis of a single country, and still more, generalisations concerning them all, confront serious difficulties, which are likely to be aggravated in the future as the individuality of each country becomes more pronounced. A detailed study of opposition in communist East Europe must therefore present a kaleidoscopic picture, the variety of which is in some degree comparable to that of the political democracies.

Generalising from these different and zigzag courses of development, one can say that integral opposition, after a climactic outburst in 1956 in Hungary, has everywhere declined, or at least does not usually express itself in overt action of serious proportions. A significant exception is the case of the Polish Catholic Church. Factional opposition, after intense activity in the early years of de-Stalinisation, especially in Hungary, Poland and Bulgaria, has also declined and where it occurs, has assumed more moderate forms. Fundamental opposition,

[17] See the author's *Communism National and International*, Toronto, 1964.

after an initial flourish in the Polish and Hungarian crises, has also somewhat subsided but it persists, and has recurred in Czechoslovakia in the 1960s. On the other hand, specific opposition, extending over a whole range of issues, has expanded in some states, as the regimes have permitted and encouraged the articulation of conflicting interests and opinions, and various occupational groups have taken the opportunity of expressing themselves vigorously on matters of public policy. On the whole, therefore (again generalising from a very complex and differentiated development), we must now deal primarily with what we may call 'loyal opposition', which seeks peaceful changes within the system, either in leadership or in policy, but not a replacement of the system as such. Unfortunately for clarity of expression and soundness of conclusions, there are exceptions to all these propositions, each of which requires more extended consideration.

THE DECLINE OF INTEGRAL OPPOSITION

Opposition of the integral kind has declined in most of the communist systems of Eastern Europe. Immediately after the death of Stalin and under the impact of de-Stalinisation, there was an outburst of such opposition in certain states, as some sections of the party apparatus, and professional groups, such as the writers and students, sought to accelerate the process of de-Stalinisation, to modify the system fundamentally and to replace its leaders. As is well-known, this took the form of violent riots, in East Germany, and of riots at Pilsen in Czechoslovakia, and Poznan in Poland, and culminated in the Hungarian revolution and the Polish unrest in 1956. The failure of all efforts at violent revolt, and the maintenance of adequate means of repression by all the regimes, has made resort to violence, as a means of integral opposition, a rare occurrence. Underground resistance has therefore appeared futile and become less frequent. From time to time conspirators are arrested and tried, but the heroic days of revolutionary resistance are over, and are likely to recur only in restricted circumstances or in conditions of extreme crisis.[18]

[18] A conspiracy trial was held in Albania in 1961, and in Bulgaria in 1965. Individual arrests and trials for conspiracy have occurred in other countries, notably Hungary, but also in Czechoslovakia, Poland and Yugoslavia.

At the same time, the decline of integral opposition reflects factors other than the continued presence of coercion. Since 1953 there has been, in varying degrees and with interruptions and reversals, a deceleration of the 'permanent revolution' imposed from above, the removal of some of the worst grievances created by Stalinism, and a series of reforms in the system designed to make it more palatable and to give satisfaction to the interests of diverse social groups. An important factor, paralleling similar shifts in some Western democracies, has been the transition from an ideological to a more pragmatic and empirical approach on the part of the leaders.[19] These changes, coupled with the futility of integral opposition, have brought about significant shifts in opinion and created a willingness to adapt to the requirements of the political system and to seek to make the best of it and to improve it. This has sometimes been reinforced, as in the case of Yugoslavia and Rumania, by feelings of national solidarity generated by resistance to the Soviet Union or, in the Polish case, to traditional enemies such as West Germany. Even, however, in a country such as East Germany, the combination of extreme measures of coercion, such as continuing Soviet occupation and the building of the Berlin wall, and policies designed to improve conditions of life, have engendered a wider acceptance of the regime by the elite groups and by the population as a whole.[20] In varying measure, all the regimes (except Albania) have sought to reach a working relationship of co-existence with the people and to cease regarding non-communists as *ipso facto* enemies or oppositionists. Kadar's slogan, 'Who is not against us is for us', epitomises this latter tendency.[21]

This is not to say, of course, that agreement on fundamentals has been achieved. In the absence of free expression of opinion and a genuine electoral process, there is no way of measuring the degree of consensus or lack of it, or the extent of integral opposition. No doubt there is widespread disaffection, and even rejection of the system as such, expressing itself in apathy, in disobedience to the regime and its requirements, and to some

[19] Cf. Dahl, *Political Opposition in Western Democracies*, pp. 354–6.

[20] Jean Smith, 'The German Democratic Republic and th ‹West', *International Journal*, XXII, No. 2, Spring 1967, pp. 231–52.

[21] In defending this policy, Kadar argued that, although Hungary had a one-party system, they should work as though there were a twenty-party system and a secret election every day (*The New York Times*, 7 March 1962).

degree in passive resistance. From time to time, in various countries, there is evidence of such attitudes among alienated sections of the youth; among some of the religious communities, such as the Catholics in Poland and the Protestants in East Germany; among the peasants, devoting their primary effort to their private plots rather than to the collective farms; among the workers in 'going slow', or even attempting to halt work; or among writers and artists, creating for their own satisfaction rather than for exhibition. Such 'opposition in principle', as Otto Kirchheimer has termed it, cannot speak out openly through any recognised vehicle of opinion and can manifest itself only in such amorphous and anomic forms.

The case of Poland constitutes an outstanding exception to the general rule in Eastern Europe. The role of the Catholic Church as an organised 'opposition' force, capable of counter-balancing party and state by claiming the allegiance of wide sections of the population and by expressing open disagreements with basic policies of the regime, is unique. The Church has been described by a Polish scholar as 'a perpetually competitive ideological force juxtaposed to the party and the state', which 'constitutes the political opposition'.[22] With Cardinal Wyszynski as the main spokesman, and with newspapers and journals, and the churches themselves, as media of communication, the Polish Church is able to challenge the ruling party not only on matters of religious policy, but also on questions of doctrine and education. During the millennial celebrations in 1966 an extraordinary confrontation of Church and state, of Cardinal and First Secretary, at meetings held during many months, testified to the political power of the Church. True, the latter denied its intention of interfering in political affairs and argued that it confined itself to matters of religious doctrine and policy. None the less, the Cardinal's statements on foreign policy and on such questions as atheism and freedom of conscience touched on sensitive political questions[23] and brought

[22] Jerzy J. Wiatr, 'Elements of the Pluralism (sic) in the Polish Political System', The Polish Sociological Bulletin, No. 1, 1966, p. 25.

[23] In a sermon, Cardinal Wyszinski stated: 'We have to stand up before the rulers, princes and authorities and calmly and bravely proclaim the Gospel. The people could be without kings, leaders, premiers and ministers, but never without its shepherd. The bishop is the good shepherd who faces the wolves, and although hurt, defends the people against hatred, falsehood and harm' (The New York Times, 31 January 1966).

accusations from the government that the Church was playing a political role in opposition to the regime and the new social order.[24]

SHIFTS IN FACTIONAL OPPOSITION

The Eastern European communist parties have never been as united as propaganda and theory assume, and leaderships have always been divided into factions seeking power and advocating conflicting policies.[25] Such factions are in a certain sense a surrogate, in a one-party state, for parties within a multi-party system. In the Stalinist past this conflict expressed itself in radical and violent purges, often dictated from Moscow and with the severest of penalties for the defeated. In the initial phase of de-Stalinisation, long and bitter struggles were waged between leadership groups in Poland, Hungary and Bulgaria, and led to the ultimate replacement of existing Stalinist leaders by more 'liberal' or 'national' communist 'oppositions'. Purges of high-ranking leaders have continued to occur in the past decade, but with less drastic personal consequences for the victims.[26] Although purge of the old type is not as 'permanent' a feature of communist rule as was once assumed, an intra-party struggle over leadership and policy is even more likely to occur now that control from Moscow is either absent, or less decisive, and the outcome is no longer fatal for the losers. Factional opposition, seeking a change in the leadership (either complete or partial), will, therefore, remain an important feature of Eastern European politics.[27] The clash between leaders and opposition takes place secretly, and exclusively within the party, at its topmost level, among the 'high command' in the presidium and secretariat. The Central Committee may come, and in some cases may already have begun, to play a significant part. As yet, there is no evidence that the process of leadership conflict is likely to be institutionalised through a representative parliament and elections, or even through a more genuine electoral process within the party itself.

[24] See Gomulka's speech of 14 January 1966, and the editorial, in *Nowe Drogi,* April 1966.

[25] See Ionescu's book, pp. 227 for a discussion of factionalism.

[26] E.g. the removal of Yugov in Bulgaria in 1962; of Ranković in Yugoslavia in 1966; of Novotný in Czechoslovakia in 1968.

[27] Skilling, *Governments of Communist East Europe,* pp. 91–7.

THE PERSISTENCE OF FUNDAMENTAL OPPOSITION

The decline of anti-system opposition has been accompanied by the persistence of intra-party opposition by individual communists or groups who are out of sympathy with a whole range of key official policies and with the leadership itself. For example, in 1964, two Polish students, J. Kuron and K. Modzelewski, illegally circulated an open letter which, in Marxist terms, denounced the entire Polish system for its bureaucratic deformations. In 1966, a leading intellectual, Professor Leszek Kolakowski, in a meeting at Warsaw University, severely censured the record of the Polish party in the decade since 1956. In 1967, a prominent Czech writer, Ludvik Vaculík, delivered an eloquent and slashing condemnation of the Prague regime and its policies on the floor of the congress of the Writer's Union. These instances of individual dissent offer testimony of the continuance of basic opposition within the system.

Important social groups may manifest chronic discontent with major policies of the regime. In Yugoslavia, and elsewhere, there has been resistance to the implementation of economic reforms and to the liberalisation of the political climate by the more conservative elements, concentrated especially within the party apparatus.[28] In Poland, in 1968, street demonstrations and mass meetings have been held in protest against literary curbs and arrests of students. In Czechoslovakia, there has been widespread criticism of what was deemed to be the conservative line of the regime in failing fully to carry through the economic reforms and in imposing literary curbs, by more 'progressive' circles among the economists, writers and other professional persons. These currents of dissent, fusing with criticism by Slovaks of Prague's nationality policies, and with student demonstrations, produced a major political crisis in 1967. Severe reprisals against dissidents intensified the crisis, and led to the replacement of Antonín Novotný as party secretary by a new leader, Alexander Dubček. In this way a tidal wave of fundamental opposition, not opposed to the communist system as such, but in basic disagreement with its major policies and leadership, was expressed in successful factional

[28] See Jan F. Triska, 'The Party Apparatchiks at Bay', *East Europe*, 16, 12 (Dec. 1967), pp. 2–8.

resistance to the established leadership and in a major change in the direction of public policy.

The national question is another source of fundamental opposition. Resistance by constituent national groups of the multinational Yugoslav state to some policies of the federal government in Belgrade has been openly and sharply expressed. The governments of the national republics and the republic parties have proved to be effective agencies for articulating the interests of individual nationalities. In Czechoslovakia, Slovak organs, both party and state, have been much weaker and unable to give adequate expression to Slovak discontents. As a result, the articulation of Slovak interests has been accomplished through professional groups, such as economists, writers and even historians. The latter, in re-assessing crucial events from the past, such as the Slovak uprising in 1943, have expressed a distinctive national viewpoint. The establishment of a new regime, headed by a Slovak, after the resolution of the crisis of 1967–8, indicated the possibility of the adoption of policies to meet some of Slovakia's grievances.

THE RISE OF SPECIFIC OPPOSITION

The most striking feature of the post-Stalin scene in some states has been the rise of specific opposition, i.e. criticism of particular policies which have been adopted or are under consideration. Where it has occurred, this development reflects a subtle, but significant, change in the attitude of the party to society and social groups, and in its conception of the process of decision-making. As we have noted, there has been no relaxation of the party's monopoly of political power and no admission of the desirability of political opposition as such. It is, however, no longer assumed that the party alone, and infallibly, knows the public interest and that all individual or group interests must be subordinated and sacrificed automatically and without question. There has been an increasing recognition that, in a heterogeneous society, some conflicting interests will exist and that there will be clashes between partial individual and group interests, and the broader national interest.[29] It is understood that public policy, if it is to be realistic and well-based, should

[29] See, for instance, articles by A. Lantay, *Ekonomický časopis*, No. 6, 1963 and *Pravda* (Slovak), 18 May 1964; and by M. Lakatoš, *Právný obzor*, No. 1, 1965.

take these conflicting interests into account and should represent to some degree a reconciliation or synthesis of them. The
party would thus perform the role of an aggregator of conflicting
interests, rather than the exclusive articulator of its own conception of the national interests.[30]

Moreover, public policy, it is increasingly recognised, must be
'scientific', in the sense of being based, not merely on Marxism-
Leninism, but also on the findings of scholarship and science.
In some cases, the party has tolerated and indeed deliberately
encouraged wide-ranging debates among experts on certain
policy issues such as economic reform or legal revisions.[31] This
kind of discussion, permitting the expression of oppositional
viewpoints on specific issues, is, needless to say, subject to strict
limits, which will be discussed later. It has, however, created a
new climate of policy-making, and without altering the essential forms of political action, and in particular the leading role
of the party, has subtly and significantly modified the actual
working of the political system.

The chief exponents of loyal opposition have been professional persons, such as economists, lawyers, social scientists
generally, natural scientists, writers and jounalists. These
'professional interest groups', as they may be called, do not have
the official power of 'bureaucratic interest groups', such as the

[30] This was the phrase used by Hendrych, in the article cited above. The Czech
theorist, Z. Mlynář, has described the leading role of the party as involving 'the
conscious embodiment of the interests of the whole society in its entirety, but
also the deliberate harmonisation of these interests'. See his article, 'Problems of
Political Leadership and the New Economic System', *Problemy mira i sotsializma*,
No. 12, December 1965, p. 98. The Polish scholar, J. Wiatr, has referred to the
party as 'the forum of the expression of the non-antagonistic classes of interests
of various socialist strata of Polish society', and as 'the platform where the divergent interests of the socialist society collide'. Although the struggle of class
interests takes place outside the party, the resolution of conflicts which harmonise
the interests of workers and their allies' takes place within the party and is guaranteed by intra-party democracy. See Jerzy J. Wiatr, 'The Elements of the Pluralism
in the Polish Political System', *The Polish Sociological Bulletin*, No. 1, 1966, pp. 22–3.

[31] Z. Mlynář, in an important article already cited, rejected 'the effort to solve
these problems without discussions and controversies, without democratic delib-
eration of various possible alternatives, without serious scientific and theoretical
elaboration of the perspectives of development' (p. 93). Cf. I. Santa, 'Debate and
Party Unity', *Tsaradalmi Szemle*, June 1967. He refers to the 'participation of
experts', 'drawing up and presenting several alternatives or ... several platforms.
This makes the comparison of differing concepts possible, a choice among them
or their eventual combination or even their rejection, as well as agreement between
the demands of expertise and democracy.' Cf. M. Soukup, 'On the Conception and
Tasks of Political Science', *Nová mysl*, XX, 18, 6 September 1966, pp. 13–15.

party *apparatchiki*, the state bureaucrats and managers, and the police.[32] They do, however, possess knowledge and enjoy a prestige which affords them some possibilities to express their views, and gives these views a certain authority and influence. No doubt, in some cases, such groups are linked with 'political leaders', who seek changes of policy and perhaps changes of leadership, and are thus involved indirectly in the struggle for power among rival factions. They may often operate, however, as 'pressure groups' primarily seeking to influence the actions of the existing leadership. They are not always organised institutionally, although they may carry on their activity within institutions, but are usually amorphous and informal congeries of individuals of the same occupation or of similar viewpoint on public issues.

Indeed, within each 'occupational group', such as the writers or the economists, there is likely to be no unanimity of viewpoint, but on the contrary, distinct cleavages, sometimes constituting ill-defined wings of more conservative or liberal orientation. Such 'opinion groups' more often express, not an exclusively selfish interest of their occupational group, but a particular conception of the 'public interest', e.g. concerning economic reform, legal changes or literary freedom. As a result, professional groups may articulate the interests of broader social groups which are unable to express their views directly through their own associations. Like-minded 'opinion-groups' may form loose and informal alliances with each other, and with groups holding similar views within the bureaucratic groups, such as the party, state and police, and with factions in the top leadership creating at least in an amorphous sense a 'conservative vs. reformist' dichotomy. On the whole, the forces making for change and reform are found primarily outside the party apparatus, among the new classes of the creative and technical intelligentsia, and the party apparatus, although divided, is frequently a conservative force. None the less, more conservative groupings also exist in most of the groups, professional and

[32] For a fuller discussion of these concepts see the introduction to the forthcoming book edited by H. Gordon Skilling and Franklyn Griffiths, *Interest Groups in Soviet Politics*. See also my article, 'Interest Groups and Communist Politics', *World Politics*, XVIII, 3, April 1966, pp. 435–51. Cf. Wjatr and Przeworski, op. cit., pp. 232–8. Ionescu (*The Politics of the European Communist States*, pp. 88–95, 226) is critical of such an interest group approach, but himself treats 'political checks' and 'dissent' as two distinct forms of interest group activity.

bureaucratic, and in rarer cases, the party apparatus and certain top leaders may espouse important reforms opposed by the former.

THE CHANGING CONTEXT OF
POLITICAL ACTION

The paradox of post-Stalin Eastern Europe has been that, although the basic structure of the political system has changed but little, and the attitude of the leaders toward opposition in the abstract has not been modified, there have been, none the less, in all countries except Albania, significant alterations in the way the system has in fact operated. The making of policy remains exclusively in the hands of the top leaders of the party, but the style of decision-making has undergone striking changes. In almost every state of the region, there has been a substantial shift in the role of the party and, in particular, in its relations with the other major bureaucratic groups, notably the police and the state apparatus, and the managerial class generally. In Poland and Hungary, and later in Czechoslovakia, where political relaxation occurred, the diminution of coercion brought with it not only a decline in prestige, and reduction in influence, of the police, but a substantial broadening of the area of permissible discussion. This in turn gave a fillip to the expression of loyal 'opposition' in these more liberal states, sometimes taking the form of significantly unorthodox specific dissent. Even in these countries the influence of the police continues to be present, however. In the 'hard-line' states, such as Albania, Bulgaria, East Germany, and Rumania, the security forces remain a significant obstacle in the path of liberalisation and discourage the expression of oppositional viewpoints. Even in Yugoslavia as late as 1966, the police resisted the course of economic and political reform and was downgraded only after the removal of Ranković and the purge that followed.

Another important development has been the broadening of the authority of the state administrators and the inclusion in the state bureaucracy, at least in an advisory capacity, of experts and specialists in the relevant fields.[33] This tendency has

[33] Carl Beck, 'Bureaucratic Conservatism and Innovation in Eastern Europe', paper presented at the American Political Science Association, September 1966, mimeo.

been most pronounced in Yugoslavia, where the role of the party has ostensibly been reduced to that of a 'guiding force',[34] but has been noticeable in varying degrees in other states where the party's traditional 'leadership' function has been maintained. The economic reform gradually being introduced in all the states, except Albania and Rumania, has further reduced the role of the party as such, and increased that of the managers and the experts in the running of industry and commerce. This has been particularly reinforced in Hungary by the inclusion of non-communists in important managerial and supervisory posts. Such developments have primarily affected the processes of 'government' or 'rule-making', but have also stimulated the utterance of 'oppositional' views and have blurred the dividing line between government and opposition. Consultation with experts, official and non-official, and the freer atmosphere of discussion generally, encourages the expression of dissent and the suggestion of alternative courses of action. The experts are increasingly expected not merely to 'advise' and 'consent', but to 'advise' and, if necessary, to 'dissent'.

ASSEMBLIES AND ELECTIONS

The changes in the context of decision-making have been least pronounced in the functioning of the representative system and the mass or societal organisations. The representative bodies in all countries, with the exception of Poland and Yugoslavia, are still deprived of the real power of policy-making, which remains in the hands of the organs of the party. In Bulgaria, Czecho-slovakia, Hungary and Rumania, there has been criticism of the inactivity of parliaments, and changes have been intro-duced to make the legislature, and particularly its committees, places of active and critical discussion. Plenary sessions have become longer and more business-like; committees are more active; question time has been introduced; the parliamentary responsibility of ministers has been proclaimed. The assemblies continue, however, to be the scene of unanimous approval of proposed legislation and do not offer a locus of serious opposition or a medium for articulating diverse interests and opinions. Only rarely, as for instance, in Czechoslovakia, in June 1965,

[34] Tito has, however, felt it necessary to stress the political role of the League of Communists. See *The New York Times*, 22 November 1966.

is there a divided vote, and in that case the legislation was passed with the clause opposed by a majority unchanged. In the Polish Sejm, however, the legislative committees play an important role in the discussion of legislation.[35] Opposition is sometimes expressed in the plenary session, notably by the Catholic deputies, and negative votes are occasionally recorded. In Yugoslavia, the assembly is an even more active arena of debate and of opposition, and the defeat of proposed legislation has from time to time occurred. In an event unique in the communist world, the government of the Slovene Republic was on one occasion compelled to resign as a result of an adverse vote, although it resumed office shortly thereafter.[36]

Efforts to invigorate the assemblies are likely to remain abortive as long as the elections themselves simply endorse the dominant position of the ruling party and exclude competition by opposition parties. In no country of the region have such parties been permitted to take part in electoral contests. A minor element of competitiveness has been introduced in Czechoslovakia, Hungary and Rumania, in the form of the legal possibility of multiple candidacies for office. So far this has not led to frequent electoral conflicts. Where other parties do exist, as in Czechoslovakia, Bulgaria, East Germany and Poland, they are in all cases allies and partners of the communist party and do not compete with it for power.[37] At the most, they may give a modest expression of the interests of certain social or religious groups and seek to influence the ruling party in these spheres. Even in Poland elections are not competitive, but constitute what a communist theorist has called 'semi-plebiscitary' or 'consent' elections.[38] As a result of the fact that

[35] See V. C. Chrypinski, 'Legislative Committees in Polish Lawmaking', *Slavic Review*, XXV, 2, June 1966, pp. 247–58.

[36] *East Europe*, 16: 1 and 2 (January and February 1967), pp. 28 and 37 resp.

[37] See Jerzy J. Wiatr, 'One-party Systems – The Concept and Issue for Comparative Studies', in *Transactions of Westermarck Society*, Vol. X, E. Allardt and Y. Littunen (eds.), *Cleavages, Ideologies and Party Systems, Contributions to Comparative Political Sociology*, Helsinki, 1964, pp. 281–90. He there argues that the Polish system is not strictly speaking a one-party system, but rather a 'hegemonical party system', in which other parties exist as well as the Communist Party, but as in the one-party states, there is no real competition for power and no political opposition.

[38] Wiatr and Przeworski, op. cit., pp. 238–9. A fuller analysis of Polish elections is given by Wiatr in his chapter on 'Elections and Voting Behaviour in Poland', in A. Ranney (ed.), *Essays on the Behavioural Study of Politics*, Urbana, 1962, pp. 237–51. See p. 239. For further discussion of the Polish system, see Wiatr, 'One-party Systems', cited above, pp. 287–9; Wiatr, 'The Electoral System and Elements of

there are more candidates than seats to be filled and voters may express preference in voting for certain candidates and certain parties, the elections provide 'an opportunity to criticise government policy by lowering the electoral acceptance of this policy'.[39] In this way, Wjatr argues, 'the consent elections do not decide who will rule the country, but they influence the way in which the country will be ruled'.[40] In Yugoslavia, where no other parties exist, but a kind of national front, in the form of the Socialist Alliance, plays a significant part, elections have also assumed a somewhat different character in that recently the number of candidates has considerably exceeded the number of seats to be filled. As a result, at least a personal competition for office takes place, although this does not represent opposition in terms of policy.[41]

Traditionally lacking in communist systems has been an effective system of parliamentary control of the executive power. The danger of 'uncontrolled power' has been recognised, and the need for a more powerful public opinion as a check on the abuse of power has been stressed.[42] As a substitute for parliamentary opposition of a constitutional kind, a question time has in some cases been introduced in the assembly, and a more vigorous criticism of administration by deputies has been encouraged, but with minimal results. Extra-parliamentary 'checks' on official actions, through the press and by special organs of popular control, have also been stressed. Paradoxically, however, the chief source of criticism of executive arbitrariness or of failures in administrative action has been the

---

Pluralism in a "One-Party" System: Poland', *Transactions of the Fifth World Congress of Sociology*, International Sociological Association, 1962, Vol. IV, pp. 381–6.

[39] Wiatr, in Ranney, op. cit., p. 251.

[40] Ibid., p. 239.

[41] This has been called Yugoslavia's '1½ party system' (*The New York Times*, 29 May 1966). A Yugoslav, M. Popović, has used the term 'non-party system'. See S. Stanković, 'Yugoslavia's Critical Year', *East Europe*, 16, 4, April 1967, p. 16. See also R. V. Burks and S. A. Stanković, 'Jugoslawien auf dem Weg zu halbfreien Wahlen', *Osteuropa*, 17, 2/3 (February, March 1967), pp. 131–46. For further discussion of elections in communist countries of Eastern Europe, see my book, *The Governments of Communist East Europe*, pp. 130–4.

[42] For instance, see the articles by Miroslav Jodl, a Czech sociologist, in *Literární noviny*, 13 November 1965, and 22 January 1966. Cf. also the Polish discussion in 1965 of Adam Schaff's book, *Marxism and the Individual*, and of his concept of the power elite and alienation under communism. The Slovak, M. Lakatoš, has written of the manipulation of the ruled by the rulers and urged genuinely free elections as a means of preventing this (*Právný obzor*, No. 3, 1966, also translated in *East Europe*, 15, No. 6 (June 1966), pp. 22–3).

party itself, especially its top leaders and its agencies, the Central Committee and the apparatus. This traditional device, used even in Stalinist times, represents a kind of 'control from above', quite different from the control from below of democratic societies. In Albania, for instance, the Central Committee in an open letter in March 1966, censured the bureaucratic elite of party and state.[43] It is a curious paradox of communist systems that an important agency of 'opposition' is, in a certain sense, the ruling party itself, which assumes the functions of supervising the actions of the executive or leading figures of government or party and subjecting them to criticism.[44]

WEAKNESS OF ORGANISED PRESSURE GROUPS

The mass or societal organisations, such as the trade unions, or the associations of women or youth, have not so far evolved as genuine defenders of the special group interests of their members or the people they claim to represent. In most countries, these organisations remain what they have always been, transmission belts employed by the party for imposing on them the party's concepts of their group interests and of the general interest of society. In few cases have they emerged as exponents of opposition or served as arenas for the expression of such views by their members. A rather novel development, in Bulgaria, Hungary and Rumania, has been the establishment of national councils or unions of the collective farms, which have given the peasants a kind of organisational representation comparable in form at least to that of the industrial workers. Whether these new institutions will have more independence and vigour than their counterparts in other fields, remains to be seen. In Czechoslovakia, there has been outspoken criticism of the mass organisations for their lack of genuine representative character and their failure to act in the defence of group interests, and measures have been suggested to make them effective.[45] In the case of

[43] *Christian Science Monitor*, 31 March 1966.

[44] The daily organ of the Hungarian People's Front, *Magyar Nemzet* (28 August 1966), used this as an argument that an opposition party was not necessary. Criticism, it declared, is 'the essence of opposition'. In Hungary, 'the party and the government criticise everything at all times where things are not going as they should' and thus 'supply the checking and criticising functions of an opposition'.

[45] Z. Mlynář (*Rudé právo*, 16 August 1966). The same writer, in the international communist organ, argued that these organisations should not serve as mere trans-

the Czechoslovak youth movement, an unprecedented claim was made on one occasion that it should be permitted to express views, if necessary, in opposition to those of the party.[46]

Even in official statements at the highest level, in some countries, there has been talk of the desirability of more vigorous expression of group interests by these organisations and of consideration of their special interests by the party in working out public policy in relevant spheres.[47] Special efforts have been made by certain states to broaden the authority of the trade unions in particular, and to encourage them to speak more genuinely for the workers, especially at the local level, and to serve as consultants, and advisers of the government and party at the national level.[48] The unions are thus expected to serve as transmission belts operating in two directions, providing information needed by the rule-makers on the attitudes of the workers, and funnelling policy decisions and directives to the masses. How far these principles will be applied is difficult to estimate, especially as the trade unions remain under the general direction of the party and are not regarded as independent pressure groups.[49] In Yugoslavia, however, the trade unions have become much more independent and more representative of the workers' interests, and have on occasion exerted a considerable influence on the course of legislation. The national plan for 1965, for instance, was rejected by the trade unions and had to be revised extensively before parliamentary approval. Moreover, strikes have occurred more than once and have been treated by the authorities as legitimate forms of opposition action. Apart from Yugoslavia, the most notable step was taken in Hungary in the enactment of a labour code, in October 1967, significantly widening the authority of the trade unions.

---

mission belts operating in one direction only (*Problemy mira i sotsialisma*, December 1965, p. 97). The Polish writer, Wiatr, has written of the dual functions of various interest groups, serving not only as 'pressure groups', which 'represent the interests of their groups vis-à-vis the Party and the government', but also as 'mobilising groups', which mobilise their members to the tasks put forth by party and government (*Polish Sociological Bulletin*, cited above, p. 24).

[46] See *Student*, No. 4, 1966.

[47] See for instance the speech by Kadar, on 26 November 1966. Cf. also the resolution of the Congress of the Hungarian Youth Union in July 1967.

[48] M. Gamarnikow, 'New Tasks for the Trade Unions', *East Europe*, 16, No. 4, April 1967, pp. 18–26.

[49] Cf. M. Pastyřík, 'Trade Unions and Participation of the Workers in the Direction of Production', *Nová mysl*, XX, 22, 3 November 1966, pp. 6–9.

THE RISE OF THE INTELLECTUALS

The most impressive development in some of these countries has been the emergence of public discussion, either in mass media, such as newspapers, and to a lesser degree, radio and television, or in the periodicals and at the congresses of scholarly institutions, or the writers' unions. Even novels, plays and poetry, and scholarly works have been vehicles for articulating oppositional views or group interests. This is in part a product of an official decision to permit freer discussion and encourage wider consultation outside the party, although measures of de-Stalinisation have created an atmosphere more favourable to such activity and even opposition. Relaxation of restrictions has often, however, meant that the professional groups have expressed radical specific criticism of facets of the regimes' programme, verging sometimes on fundamental opposition. The consequences have sometimes been official censure and renewed restrictions.

For instance, during the critical early years of de-Stalinisation in Hungary and Poland, the writers and journalists emerged as a powerful force seeking an acceleration of the process of liberalisation and constituted a radical opposition to the existing regimes. In the case of Hungary, the literary community, together with other sectors of the intelligentsia, formed the spearhead of the subsequent revolution. Although the revolt was crushed, the liberal writers continued to act as an opposition, at first refusing to write for publication, and later, acting as spokesmen for greater freedom of expression. Similarly, the Polish writers, and intellectuals generally, without taking the road of violent revolt, were in large degree responsible for the events of October 1956, and continued to express their own views vigorously for several years thereafter. Even after the regime reverted to stricter control of literature and the arts, the writers have on more than one occasion defended their interests and protested against government actions.[50]

In Czechoslovakia, in the 1960s, writers and journalists became a significant political factor, pressing, in their associations and in their journals, for de-Stalinisation and greater freedom

[50] For instance, in 1964 the letter to the government of thirty-four writers protesting against the censorship and paper restrictions, and the mass demonstrations by Polish students in 1968.

of expression, and in some cases, directly challenging the government and individual leaders.[51] The most celebrated case was the courageous attack by the Slovak journalist, M. Hysko, on the Prime Minister, Široký. Although he was sharply censured by no less a person than the President and First Secretary, Novotný, the removal of Široký testified to the effectiveness of Hysko's opposition. Most significantly, his article had been published in the organ of the Slovak Communist Party, *Pravda* which, on that and on other occasions, served as a vehicle of oppositional attitudes. Other literary periodicals, in particular *Literárni noviny* and *Kulturní život*, continued for years to be in effect organs of opposition, publishing critical articles dealing with all aspects of Czech and Slovak life, and bringing down on their heads torrents of official disapproval.[52] In 1967, the congress of the Writers' Union was the occasion for outspoken criticism of the prevalent policies, including even the regime's support of the Arab states in the war with Israel, and of censorship. Retaliation in the form of expulsion from the party of three prominent writers and curbs on the activities of the organisation did not eliminate the problem and created a political crisis shaking the Novotný regime to its foundations.

Similarly, social scientists and other scholars have begun to play a more important role in the political life of certain countries. Like the writers, lawyers, economists, sociologists, and even historians and philosophers have acted as influential interest groups in their respective fields. 'Opinion groups' within these categories, conservative as well as liberal, have voiced conflicting opinions and thus represented oppositions of varying outlook. In particular, the economists have played a significant role in criticising the older planning system, in advocating economic reforms, and often in complaining about the slowness of the reforms officially adopted. Sharp cleavages on the nature of the reforms have manifested themselves among the economists, and between economists and bureaucratic groups.[53]

[51] See my book, *Communism, National and International*, Toronto, 1964, Chap. 7, for a detailed discussion of the events of 1963.

[52] See the Central Committee resolution on the cultural periodicals, *Rudé právo*, 4 April 1964, and subsequent official denunciations. In early 1966, the party organ, *Život strany* (No. 1, January 1966) had to refer again to 'disquieting tendencies' in these periodicals and to charge them with failing to eliminate their shortcomings. In 1967 *Literárni noviny* was taken out of the hands of the union, and placed under the Ministry of Culture. In 1968 the union began to publish a new organ, *Literárni listy*.

[53] Note the role of, for instance, Ota Šik, E. Loebl and R. Selucký and other

Similar controversies among historians, in attempting a more objective re-evaluation of the past, have often had direct political relevance. Lawyers have been less influential, but have actively contributed to the discussions of legal and political reform. The rise of the discipline of sociology has introduced a new element in scholarship capable of serving as an instrument in the formation of policy. A unique feature of certain countries has been the part played by philosophers in the expression of dissident views and the advocacy of greater freedom of discussion.[54] Indeed, the need for greater freedom of expression has been the common concern of scholars in many fields, some even demanding unlimited freedom.[55]

CONTINUING LIMITS ON DISSENT

It should be emphasised that opposition of the kinds we have been discussing differs greatly from what would normally be regarded as legitimate opposition in a democratic political system. Such dissent has perforce to operate within strict limits, although not as strict as has customarily been assumed and as was once the case. The party's monopoly of the instruments of coercion can prevent violent revolutionary opposition. In any case, after the fiasco of Hungary, such a resort to force is not likely to occur, except in extraordinary circumstances. Moreover, although the coercive power of the regimes is exercised more lightly than in the past, and not usually in the form of ruthless terror, its presence still inhibits non-violent opposition of a fundamental or integral kind. Similarly, the nature of the electoral system and the domination of a single party rules out effective parliamentary or electoral opposition. The centralised and unified nature of the party sets strict limits on factional opposition, although this does not exclude the possibility of conflicts of leadership groups within the Politburo. The party's continuing claim to control all facets of society circumscribes

---

reform-minded economists in Czechoslovakia. Similar discussions occurred in Bulgaria, Hungary and Yugoslavia.

[54] For instance, note the role of Prof. L. Kolakowski, dissident Polish Marxist philosopher, or that of the East German, Wolfgang Harich, imprisoned in 1965 for his revisionism. Cf. the expression of dissident Marxist views by the Slovene theoretical journal, *Praxis*.

[55] Note such demands by the Czech economist, Loebl; the Slovak writer, L. Novomeský; the Polish scientist, T. Kotarbinski; and the East German scientist, R. Havemann.

the overt and autonomous action of organised interest groups, but does not entirely prevent it. Adherence to a single official theory, Marxism-Leninism, restricts the expression of oppositional views and compels dissent to be expressed in doctrinal terms, but does not exclude significant divergence, for instance with reference to economic reform.

The party's monopoly of the means of communication also does not rule out the expression of diverse views on sensitive issues such as literary or scholarly freedom, economic or legal reform. The party, while paying homage to the idea of freedom of discussion, never fails to stress that this freedom cannot be an absolute one, and that criticism, or dissent, must be conducted within the framework of Marxism-Leninism and the general party line, and may not express 'bourgeois' or 'anti-communist' views.[56] When necessary, the party can resort to 'administrative' sanctions, such as closing down of a periodical, the removal of an editor, public censure of an offending critic, expulsion from the party, dismissal from posts held, or in the most extreme cases, arrest and trial.[57] This in turn may sometimes lead to continued resistance by the person in question and perhaps protests by his colleagues, and may on occasion prepare the ground for major changes of leadership and policy, as in Czechoslovakia in 1968.[58]

THE FUTURE OUTLOOK

How the process of opposition will develop in Eastern Europe in the future is difficult to predict. There has been speculation

[56] The Czech, J. Hájek, distinguished between 'liberalisation' and 'democratisation' and rejected the former because it permitted all kinds of opinion and afforded 'equal rights to the opposition' (*Rudé právo*, 1 April 1966).

[57] The case of *Literární noviny* in Czechoslovakia has been mentioned. Earlier, in Poland, the newspapers, *Po Prostu* and *Kultura*, were closed down: in Yugoslavia, in 1964, *Perspektive*, and in Czechoslovakia, in 1966, *Tvař*, were stopped. A prominent case of expulsion was the Polish philosopher, Kolakowski. In East Germany, Professor Havemann was deprived of his posts in the University, but remained at liberty. In 1964–5, in Poland, Kuron and Modzelewski were imprisoned for their opposition activity. In Yugoslavia, in addition to the well-known case of Djilas, that of Mihajlov has already been referred to. In Czechoslovakia, three prominent writers were expelled from the party in 1967, and another, L. Mnačko, who left for Israel, was also deprived of his citizenship.

[58] A notable case was the resistance to Kolakowski's expulsion by students and intellectuals. Letters of protest by writers led to further expulsions and resignations from the party. Heated criticism was reportedly expressed at party meetings in Warsaw University, the Academy of Sciences, and the Writers Union.

in the West as to the possibility of the emergence of a kind of
political pluralism and even of an institutionalising of opposition in the communist systems.[59] The most optimistic forecast
is that made by Ghiţa Ionescu who, in his recent book, has
analysed the growth of 'checks' and 'dissent' in the European
communist states and predicted their 'institutionalisation'.[60]
This he regards as 'an irreversible trend', likely to continue
where it has not yet manifested itself. In his opinion, this
development reflects the necessities of a rapidly developing
industrial society, which, in its concern for 'efficiency', must
replace 'coercion' by 'consultation'. He also expresses the conviction that in the 'European' communist states, as he calls
them, to distinguish them from the Soviet Union, this process
will be swifter and more marked than in the latter, owing to
the relatively short period communism has dominated these
countries and their relatively recent experience of pre-communist political pluralism.[61]

There is no denying that in certain countries of Eastern
Europe there has been a notable development of oppositional
tendencies, and as a result, a significant modification of the
actual operations of the one-party systems. There seems to be
nothing inevitable about this tendency, however, nor does it
seem to be closely correlated with the degree of economic
development of a given country. In all countries, communist
and non-communist, there are many sources of discontent from
which opposition of varying kinds may develop. Economic and
social conflicts of interests, or national cleavages, may lead to
sharply differing conceptions of the most appropriate policy
solutions. Economic development may, it is true, encourage

[59] See the discussion on the future of monolithic parties in the special issue of
Government and Opposition, cited above, n. 2. Cf. my book, *The Governments of Communist East Europe*, concluding chapter. See also Ionescu, International Conference
of Futuribles (Paris, 1965), mimeo., where he speculated concerning the possible
emergence of other parties, and of a more genuine parliamentarism, and a greater
role in decision-making by specialised bodies and associations. 'An a-political
pluralism of the future could replace the political pluralism of the past', he wrote
(p. 17). See also J. J. Wiatr, 'The Future of Political Institutions under Socialism,'
at the Conference on Futuribles, 1965, mimeo, pp. 22–6. Cf. A. Brown, 'Pluralistic
Trends in Czechoslovakia', *Soviet Studies*, XVII, 4, April 1966, 453–72. Carl Beck,
in the paper cited earlier, wrote that 'the thrust of the discussion and of institutional reform has been toward a greater degree of participation by a variety of
political actors and social forces in the entire political systems' (*sic*) (p. 15).

[60] *The Politics of the European Communist States*, pp. 80–5, 166–9, 190, 271–8. See
above, n. 13, for Ionescu's definition of these terms.   [61] Ibid., pp. 5–10, 272.

opposition by contributing to social differentiation and to the emergence of important elites playing an indispensable role, in the economy or in society. But the very nature of the communist system also produces profound differences of outlook, with regard not only to the proper strategy of economic action, but also the course to be followed in regard to culture and society, and to the political process. Thus opposition may be generated on such issues as these which are not necessarily the result of economic development.

Moreover, the character of the system at a given time determines the degree to which opposition may express itself and affects the form it will take. The leadership retains its monopolistic control of the means of coercion, economic resources, and the media of communication, but may exercise these powers in a *more*, or *less*, coercive and total manner, thus inhibiting, *or* stimulating, dissent. In some cases, leaders have encouraged, and in other cases, discouraged, the expression of dissent by individuals or groups. In some cases, the latter have been more active and daring, and in other cases, less so, in criticising official policy. As a result the development of opposition has varied greatly from country to country, and from time to time, and has proceeded in fits and starts, in a zigzag manner, rather than in a predetermined and unilinear direction. As the national traditions become more influential factors in the political culture of each country, the evolution of opposition is likely to reflect the diversity of pre-communist traditions, and to take special forms in each case. In some, it may surpass, in others, lag behind, the Soviet system, which is itself undergoing somewhat similar tendencies towards political pluralisation.

Opposition in communist countries is likely to differ substantially in form and content from that which occurs in a constitutional order. The terms 'liberalisation', 'pluralisation', or 'institutionalisation', are indeed not entirely appropriate to describe the process of change in communist systems. The likelihood of the emergence of an advanced form of pluralism in the form of an effective multi-party system or a fully democratic exploration of policy alternatives, with wide and unlimited opportunities for dissent, seems to be remote. Nor can one foresee a fundamental change in the electoral system, or in the role of parliaments and courts, or a freedom of expression and association comparable to that of a fully constitutional system. In certain countries, if present trends continue, there will probably be expanded opportunities for non-governing groups to express dissent and to influence public policy through private pressure and public discussion. There may be a somewhat greater participation by the legislatures in policy formation; a somewhat more effective parliamentary control of executive action by the assemblies; perhaps, limited electoral competition; and a greater role in decision-making by organisations such as the trade unions and professional associations. The tradition of the monolithic party and of the party's monopoly of power is, however, likely to die hard and to set strict limits to the expression of opposition. The single party seems destined to remain the chief mechanism of political control and rule-making although it may to an increasing degree become a kind of arbiter among conflicting interests and viewpoints, or even in some cases, agency of conciliation and mediation. Opposition, therefore, will continue to express itself primarily in non-institutionalised ways, such as those described, through factional conflicts, and informal group actions, and only to a limited degree, as in Yugoslavia, in more institutionalised forms.

The unanswerable question remains: how far will the process of opposition develop and what effect will it have on the system as a whole? It is impossible to predict the degree to which the regimes will tolerate opposition and the extent to which the oppositional tendencies will go in expressing specific dissent. Full tolerance of opposition is hardly likely, and, at present, complete rejection of the communist regime by the opposition is also not probable. There is, however, a propensity for dissenters to go beyond the specific cause of their opposition to more fundamental opposition, and even in some circumstances, to integral resistance. There is also a tendency on the part of the regime to fear even moderate dissent, and to curb criticism if it goes too far. The future of opposition, and of the regimes themselves, will depend therefore on conscious acts of human will, the outcome of which cannot be predicted. An excessive curbing of opposition, or too generous a toleration of it, might produce a situation of radical conflict and in certain circumstances conceivably lead to a collapse of the system. On the other hand, dissenters may be unwilling to take the risks of active or open opposition, thus producing a passive and stagnant situation, or they may exploit opportunities for dissent too recklessly, provoking the regime to reprisals and creating a dangerous crisis. Stable development therefore depends on a kind of equilibrium of mutual tolerance by regime and opposition which is extremely difficult to maintain and may easily be disturbed on either side. It is on this subtle balance of human factors, in Eastern Europe as in other countries, that the future of opposition will depend.

Hugh Seton-Watson

Czechoslovakia – 1938, 1948 and 1968*

THE MUNICH AGREEMENT HAS BEEN THE SUBJECT OF a vast literature. There are only a few points which I should like to make. The first is that for the Czechs the main horror of Munich was not that it deprived them of valuable territories, but that it was imposed on them by their allies. The Anglo-French ultimatum of September 1938 profoundly wounded President Beneš and the whole Czech nation. If they had had no friends at all, the Czechs might have fought alone and perished, or they might have surrendered, the tragedy would have been simple. But their false friends told them that if they resisted they would be in the wrong, they deprived them even of the chance of defending themselves. This was to have lasting effects on their national morale.

The second point is that, if the British nation wronged the Czechs in 1938, it is also true that between 1939 and 1945 they repaid their moral debt to them. Britain was the only country which fought Hitler for the whole six years.

The third point is that though the Soviet government behaved correctly in 1938, it did nothing to help Czechoslovakia. It was of course bound by two obligations: to go to war if France went to war in defence of Czechoslovakia, and to join in any action against aggression ordered by the League of Nations. Neither obligation arose. The Soviet leaders certainly had nothing to reproach themselves with. However, the assertion often made by Soviet propaganda, that the Soviet Union would have fought Germany alone if Beneš had decided to ignore the Western Powers and fight, is supported by no evidence known to me, or to any specialist whom I have consulted.

In liberated Czechoslovakia after 1945 the forces frozen by Nazi rule began to thaw. There was a multi-party democracy,

* Vol. 4, No. 2, Spring 1969.

a free press, a reviving cultural life. The fact that Czechs and Slovaks are two nations was now officially recognised, and honest attempts were being worked out to put their relations on a new basis. Revisiting Czechoslovakia in 1946 and 1947 I was impressed by the same intellectual vitality and energy, the same curiosity and passion for knowledge about the whole world which had delighted me in the visits of my undergraduate days, in 1937 and 1938. The Czechs and Slovaks now accepted the need to co-operate closely in foreign policy with the Soviet Union: indeed they positively desired such co-operation. But they also wished to conduct their internal affairs in their own way, to introduce socialism certainly, but on the foundations of democratic liberty as Masaryk had shown it to them.

It was precisely this that the Soviet leaders would not allow them. The Czechoslovak communists were told to change their tactics, they seized power and deprived their former associates of liberty. The single event which most eloquently symbolises the tragedy of the whole Czech people is the death of the son of the President-Liberator, Jan Masaryk, the Foreign Minister of the Republic, who was found dead under the window of his apartment in the Czernin Palace on 10 March 1948. Whether his murder was direct or indirect we still do not know.

The next years brought economic exploitation and political terror, different from that of the Nazi period but not less cruel. One single political orthodoxy was imposed by force; contact with Western countries became treasonable; Slovak autonomy was reduced to a fiction, and Slovak patriots were persecuted as bourgeois nationalists even if they were communists. In the early 1950s came a purge of the ranks of the Communist Party itself, more far-reaching and more bloody than had been seen outside the Soviet Union itself.

In the 1950s Czechoslovakia presented a gloomy spectacle to its foreign friends. There appeared to be less resistance to totalitarianism than anywhere else in Eastern Europe, even than in Bulgaria. It looked as if the spirit of Hus and Masaryk had finally died out, as it had appeared that the spirit of Luther and Goethe had died out under the Third Reich.

Yet the appearance was misleading. Forces were gathering under the surface. A new generation was growing up, which had known only totalitarianism, yet which looked back to the heritage of Masaryk. Slovak national feeling revived and found open expression, industrial managers began to demand reforms, there was a new flowering of the arts and literature, and writers put forward bold political demands. The ferment spread to the Communist Party, and then suddenly the whole structure of Novotny's despotism began to crumble. The leaders of the Communist Party became a party of democratic socialism.

Once more the Czechs and Slovaks proclaimed their loyalty to their alliance with the Soviet Union, and their devotion to socialism, but once more they asked to be allowed to manage their own affairs in their own way. The Soviet answer was the same as in 1948: a brutal refusal. In 1948 they had had their agents willing to do their bidding. In 1968 they had to send in their armies. Continuity with 1938 was maintained by the presence of German troops sent by Ulbricht, and also by the intervention of Poles and Hungarians. The Polish action deserves a brief comment. In the 19th century Polish troops were often to be found on foreign battle-fields, in defence of some struggle for national freedom. Their motto, known to every Polish child for generations past, was 'For our freedom and yours!' As far as I know, 1968 is the first time that Polish troops have marched into another country with the avowed object of imposing censorship and suppressing freedom of speech, and it is certainly the first time that they have marched in the simultaneous company of Russians and Prussians.

Another common feature of 1938 and 1968 was the demonstration of friendship for Czechoslovakia by the Yugoslavs and Rumanians. I was in Prague in July 1938, during the last rally of the Sokols, the great gymnastic society which played a leading role in the Czech national revival of the 19th century. The enthusiasm with which the crowds greeted the large number of Yugoslav and Rumanian athletes who came to take part in the public ceremonies is something I shall not forget. During that summer tens of thousands of Yugoslavs were volunteering to fight in the Czechoslovak army, but the Yugoslav government, under Stojadinović, had gone over to the German side. The Rumanian government, on the other hand, maintained a helpful and honourable attitude throughout the crisis. In 1968 both the governments and the peoples of these two countries showed their sympathy for Czechoslovakia, at a risk to themselves which it is hard to estimate, and of which we may hear more in the future.

Would the Czechs and Slovaks have fared better if they had resisted? In 1938, 1948 and 1968 their leaders accepted defeat without fighting. Were they right to do so?

Let us first state certain things clearly. The Czechoslovak surrender was extremely convenient to the Western governments on all three occasions. In 1938 the apologists of Munich were even so good as to take a little time off from their dithyrambs to Chamberlain, in order to praise Beneš for his realism. In 1948 and 1968 the Western sighs of relief were positively deafening. But Western praise, based on bad consciences, proves nothing about Czech and Slovak interests.

It is equally clear that Western blame for Czechoslovakia's surrender would be sheer impudence. It was the Anglo-French ultimatum of September 1938 which forced Beneš to yield. In 1948 the West did not betray Beneš, but no encouragement was offered. In 1968 the Western attitude has varied from the helpless distress of the West Germans and British to the more or less contemptuous indifference of the United States and France.

But regardless of Western attitudes, the question remains. I remember that in the spring of 1939 I asked the late Hubert Ripka[1] what he thought. His reply was: 'I as a Czech have the right to reproach Beneš, but no Frenchman or Englishman has that right.' I agreed with him then, and agree still. But after thirty years it is clear to me that the historian, whatever his nationality, has to raise the problem. Let me put a number of hypothetical questions. If Czechoslovakia had fought alone in 1938, could it have held out for some weeks, and if so, would France and Britain have been forced to join in? If Beneš had ordered the Czechoslovak army to suppress the communist *putsch* in February 1948, would the Soviet army have invaded Czechoslovakia? If the Soviet leaders in 1968 had not known beforehand both that the Czechoslovak forces would not fight, and that the United States was completely indifferent, would they have ordered the invasion? If they had invaded, and there had been large-scale fighting in Bohemia, can any one know what would have happened? Finally, did the surrender of 1938 so demoralise a whole generation of political leaders that the

[1] A close friend of President Beneš, for many years foreign editor of the liberal newspaper *Lidove Noviný*, during the war Deputy-Minister of Foreign Affairs in exile, in 1945–8 Minister of Foreign Trade, from 1948 until his death again an exile.

surrender of 1948 was inevitable, and did the surrender of 1948 predetermine the surrender of 1968? I cannot answer any of these questions, but I am sure that they will be asked by historians, and by Czech and Slovak men and women who care for their country, for long years to come.

I might however comment briefly on the last question. It may well be argued that in 1968 there was no surrender, that the Czechs and Slovaks gave such a demonstration of unity, and of contempt and hostility towards the invader, as has never been seen before. It may also be argued that a young generation has grown up which has not been accustomed to surrender. In 1945 the Czechs and Slovaks were demoralised by years of humiliation and by guilt complexes about collaboration with the enemy, and they were misled by illusions about their Russian big brothers. These things were especially true of men in their twenties, who had been children when the First Republic was destroyed. Today things are different. The illusions have gone, and the young generation is one which has been struggling for some years, with growing success until now, for freedom and human dignity. It is a realistic generation, which knows better than its parents what it means by liberty, which accepts socialism but does not accept its interpretation by the scribes and Pharisees of Moscow. It is also a generation capable of heroic self-sacrifice. The terrible act of the student Jan Palach recalled the fate of Jan Hus at Constance and of the Buddhist monks of Saigon. The world-wide horror, admiration and compassion for the martyr and his people left no mark on the hearts of stone and minds of mud which serve the members of the Soviet Politburo. But the fortune of young Czechs and Slovaks in their own country, and their effect on its occupiers, are something which even the men in the Kremlin, the self-appointed sole interpreters of Marxist-Leninist science, may hesitate to predict.

Finally, we may perhaps recall the words of the great Czech hitorian Palacky, the leading spokesman of the Czech people in the mid-19th century. Palacky believed for most of his life in Austria: he believed that the Czechs belonged in the Habsburg Monarchy and that the emperor was their sovereign and protector. It was he who invented the phrase: 'If Austria had not existed, it would have been necessary to invent her.' His belief brought him many disappointments, and in the end he gave it up. He spoke the words known to every Czech school-child: 'Before Austria was, we were, and when she has ceased to exist, we shall still be there.' Half a century later, Palacky's words were proved true. The generations of Czechs who followed Palacky put something of the same trust in Russia as he had put in Austria, and it has proved no less misplaced. Long before Moscow was built, the Czechs existed and Bohemia was a civilised state. The speed at which empires crumble has quickened in this century of ours. We need not doubt that the Czechs and Slovaks will outlive the Muscovite Empire, and it may well be that some of us will live to see that day.

A. H. Brown

Political Change in Czechoslovakia*

IN A RECENT ISSUE OF *Government and Opposition* AN AT-
tempt was made to answer at an abstract level the question,
'Why Political Systems Change'.[1] The aim of this article is more
limited. It is a tentative preliminary attempt to explain why
important changes took place in a particular political system –
that of Czechoslovakia – in January 1968 and to examine the
changes themselves and what remains of them in the wake of
the Soviet intervention.

It must be emphasised straight away that the January changes
in Czechoslovakia were not so sudden as their treatment by the
western mass media perhaps implied. For something close to
five years before the January reforms pluralistic developments
could be discerned in Czechoslovakia. Limited though they
were, they expressed themselves in the form of a less severely
censored press, greater scope for interest group activity, a slight
relaxation of detailed central party control over the National
Assembly and local government ,and in more debate within the
ranks of the Communist Party.[2] The pre-January changes were
perhaps more atmospheric than institutional. Thus, the intellectual and cultural climate in, say, 1965 was very different
from that of 1960. Diversities of view had become vocal and a
spirit of critical inquiry found expression in films, the theatre,
the literary journals and in radical innovation in the curricula

[1] David Apter, *Government and Opposition*, III, No. 4, Autumn 1968.
[2] For further discussion of aspects of these developments see Edward Táborský:
'Czechoslovakia: out of Stalinism?' in *Problems of Communism*, May/June 1964;
A. H. Brown, 'Pluralistic Trends in Czechoslovakia' in *Soviet Studies*, April 1966;
Morton Schwartz, 'Czechoslovakia: Towards One-Party Pluralism?' in *Problems
of Communism*, January/February 1967; and H. Gordon Skilling, 'Background to
the Study of Opposition in Communist Eastern Europe', pp. 72–103 above.

* Vol. 4, No. 2, Spring 1969.

of higher educational institutions. (Particularly pertinent were the new developments in the social sciences, philosophy and history.) Perhaps the most concrete and overt of all pre-January changes was the economic reform which was accepted in principle by the January 1965 plenum of the Central Committee of the Czechoslovak Communist Party.

Though insufficient attention has in general been paid to the pre-history of the January events, it is, nevertheless, entirely reasonable to regard the plenary session of the Central Committee of the Czechoslovak Communist Party within the first week of 1968 as an important turning-point. It was at this meeting that the offices of President of the Republic and First Secretary of the Party Central Committee were separated and Alexander Dubček succeeded Antonín Novotný as First Secretary. Proposals for further change and many actual changes subsequently became almost daily events, but the most basic of the changes which were initiated or carried further can be easily summarised as follows:

1. *Inner-party democratisation.* The wide range of opinion and the reformist tendencies within the party which had struggled for expression before January were articulated as they had never been previously in the post-1948 history of the Czechoslovak Communist Party. From the highest party organs to the lowest there was real debate, and pressure from below played a considerable part in influencing higher party appointments. The draft party rules which were published shortly before the invasion were designed to give official ratification to the new reality whereby, for instance, the individual party member not only had the right to his own opinion but the right to attempt to convert others to his view.

2. *Freedom of expression for the mass media.* Censorship virtually withered away in the post-January atmosphere and newpapers began to develop a distinctive character and line of their own. Editors were still appointed by the top party leadership but the latter no longer determined the contents of the paper. There was a virtual explosion of information, and the press, radio and television helped to stimulate a new level of political awareness with their revelations and questioning. (Czechoslovak political scientists as well as journalists made use of weeklies such as *Literárný Listy* to publish political critiques which were both pungent and perceptive.)

3. *Federalism.* Though the new federal structure of Czechoslovakia was only finalised in the post-August period and officially came into operation on 1 January 1969, the decision to federalise was one of the most important decisions taken soon after the January change. Whether the doctrine of democratic centralism and the centralising tendencies which have characterised communist parties even more than other ruling parties would have allowed Czechoslovakia to approach near 'ideal type' federalism is perhaps doubtful. Plans were, however, made to create separate party organisations within the framework of a federal party. This would have involved creating a separate party organisation for the Czech lands of Bohemia and Moravia to match the already existing Slovak Party and at the same time according the Slovak Party a greater measure of autonomy.[3] State, as distinct from party, bodies have in fact become federative.

4. *Changes in the relationship of the Communist Party with other institutions in society.* Other elements within the National Front besides the Communist Party (for example, the trade unions and the Socialist and People's Parties) were allowed to establish a more clearly separate identity. New organisations were able to develop which were completely free from Communist Party tutelage, prominent among them being KAN (the Club of Committed Non-Party Members) and Club 231 (of former political prisoners). The grievances of the churches began to be redressed and a genuine religious freedom was re-established.

5. *Recognition of role of public opinion.* While the leadership of the Czechoslovak Communist Party made clear that it did not intend to relinquish its 'leading role' in society, the reformist elements in the Central Committee distinguished leadership from dictation. In rejecting a high level of coercion, they committed themselves to listening to (and taking account of) popular opinion and the views of particular sectional interests.[4] Dubček personally acquired the reputation of being a good

[3] The intention to federalise the party has not, in fact, been carried out. See pp. 127, 128, where I discuss what remains of the reforms.

[4] This point links up with David Apter's Information-Coercion Relationship ('Why Political Systems Change', op. cit.). Though this aspect of the Apter model strikes me as relevant and illuminating, I have very serious reservations about the explanatory value of his conceptual construct as a whole. Among other things, his blurring of the distinction between technical information and political opinion is unhelpful.

listener and popular opinion was given an opportunity to express itself – for example, in the form of public opinion polls which did not shirk the most sensitive political issues and which were publicised by the mass media. There was official recognition, too, for the useful part which the organised interests might play in reflecting sectional opinion and providing specialised knowledge as an aid to decision-making.[5]

6. *The curb on secret police powers.* The Ministry of Interior came under the control of a reformist minister, Josef Pavel. Some of the worst past offenders in the ministry lost their jobs and an attempt was begun to convert the ministry from a secret police machine into the more limited kind of guardian of national security which exists in any state.[6] Investigations into past violations of justice in which the Ministry of Interior had played a prominent part put its officials very much on the defensive between January and August. They were in no position to carry out the arrests which the Soviet Party leaders (and some old-style Czech party functionaries) felt were required. At the same time control of prisons was transferred from the Ministry of the Interior to the Ministry of Justice. The developing independence of the judiciary was a significant check in addition to that of public opinion.

7. *Change in the role of the National Assembly.* Prior to January 1968, the National Assembly came close to being a rubber-stamp legislature on the lines of the Supreme Soviet. In the post-January period it played a much more vigorous role in critically examining legislation. Especially following the appointment of Josef Smrkovský as chairman of its Praesidium, the National Assembly became a political force to be reckoned with. Its increasing tendency to scrutinise government proposals

[5] Interest group activity was accepted by the Action Programme of the Communist Party approved in early April. Earlier Zdeněk Mlynář, one of the authors of the Action Programme and a theorist who had long recognised the role which interest groups might play in the decision-making process, had urged (*Rudé Právo*, 13 February 1968) that 'every institutional component of the political system must also be an independent political agent: the state (its agencies), the Party, and the many social organisations which represent various interests of people (the interests of producers and consumers, various professional groups, and of various types of labour, the interests of specific generations, cultural interests, etc.)'.

[6] The Action Programme of the Czechoslovak Communist Party argued that it was necessary to divide the security forces into two independent bodies – one concerned with combating external threats and the other with maintaining public order at home. The individual Czechoslovak citizen's political opinions were to be of no interest to either body.

rigorously was not universally welcomed, and in the post-August period Dubček was among those who, in retrospect, criticised the National Assembly for its tardiness in passing necessary legislation.

8. *Important changes of personnel.* The most important change of personnel was the removal of Novotný from his offices of First Secretary (in January) and President (in March) and his replacement by Alexander Dubček and General Ludvík Svoboda. But part of the importance of this lay precisely in the fact that it opened the path of promotion to men, more radical than Dubček, who had definite ideas on reform of the poitical system. Thus, for example, in early April Zdeněk Mlynář and Čestmír Císař were appointed to the Secretariat of the Central Committee of the Communist Party, while František Kriegel and Josef Smrkovský were appointed to its Praesidium. At the same time the Central Committee recommended Smrkovský as chairman of the Praesidium of the National Assembly and Kriegel as chairman of the National Front. Within a few days the enlarged Central Committee of the National Front unanimously elected Kriegel as its chairman and in the middle of April the National Assembly accepted the resignation of its chairman, Bohuslav Laštovička, and elected Smrkovský in his place. A significant appointment in the government formed by the new Prime Minister, Oldřich Černík, on 8 April was that of Ota Šik as one of the five vice-premiers.

Taking the changes as a whole, it may be said that the 'new men' in the party and government leadership included not only able young intellectuals (e.g. Mlynář) but steadfast party veterans (like Kriegel and Smrkovský) who had suffered at the hands of the Stalinists. It is worth noting that personnel changes were greater at the top than at the middle and lower levels of the party. At these levels the great majority of party officials succeeded in retaining their posts.

THE ACTION PROGRAMME

The most significant document to emerge in Czechoslovakia during 1968 was the sixty-four page Action Programme of the Communist Party published on 5 April. Some of the changes which it advocated have been touched upon in the points enumerated above, but the Programme is sufficiently important to merit some separate consideration. It was a compromise document in which the reformists, in the face of strong conservative opposition, had to make some concessions. Yet no ruling Communist Party has ever produced a programme containing more fundamental self-criticism or more radical proposals for reform of the political system.

The programme speaks of the 'unthinking adoption and dissemination' (in the early 1950s) 'of ideas, habits and political concepts which conflicted with our circumstances and traditions. The leading organs and institutions of the Party and state at that time bear full responsibility for this unthinking adoption.' It speaks of the gradual development of a 'bureucratic system'. 'The internal life of the republic was plagued by sectarianism, suppression of popular democratic freedom and liberty, legal violations, and evidence of dogmatism and misuse of power. . . .' The economic failure of the 1960s is noted and it is admitted that economic policy was implemented by 'arbitrary administrative methods' which 'no longer corresponded to the economic needs and opportunities of the country'. The programme states that 'the people became more and more embittered' and seeks the source of the trouble within the party itself. Among the defects it observes are unjustified interference with state organs, a 'cult of mediocrity' and 'ill-advised anonymity'.

In the past, the programme states, 'the leading role of the Party was often understood as a monopolistic concentration of power in the hands of the Party organs. This was in keeping with the false thesis that the Party is an instrument of the dictatorship of the proletariat. This harmful concept weakened the initiative and responsibility of state, economic and social institutions, damaged the authority of the Party, and hindered the Party in the performance of its proper functions.' This exposure of what the 'leading role' of the party had meant in practice is followed by proposals for the future which bear signs of compromise between those who believed that the party must be forced to justify itself in the political market place and those who were concerned to ensure that its apparatus would retain its controlling position. On the one hand, the need for 'systematic persuasion and personal example' on the part of communists to win over the working people is stressed. On the other hand, the programme states that 'the Party must not be turned into an organisation which exerts influence on society merely by its ideals and programmes. Through its members, organisations and organs, the Party must perform the practical organisational function of a political force in society. The political-organisational activity of the Party co-ordinates the practical efforts of people to ensure that the line and programme of the Party are implemented in all sectors – that is, in the social, economic and cultural life of society.' However, the programme greatly stresses the need to develop inner-party democracy. For example: 'The basis of the Party's ability to act under the new conditions lies in ideological and organisational unity, built on a foundation of broad democracy within the Party. The most effective way to prevent the introduction of methods of bureaucratic centralism into the Party is to strengthen the influence of Party members on the shaping of the political line, and to strengthen the role of organs elected in a really democratic way. The elected Party organs must guarantee, in the first place, that all rights of members are respected, and that decisions are made collectively and power is not concentrated in one person's hands.'

An important section of the Action Programme is devoted to 'the division and control of power – a guarantee against dogmatism'. It is argued that the government must be responsible to the National Assembly for its actions and that it must avoid shifting responsibility on to the party. The Programme does not advocate a 'separation of powers' but a 'system of mutual control'. Throughout the political system there should be no excessive concentration of power in any 'one link, apparatus or individual'. It is within this context that the Ministry of Interior comes under fire as one of the most obvious examples of an 'excessive concentration of functions'. In an attempt to put the security organs firmly in their (subordinate) place, the Programme goes on: 'The Party openly declares that this apparatus must not be used to resolve domestic political questions and conflicts within socialist society.' It also advocates a clearer definition of governmental control over the Ministry of the Interior and a clarification of its legal relationship with the National Assembly. As a further important safeguard against arbitrary executive action, the independence of the judiciary is upheld. 'The Party's legal policy is based on the principle that in law disputes, including those concerning administrative decisions of state organs, the basic guarantee of legality is court procedure which is independent of political factors and bound solely by law.' In general, in the view of the authors of the programme, the role of the courts in Czechoslovak society needs to be enhanced.

In the section of the Programme on external relations, Czechoslovakia's adherence to the Warsaw Pact and Comecon is emphasised. But the deepening of fraternal contacts with the Soviet Union and the other communist states is to be based upon 'mutual respect, sovereignty, equality of rights, mutual esteem, and international solidarity'. American aggression in Vietnam is condemned and the struggle against imperialism in general is to be waged, but there are signs in the Programme that, in spite of a broad area of agreement with the Soviet Union on questions of international relations, a more independent Czechoslovak foreign policy was beginning to emerge. No doubt in response to the very widespread sympathy with Israel which exists in Czechoslovakia, reference is made to the intention to seek a political solution of the Middle East crisis and there is no criticism of Israeli action in the Six Day War or following it. Czechoslovakia's intention of playing a more active part in the United Nations is explicitly stated and a more active future role for the Czechoslovak Communist Party within the international communist movement is predicted.

Among the many other questions of great importance taken up by the Programme are the necessity for factual discussion and clash of opinion as an aid to decision-making; the need for voluntary associations and interest groups to express the interests of their members (and independently choose their own representatives); the need for a two-way flow of information between government and the governed which would include the systematic use of public opinion surveys; the right of citizens to foreign travel and the need to make available more foreign literature and study trips for students; the rights of national minorities and, in particular, those of the Slovaks; the need to work out a new electoral system which would be in harmony with the other political changes and the principles of a developed socialist democracy; the need to give young people a greater chance to participate in decisions on matters affecting them; the aim of adjusting prices to accord more with the world market and ultimately to facilitate convertibility of the currency; and the development of the social sciences and the help that the social sciences may provide in the tackling of social problems. The list is far from complete, but sufficient, perhaps, to substantiate the claim which the Programme makes that its proposals are far-reaching and that their realisation would deeply affect the life of the country. In view of what has gone before, the bold statement of intent made towards the end of the Programme can lay claim to be more than empty rhetoric: 'We want to embark on the building of a new model of socialist society, one which is profoundly democratic and conforms to Czechoslovak conditions.'

The Soviet White Book on events in Czechoslovakia does not explicitly attack the Action Programme of the Czechoslovak Communist Party. The document which it regards as the manifesto of counter-revolution is the *Two Thousand Words*, published on 28 June. This manifesto was written by the novelist and party member, Ludvík Vaculík and sponsored by a distinguished group of Czech scholars and writers who included both Communists and non-Communists. In the Soviet view, 'the document is a frank (if thinly camouflaged with pro-socialist mouthings) platform of those forces in Czechoslovakia and abroad which under cover of talk about "liberalisation", "democratisation", etc. sought to cross out the history of Czechoslovakia from 1948 onwards, to nullify all socialist gains of the Czechoslovak working people, to subvert the friendship between the Czechoslovak people and the people of the fraternal socialist states.'[7] The *Two Thousand Words* document, in fact, makes many of the points which are contained in the Action Programme, with the difference that it never minces its words. Criticism of the sins of omission and commission of the Communist Party of Czechoslovakia is more biting. Credit is given to the party for starting the 'regenerative process of democratisation' of 1968, but it is qualified by the view that there was nowhere else that the process could have started since 'it was only communist criticism which had any impact on courses of action'. Support is given to the reformers in the Communist Party and anxiety expressed at what is seen as a slowing-down in the democratisation process. Public sessions of local national

[7] *On Events in Czechoslovakia: Facts, documents, press reports and eye-witness accounts*, Moscow, 1968, p. 23. A full English translation of the *Two Thousand Words* is included as Appendix 3, pp. 227–34, of the recent book by Kurt Weisskopf, *The Agony of Czechoslovakia '38/ '68*, London, 1968. The same author provides a translation of some of the major points of the Action Programme.

committees are demanded and the more radical suggestion is made that citizens should spontaneously set up civic committees and commissions to investigate questions which no official organ will look into. The document can be seen as one of support for the most radical elements within the Czechoslovak Communist Party, and though it was singled out by the Soviet White Book for particular attack, it is doubtful if this unofficial statement was anything like as alarming for the Soviet leadership as the statement of intentions of the Czechoslovak Communist Party itself.

SIGNIFICANCE OF THE CHANGES

Before any attempt is made to find reasons for the reforms which took place in Czechoslovakia in 1968 and for the invasion which interrupted them, an attempt must be made to assess their significance. The highest estimate of the significance of the changes comes from those who believe that the Czechoslovaks were developing a political model worthy of universal application. My own view of the post-January developments is that they may have had at least a European relevance. But a certain reluctance to go beyond that is engendered (a) by the fact that this new-model communism was still at a very transitional stage; and (b) the notorious difficulties involved in successfully transplanting political institutions. If the Czech students who predicted that their country was going to become 'the world's first democratic socialist state' were right, then not for the first time, a small state might have acquired a quite disporportionate influence in world politics. But the experiment remains incomplete and there are no other equally promising laboratories in sight.

Whatever the significance of Czechoslovakia for the outside world, there was no doubt of the significance of the post-January changes for the Czechs and Slovaks themselves. The disillusionment which existed inside the party and the apathy, in many quarters amounting to alienation, outside it which was characteristic of the later years of the Novotný era gave way to enthusiasm and involvement.[8] The real unity which the Czecho-

---

[8] The enthusiasm – so vividly displayed, for example, on May Day 1968 – was beautifully captured by a Czech documentary film, 'In the Heart of Europe', made to celebrate the fifty years of existence of the Czechoslovak state. The film

slovak people showed in the last days of August was built on
the foundation of the freedom to disagree which had preceded
it. With this had come a renewed sense of being a participant in
the political process. The significance of the reforms for the
Czechoslovaks must be seen in conjunction with the extent to
which a Czech tradition of humane and democratic values had
been subordinated to the very different Soviet paradigm. Only
eight years ago Professor Táborský could write in his major
scholarly study of Czechoslovak communism that the 'combination of Western parliamentary form with Marxist-Leninist
totalitarian substance is the only contribution of at least a
certain originality which the Czechoslovak communists have
made to political theory, and even this contribution has been
sharply depreciated by the stepped-up sovietisation of recent
years'.[9] As perceptive an observer as Táborský could conclude
on the basis of the evidence available at that time that the 'inner
weakness of Czechoslovak communism will undoubtedly prevent any meaningful democratisation in the foreseeable future
in the political system or in economics and culture'.[10]

   The significance of the post-January changes in Czechoslovakia for the Soviet Union and other communist states lay
precisely in the deviation they represented from the Soviet
model. The eight points already enumerated in this article (by
no means a comprehensive list) could be sharply contrasted
with Soviet practice in the equivalent areas of political life.

THE PROCESS OF CHANGE IN CZECHOSLOVAKIA

Until very recently remarkably little attention was given to
what (to coin an unwieldy neologism) may be termed the *dynamics of detotalitarianisation*. No doubt this omission was associated
with the common identification of real – and therefore incom-
pletely – totalitarian states with a near Orwellian model of
totalitarianism. By definition, any internal evolution other than
that sponsored by the leaders of the ruling monolithic and monopolistic party could be discounted and definition was thus

was completed before the intervention and at the time of writing – December
1968 – is still being shown in Czechoslovakia.
   [9] Edward Táborský, *Communism in Czechoslovakia, 1948–1960*, 1961, p. 603.
   [10] Ibid., p. 606.

substituted for political analysis. Yet any attempt to explain why Czechoslovakia deliberately set about dismantling the apparatus of totalitarianism while the Soviet Union, after moving away from the near ideal-type version achieved by Stalin, has still not moved anything like so far, involves theoretical consideration. The theoretical aspect I shall touch upon later in the article, but, first of all, it is desirable to examine the concrete forces which were at work in Czechoslovakia.

The factors involved were both endogenous and exogenous to the Communist Party. The main exogenous factors, which cannot, however, be entirely separated from the *internal* crisis in the party, were three (and it is extraordinarily difficult to weigh their relative significance):

1. *Economic failure.* 'The greatest stimulus to change', remarked the late Pavel Eisler in 1965, 'is failure'.[11] The *economic* failure (which was what Eisler had in mind) was real enough. To the qualitative deficiencies of Czechoslovak industry (which the party had learned to live with) was added in the early 1960s quantitative failure which turned out to be a much more traumatic experience for Czechoslovak society as a whole and the party decision-makers in particular. The seriousness of the situation which was recognised at the time in Czechoslovakia was also expressed quite bluntly for Soviet readers by Ota Šik writing in 1967: 'In 1962–1963 the growth of productivity of labour actually stopped.'[12]

2. *Czech–Slovak relations.* Though dissatisfaction in Slovakia had grown, this discontent was reasonably distinct from the economic trauma already mentioned. Slovak grievances were more than economic and, indeed, there were Czechs who felt that the attempt to industrialise Slovakia had been at the expense of necessary reinvestment in Bohemia and Moravia. The Slovak discontent was essentially nationalist and opposed to centralisation of decision-making in Prague. There were also specific grievances such as the under-representation of Slovaks

---

[11] I should personally prefer to rephrase the statement as follows: 'The greatest immediate stimulus to change is economic failure when expectations are high.' It is a generalisation which at least arguably applies to Czechoslovak developments in the 1960s. It would be easy to find examples of situations where it did not apply, for no single-sentence, unicausal explanation of political change could conceivably do justice to the complexity of social and political reality.

[12] V. F. Terekhov and V. M. Shastnitko (eds.), *Ekonomicheskiye reformy v sotsialisticheskikh stranakh*, Prague, 1967.

in high public office (e.g. in top party posts and the diplomatic service). The scant respect which some Czech party leaders – and most notably Novotný himself – paid to Slovak national traditions and their distinctive culture increased Slovak disquiet.

3. *Disillusionment of specific social groups.* The intelligentsia was the social group most thoroughly disillusioned and determined to seek change. Within this group, writers, social scientists and students were particularly significant elements. (To classify the Czechoslovak January as a 'student revolution' – which some commentators have done – is, however, grossly to exaggerate the specific role of students in stimulating the change.) There was less pressure for change from the workers than from the intellectuals, but there was very considerable working-class apathy during the later stages of the Novotný regime and a lack of positive identification with it. There was certainly no substantial working-class support for Novotný personally. Had there been, the reformers' task would have been rendered extremely difficult, if not impossible.

Within the party the intellectuals were a basic link between the endogenous and exogenous forces of change. The *party intelligentsia* played a crucial part in initiating change, partly by influencing public and party opinion in the country as a whole and also more directly in important party meetings and through their access to members of the party *apparat*. The changing role of the Communist Party in Czechoslovak society and the gradual acquisition of heterodox ideas by the party intellectuals (and, to a lesser extent, by the higher party *apparat*) is crucial to an understanding of the January changes.

Prior to the 1968 reforms there were two major attempts from within the party to bring about political change – in 1956 and 1963. In 1956 there was a limited response from the party leadership to Khrushchev's speech to the 20th Congress of the Soviet Communist Party. But it was a carefully controlled response calculated to ensure that change would not get out of hand in Czechoslovakia. The response was insufficient to satisfy many party members and there was a strong demand for the convening of an extraordinary party congress. The violent explosions in Hungary and Poland gave the party leadership the excuse they needed to reject such demands and many party members who had called for an extraordinary congress were expelled from the party. Other party members more or less voluntarily lapsed into orthodoxy, having been seriously disturbed by the Hungarian developments.

In the years immediately following the Hungarian uprising, memories of the Soviet reaction acted as a strong disincentive to any kind of political pressure from below in Eastern Europe. In Czechoslovakia it is probable that an additional major reason why ideas of political reform fell on stony ground in the late 1950s was that the economy was still booming and there was comparatively little working-class dissatisfaction. But in the early 1960s, as the economy stopped expanding, discontent grew. There is a case for regarding 1963 as the year in which the political thaw began. Under pressure, Novotný dismissed a number of 'Stalinists' from the leadership, including the Prime Minister, Viliam Široký. It was in 1963 that foreign travel became slightly easier (certainly for party intellectuals if not for the population as a whole) and in the course of the next five years, despite many vicissitudes, the political atmosphere became more relaxed and discussion and criticism within the party grew. In 1963 Novotný succeeded in stemming a revolt in the party, but he could not stop the process of disillusionment among the party intellectuals. The economic failure helped to promote scepticism among non-intellectuals also about the party leadership's handling of affairs.

In this period the party reverted to its pre-1948 practice of setting up commissions composed of members of scientific institutions as well as party functionaries to investigate particular problem areas. An *ad hoc* commission under the chairmanship of Šik worked out detailed proposals for economic reform, and in 1963–4 five permanent commissions of the Central Committee of the Party were set up. They were concerned with ideology, law, the economy, agriculture and living standards and became a medium through which party intellectuals sought to influence the party's top decision-makers. In theory, the commissions were free to present their views directly to the Praesidium of the Central Committee of the Party. In practice, they had to go through the relevant department of the Central Committee *apparat*. By the time their analyses and proposals reached the Praesidium, they had generally been considerably diluted along the way. But *something* got through, and in the meantime the more intelligent members of the *apparat* were being influenced by the reformers.

So far as the work of Šik's commission is concerned, the
economists won round the rest of the party intelligentsia to
strong support for the proposed reforms and eventually the
party leadership was persuaded. Novotný and some of his
colleagues were unenthusiastic to say the least, regarding some
of the reforms as revisionist. But since they recognised that the
economy was in serious trouble, and since they had no alternative theory on how to put things right, they reluctantly
acquiesced with the proposals of the economists. The economic
reforms had no sooner been officially approved in 1965, however, than party vested interests set about diluting them. As a
consequence, the economists were not alone within the party in
thinking that a socialist market economy would not work
so long as the political system remained unreformed and
well-ingrained habits of bureaucratic interference continued un-
checked. It was Šik who first gave clear *public* voice to this position – that the economic reform could not work without political
reform – on the last day of the 13th Congress of the Czechoslovak Communist Party in the summer of 1966. The widespread
discontent which already existed within the party ranks was
fertile soil for such an idea and it quickly gathered strength.

Besides Šik's large group of economists, there were two other
academic teams at work whose influence inside the party
intelligentsia was considerable. One was headed by Zdeněk
Mlynář at the Academy of Sciences and was concerned with
analysing the workings of the political system in Czechoslovakia
and working out an optimal political model for the country.
A good many of the ideas which were publicly aired in Czechoslovakia for the first time in 1968, some of which were included
in the party's Action Programme and were in the process of
becoming institutionalised, were the product of work by members of this team. The other group was an inter-disciplinary
team headed by Radovan Richta which investigated the effects
on society and implications for socialism of the scientific and
technological revolution. Richta's team told the party leaders
what they wanted to hear: namely, that socialism had all the
pre-requisites for carrying out the scientific-technological revolution and could do the job better than capitalism. At the same
time they argued that to a completely new degree they would
have to take account of scientific findings and the results of new
technology. Many members of the party *apparat*, rightly or

wrongly, drew the conclusion that this aim which they saw as desirable was unlikely to be realised under the leadership of Novotný.

Criticism at the Writers' Congress in June 1967 and harsh suppression of a student demonstration later in the year provoked new pressures inside the party. Inner-party life was on the verge of collapse, so great was the rift between the leaders and members. For some time there had been members of the higher *apparat* who were failing to carry out the spirit or letter of certain instructions which they regarded as unenforceable or too stupid to be worthy of implementation. By January 1968 there was something approaching a consensus not only in the party intelligentsia (for whom this had long been a commonplace) but also in the higher *apparat* that Novotný's capacities were too limited for the office of First Secretary which he held. To this feeling was added the three basic sources of discontent (or exogenous factors) which I have already touched upon – the frustration of the economic reform, the Czech–Slovak tension (which Novotný's tactlessness had exacerbated), and the widespread intellectual opposition to official party policy.

The temporary coalition which ousted Novotný from the First Secretaryship in January was, like most coalitions, composed of very different elements – of people whose aims did not go beyond limited personnel changes,[13] with perhaps an improved position for themselves, and those who had far-reaching reforms in view. Within the Praesidium even the voice of such a hardliner as Jiří Hendrych (who by early April 1968, had himself resigned from the Praesidium, Secretariat and Chairmanship of the Ideological Commission of the Central Committee of the Party) was raised against Novotný. Novotný himself, when he found that there was no hope of retaining his position, proposed Prime Minister Josef Lenárt for the First Secretaryship, but there was majority support for the lesser known Alexander Dubček. Within the Central Committee as a whole, there was some support for both Černík and Smrkovský as candidates for the First Secretaryship, but again Dubček was accepted as a compromise candidate. Though he was subsequently to gain

[13] Alois Indra probably fell into this category. An abler man than Novotný, he had little respect for the latter's limited ability. On the other hand, as Indra's subsequent record was to indicate, his opposition to Novotný was not based on the extent to which Novotný was compromised by his past.

immense public popularity, his assets at the time were the more
limited ones that nobody had anything against him and that he
was a Slovak. His nationality helped in view of the extent to which
Slovak nationalism had been a contributory factor in the crisis.

Dubček had no personal programme of reform, nor any
knowledge of the speed with which the reform movement was
to gather force.[14] But, unlike his predecessor, he was very willing
to take advice from the party intellectuals. It is worthy of note
that the two men at present in the highest party offices –
Dubček and Gustav Husák, the First Secretary of the Slovak
party organisation – and the two men in the highest state offices
– President Svoboda and Prime Minister Černik – were not
the principal authors of the Action Programme of the Czechoslovak Communist Party nor the initiators of the process of
political reform. The main qualification to that statement must
be that Husák was one of the chief authors of the project of
federalisation.[15] But that apart, it is not unfair to say that the
leaders were carried along by a movement of reform which they
did not begin[16] and which they could not have stopped without
losing moral authority. To that extent the Soviet leaders were
right. Though there was comparatively little risk of the
Czechoslovak Communist Party losing majority support in the
forseeable future[17] (its popularity increased enormously after

[14] Some armchair criticism of Dubček on the grounds that he allowed the mass
media to demand too much too soon is beside the point. Though there are *degrees*
of freedom, a basic test of a free press is whether or not political rulers can prevent
it from publishing something they do not like. The liberalising movement in
Czechoslovakia acquired its own momentum. Dubček could only have imposed
his more cautious judgement on the most outspoken journals by resorting to precisely those methods from which the new party leadership was trying to escape.

[15] Husák only became First Secretary of the Slovak Party *after* the invasion.
Dubček's successor as head of the Slovak Party organisation in January was Vasil
Bilák, an even more conservative communist than Husák. Husák set enormous
store by federalisation. Indeed, he annoyed many Slovaks by his insistent references
to Slovak rights in the first months after the Soviet intervention, a time when
Slovaks in general felt more united with the Czechs than ever before.

[16] This point becomes a substantive one for those Czechoslovaks who believe
that too much has been conceded by their leaders under Soviet pressure in the
post-August meetings. Some Czechs claim that there is an unfortunate significance
in the fact that those who have had to defend the post-January gains in successive
confrontations with the Soviet leaders were not those who initiated the radical
reforms. They would have preferred as negotiators Mlynář, Šik or Smrkovský to
Černik and Husák.

[17] What might have happened in the very long run is anyone's guess. But does
the Soviet Union, any more than other states, base its foreign and defence policies
upon the very long run?

the January changes), the party leaders were not in full control of the reform movement.

REFORM VERSUS INTERVENTION

An attempt to explain the Soviet intervention would involve detailed consideration of political, military and psychological factors. It seems likely, however, that the most basic factor was Soviet fear of the potential political influence of the Czechoslovak model of a socialist state. If the Czechoslovaks could have combined their democratisation with the economic progress they anticipated, it was not an unreasonable assumption that this would have been a very attractive formula for other communist states. In the first place it would have increased the pressures on the party leadership in Poland and East Germany (hence the hard line adopted towards Czechoslovakia by those two regimes) and ultimately its influence would have been felt within the Soviet Union itself. There is, after all, much more cultural communication and cross-national contact among members of the Warsaw Pact (and Comecon) than between the Soviet Union and the West.

Successive rejections of the Soviet political model and Moscow leadership on the part of other communist states must have been bitter blows for the Soviet leadership. For them to watch helplessly while Czechoslovakia added itself to the list of Yugoslavia, China, Albania and (to a lesser extent) Rumania would have required a considerable exercise in self-control. Such restraint might have called in question the credibility of the Soviet Union as the dominating force in the system of communist states.[18] By accepting the odium inseparable from armed intervention, the Soviet Union indicated to its Warsaw Pact partners that it would tolerate no further serious deviation from the *status quo*. In this sense the intervention was a defensive reaction – a backlash against the theory and practice of polycentrism.

What remains of the Czechoslovak reforms in the postintervention period is difficult to state precisely, for the conflict

[18] The invasion itself did great damage to the moral authority and influence of the Soviet Union within the world communist movement. But it would appear that the interests of this *movement* come much lower on the list of Soviet priorities than concern with developments in the European *communist states*.

of wills persists and the situation is one of flux. Immediately after the invasion, in the face of almost total non-co-operation on the part of Czechs and Slovaks, the Soviet Union failed to achieve all its objectives. The 'Moscow Agreement' of 26 August was a compromise between the Czechoslovak and Soviet positions, notwithstanding the fact that the former were forced to negotiate under duress.[19] Subsequently, however, the Soviet leaders have pressed for obedience to the demands made at Dresden, Cierná and Bratislava and have demanded changes which go beyond those 'agreed' in Moscow on 26 August.

The four basic demands which were made by the Soviet Union when Soviet and Czechoslovak Party leaders met in Moscow in early October were in effect: (a) that the Czechoslovak Party should give up its Action Programme as revisionist; (b) renew the leading role of the party along the lines of the early 1960s; (c) intimidate all those pursuing an 'anti-socialist' policy, and introduce a severe censorship; and (d) carry out a personnel policy whereby there would be room only for 'dedicated comrades'.

The last point is linked to one of the most basic Soviet objections to the Czechoslovak Communist Party which is that it is much too large. The Czechoslovak Party, with over one and a half million members, has more than 12 per cent of the total population within its ranks. The Soviet leaders consider this to be at least twice as large as it should be – not surprisingly, since the Soviet Communist Party accounts for only five and a half per cent of the Soviet population. The Moscow view (and it is probably correct) is that the larger a party gets, the harder it is to maintain strict discipline and to prevent fundamental diversity of view from arising. To a much greater extent than the CPSU the Czechoslovak Communist Party has been – and remains – a *coalition* of socialists who disagree on much, including the definition of socialism. In particular, the question, 'Where do we go from here?', has divided the Czechoslovak Communist Party over the past few years.

The remarkable unity of the overwhelming majority of the party in the face of armed intervention could not be a permanent

[19] It is clear that one of the minimum Soviet objectives was the replacement of Alexander Dubček as First Secretary of the Czechoslovak Communist Party. The deep hostility of the Soviet leaders to Dubček was confirmed by *Pravda*'s reference to him on 22 August as the leader of a minority group within the Praesidium who adopted a 'frankly right-wing opportunist position'.

feature of party life. The November plenary session of the Central Committee of the Party showed the considerable degree to which the Central Committee itself was split between 'conservatives' and 'progressives' and a similar division of opinion persists in the twenty-one man Praesidium. At the November plenum, the position of the most radical party leaders was somewhat weakened. One of them, Zdeněk Mlynář, resigned from the Praesidium and Secretariat. Josef Smrkovský, whose standing in the party as a whole and the country increased enormously after 21 August, remained, but his position within the leadership seemed less secure. A new Executive Committee of the Praesidium was set up in which a rather careful balance was struck between the opposing tendencies in the Central Committee. This eight-man body includes conservatives, though not Alois Indra nor Vasil Bilák [20] (the open collaborators of August) and only Smrkovský of the radicals. In spite of the apparently great support for them which still exists in the country, the radicals fared less well in the nine-man party bureau which was appointed to control party work in the Czech lands. It is known that the chairman of the Czech Party Bureau, Lubomír Štrougal (the Minister of Interior from 1961 to 1965), was the Soviet choice for the post, the original Czech choice having been Josef Špaček. Špaček, the regional secretary of the South Moravian party organisation, surprisingly enough, was not made a member of the bureau, though he retained his position as member of the full Praesidium and of the Secretariat of the Central Committee.

It is perhaps unlikely that the Czech Party Bureau will play a very significant role in relation to the Praesidium and Secretariat of the Central Committee, but only time will tell. What does appear to be the case is that Soviet pressure has been successful in preventing a fuller federalisation for this would have involved the creation of a separate Czech Party. A distinct party organisation for the Czech lands other than the bureau now appears unlikely.

Federalism in the fullest sense is by no means all that has been lost. The process of democratisation within the party would

[20] Indra was, however, confirmed in his post as Secretary of the Central Committee and Bilák is a member both of the Praesidium and of the Secretariat. The members of the Executive Committee of the Praesidium are Dubček, Prime Minister Černík, President Svoboda, G. Husák, E. Erban, S. Sadovský, J. Smrkovský and L. Štrougal.

appear to have been halted as the party leaders, under Soviet
pressure, have found themselves taking many steps which were
against the wishes of the majority of party members, among
them the suspension of the new and outspoken theoretical
journal of the Central Committee, *Politika*. The freedom of
expression of the mass media has been severely curtailed, though
the press still remains a good deal less than monolithic. Organisations such as KAN and Club 231 have been banned and the
National Assembly is once again playing a more subordinate
role, though it has not yet abandoned free speech.

So far as personnel in leading positions are concerned, there
have been concessions to the Soviet point of view. The resignation of Mlynář in November has been mentioned and to it can
be added an already significant list which includes the resignation at Soviet insistence of František Kriegel from all his political
offices immediately after the August return of the Czechoslovak
leaders from Moscow, the resignation of Foreign Secretary Jiří
Hájek and Vice-Premier Ota Šik, and Císař's move from the
Secretariat of the Central Committee to the chairmanship of
the Czech National Council. Also of significance were the removal of Josef Pavel from the Ministry of Interior and the
resignation of the heads of television and of radio, Jiří Pelikán
and Zdeněk Hejzlar. More conservative elements have re-
asserted themselves, the promotion of Štrougal having been
particularly rapid. The most important element of continuity
in the party leadership (and it is upon this that its continued
popular support depends) is the presence of Dubček, Smrkovský, Svoboda and Černík in key positions. Černík, however,
like Husák, has been willing to modify his former reformist
position very considerably in response to Soviet pressure, though
Smrkovský has stubbornly clung to the post-January policies.
Dubček has appeared to take a middle course between Husák
and Smrkovský and has succeeded in retaining popular trust
and affection. Dubček's distinctive contribution between January and August lay not so much in his programme (for the programme was 'his' only in a rather formal sense), but in his
integrity and 'style'. Most Czechs and Slovaks firmly believe
that he has retained the former, though his style has been
adapted to the new conditions. Openness and accessibility
have been discarded. But Dubček has refused to be a party to
political arrests (there have been none to date) and the policy

of rehabilitation of those unjustly accused in the political trials of the 1950s has continued.

POLITICAL CULTURE AND POLITICAL CHANGE

By the time of the Soviet intervention, it is fair to say that political dissent had been to a higher degree institutionalised in Czechoslovakia than in any other communist state, not excluding Yugoslavia. Though the Yugoslavs began to reform their system, which up to and beyond their expulsion from the Cominform in 1948 was strongly 'Stalinist', much earlier than the Czechs, the Czechoslovak reforms, once begun, acquired momentum more quickly. 'Pluralistic socialism' had become a reality, though it still fell some way short of the fully 'democratic socialism' which was the goal of many political activists both inside and outside the Czechoslovak Communist Party.

Why this should have been so – the deeper reasons for the Czechoslovak political change – is a question of considerable theoretical interest. The most useful framework for understanding why radical political change took place in Czechoslovakia rather than in the Soviet Union, for example, is not, in my view, 'modernisation' theory as developed by Apter and others, but 'comparative political culture'.[21] The enormous differences in the political cultures of, say, the Soviet Union,

[21] 'Comparative Political Culture' is the title of an essay by Sidney Verba which forms the last chapter (pp. 512–60) of Pye and Verba, *Political Culture and Political Development*, 1965. The concept of political culture had earlier been developed by Gabriel Almond and Samuel Beer, but Verba's lucid and judicious essay is the best treatment of the concept I have seen. It would not be totally unfair to say that 'political culture' is but a new name for the kind of relevant information which political scientists have traditionally studied under some such heading as 'historical background'. But the recent elaboration of the concept has been of value in clarifying the relationship between history and politics and for its stress upon the influence of society upon the way political institutions function. It has been made 'operational' by the collection of quantitative data and it is at this point that any attempt to apply the concept to communist states runs into difficulties. It is unlikely that Western political scientists are going to be allowed to carry out surveys in East Europe on the scale of those employed by Almond and Verba for *The Civic Culture* (1963). There is perhaps, however, future significance in the fact that *The Civic Culture* is among the works of western political science which have been translated in very limited editions in Czechoslovakia (for distribution only to professional students of politics). Indeed, at least one Czech political scientist was still tentatively hoping in the autumn of 1968 that it might be possible to carry out a comparative study along the lines of *The Civic Culture* in Poland, Czechoslovakia, Rumania, Yugoslavia and East Germany. Already some

Poland and Czechoslovakia are fundamental to an understanding of recent trends (and helpful for guessing future prospects) in these countries.[22]

It is true that the previous diversity of the countries of Eastern
Europe did not prevent them from attaining a fairly high degree
of uniformity in the 1950s. Even today, to a considerable extent, common political institutions are to be found in the
European communist states. Yet it is certainly wrong to suppose
that a political *culture*, though amenable to change, can be
changed overnight. Beliefs, values, focus of political identification, degree of attachment to political symbols and institutions,
political myths and political history, political knowledge and
expectations vary considerably from one communist state to
another. When an atmosphere conducive to change is created
by more immediate stimuli (e.g. economic failure), it is likely
that the direction of change will be influenced by factors closely
related to the prevailing political culture of the particular country.

Jiří Hochman, writing in the journal of the Czech Union of
Journalists, *Reportér*, as recently as October 1968, explicitly
recognises this basic point: 'The tempo of development of
democratic forms is influenced by historical tradition, national
mentality and by previous political experience. In contrast to
Czechoslovakia where for more than a hundred years a bourgeois parliamentarianism gradually evolved, the rest of Eastern
Europe has had a minimal experince, or no experience at all of
bourgeois democracy. In Germany the Weimar Republic was
but a short episode. Up to their liberation in 1944–5, Poland,
Hungary and Bulgaria had backward, semi-feudal regimes,
which in the case of Hungary and Bulgaria were so reactionary
that these two countries were both on the side of Hitlerite
Germany in World War II'.[23]

In terms of political culture, it is first of all, then, the *political
experience* of Czechoslovakia which sets it apart from its neigh-

---

fairly precise data on political attitudes in Czechoslovakia are available as a result
of the work of the Czechoslovak Institute for the Investigation of Public Opinion
of the Academy of Sciences.

[22] Apter, in his most recent article (op. cit.), takes the view that what these
states have in common as 'socialist industrial countries' is more important than
the differences. But even if they were at precisely the same stage of economic
development (which they are not), my scepticism about the value of such a
political indicator would remain.

[23] Jiří Hochman, 'Jaká východiska' in *Reportér*, No. 38, 1968.

bours. Even before the creation of the Czechoslovak republic in 1918, the Czechs had some experience of self-government within the framework of Austrian hegemony (unlike the Slovaks for whom Magyar domination was much greater than that of Vienna over the Czechs).[24] For Czechoslovakia as a whole, the First Republic provided even more relevant experience. A pluralistic democracy with universal suffrage, many parties and an abundance of organised interests provided a framework for popular participation in the political process. From the point of view of the Slovaks (and other national minorities), the main trouble was that the principal decision-makers too often were Czechs. The nationalities problem was both a major pluralistic element in the state and a severe strain on its cohesion, this despite the fact that official Czech nationalities policy was incomparably more enlightened than that of its eastern and (later) German neighbours. The essentially non-repressive nature of the First Republic is of continuing importance. In an article published in Prague last summer, a Czech social scientist made the observation that capital punishment was carried out on only eight occasions in the First Czechoslovak Republic. The contrast with the early 1950s did not need emphasis, and it is not surprising that so much importance has been attached in recent times in Czechoslovakia to the rehabilitation (even when posthumous) of the victims of the Stalinist purge.

Related factors are the *political knowledge* and *expectations* of Czechs and Slovaks. For people with experience of free elections a parliament in which debate on basic issues took place, a political environment in which parties had to compete for office and in which citizens could give vent to their varied and conflicting views on political and social issues, the attempt to give a Stalinist meaning to such familiar concepts as elections, parliament, democracy and freedom could not be wholly successful. Many Czechoslovaks recognised the problem of language of political discourse to be a substantive, not pedantic, one and devoted considerable attention to it.

[24] Two useful brief accounts of the nature of Czechoslovak political experience prior to the communist period are to be found in Miloslav Rechcigl, Jr.: *The Czechoslovak Contribution to World Culture*, 1964 (the essay by Václav Beneš, 'Background of Czechoslovak Democracy', pp. 267–76) and Paul E. Zinner: *Communist Strategy and Tactics in Czechoslovakia, 1918–48*, 1963 (Chapter 1, 'The Political Character of Czechoslovakia', pp. 5–24).

Political knowledge in Czechoslovakia was, of course, sharply reduced in the years after 1948 with the cutting off of foreign contacts other than those with communist countries. The extent of the 're-education' and the blocking of inexpedient information should not be underestimated. It is sufficient to note that for many rank and file communists and a considerable section of the Czechoslovak people the revelations of Khrushchev at the 20th Party Congress of the Soviet Communist Party came as a great shock. Many who had accepted the Czechoslovak show trials at their face value realised only in the late 1950s the extent to which they had allowed their critical faculties to be dulled in the atmosphere of the early Cold War.

Yet in a country so close to the west geographically and culturally as Czechoslovakia the process of isolation and re-education was, necessarily, far from complete. In Czechoslovakia, rather more than in most communist states, there was widespread awareness of the nature of Western political institutions and of the economic progress of Western Europe in the post-war period. By the early 1960s, *expectations* in Czechoslovakia were high, partly because Czechoslovakia had already obtained solid experience as an industrial country between the wars, partly because the economy had done well in quantitative terms throughout the 1950s, and also in view of the knowledge that a higher standard of living was being enjoyed by many West European countries who had started the post-war period from no more developed an economic base than Czechoslovakia herself.

Traditional values and *political symbols* are important elements of a political culture and in this context it is of significance that 19th-century Czech nationalism involved a rediscovery of Jan Hus and placed a particular emphasis upon democratic as well as libertarian values. The emphasis which the 19th-century Czech historian, František Palacký, put upon the Hussite Revolution and its anti-authoritarian nature left, it has convincingly been argued, 'a permanent imprint on the Czech national consciousness'.[25] Democratic and libertarian values (together with his Christian humanism) were also absolutely central to the philosophy of T. G. Masaryk, the founder and first President of the Czechoslovak state. It is a significant fact that Masarykism, as a coherent and attractive ideology, re-

[25] In Rechcigl: *The Czechoslovak Contribution to World Culture*, op. cit., p. 269.

mained in the Czech national consciousness as an alternative to the official ideology imposed after 1948. Though none of Masaryk's works were republished in Czechoslovakia between 1948 and January 1968, attempts on the part of the regime to discredit him failed. This led to a change of approach in the 1960s whereby the 'positive' features in Masaryk's life and thought, such as his contribution to the moulding of a unified Czechoslovakia, were singled out for praise. By the summer of 1968 his rehabilitation was complete. Photographs of Masaryk were being sold in the streets and his values could be publicly asserted.

Political culture, however, cannot be considered purely in terms of developments in one country without regard to external influences. In the case of Czechoslovakia the influence of foreign models is not hard to detect. Between 1945 and 1948 the Czechoslovak Communist Party was the largest single party in Czechoslovakia and enjoyed genuine mass support, particularly from the working-class. Though this did not imply mass support for, nor anticipation of, the events of the early 1950s, it did imply a conscious acceptance of affinity with the Soviet Union and a rejection of those western governments (in reality their somewhat different successors) who had failed Czechoslovakia in 1938. Acceptance of the Soviet Union as a more reliable ally than Britain or France had its profound influence upon the Czechoslovak form of government. After the communists had obtained power in Prague, assimilation to the Soviet model continued to be a voluntary activity for a large part of the Czechoslovak Communist Party and a by no means negligible section of the people.

In more recent years this process has been almost reversed. There has been a conscious rejection of the Soviet Union as a political model by the party intelligentsia and, as a positive influence, Yugoslavia has assumed a new importance. Many, though not all, of the features of the Czechoslovak reforms (for example, limitation upon party interference with industrial management, federalisation and the socialist market economy) were already more of a reality in Yugoslavia. Some of the most prominent of the Czechoslovak reformers were explicit admirers of the Yugoslav political model, though there were others who demanded more radical change. They were more attracted by Western European political institutions (for example, the

Scandinavian and British) though they believed that in
Czechoslovakia a much fuller form of democracy could be built
upon the socialist foundation of the Czechoslovak economy.
(The increasing opportunities for foreign travel and of access to
western information helped to bring Western European influence to bear.)

Political crises can be particularly important factors in the
formation of a political culture. A crisis can strengthen certain
elements in a nation's political culture at the expense of others
and in the case of Czechoslovakia in 1968, this assuredly happened. A movement which in January had the really active
support of only the intelligentsia had by August been joined by
almost all social groups, the main exceptions being those party
functionaries and placemen who owed their threatened positions entirely to the old order. In a period of less than eight
months information about Czechoslovak politics in the preced-
ing twenty years appeared almost faster than it could be assimilated. Yet the signs are that it *was* assimilated. Industrial
workers and farmers subsequently pressed no less strongly than
the intellectuals for a continuation of the process of democratisation.

The Soviet intervention strengthened this tendency instead
of checking it. In the period since 21 August massive working-
class support for the reformist movement has become increasingly overt. Factory resolutions and threatened strikes (in the
event, for example, of the dismissal from political office of the
leading radical, Josef Smrkovský) have become a new factor in
the political situation. Thus, on the one hand, the most conservative elements in the Czechoslovak Communist Party have
achieved a prominence in recent months which they were unable to win at any time between January and August 1968. In
the immediate future, it cannot be ruled out that the position
of these elements within the party may be strengthened either
by a purge of the reformists or by mass desertion of the party
by its liberal elements. But, on the other hand, the same conservative party leaders are going to have to reckon with a
society very different from that of the 1950s when they were
fortified by the loyalty of the greater part of the working-class.
It will not be easy for them to regain that support.

The events of 1968 are going to remain in the Czechoslovak
national consciousness. (In the course of time they will be trans-

formed into national mythology.) They have reaffirmed and strengthened values which were an important part of Czechoslovak political culture. Any regime which does not take account of these values and the reawakened national consciousness will find Czechs and Slovaks very difficult people to rule.

Winston M. Fisk

A Communist *Rechtsstaat*? – The Case of Yugoslav Constitutionalism*

PLATO'S ACCOUNT OF THE PLACE OF LAW IN THE political order is in two phases. One is found in the *Republic*. The *Republic* is utopian; it describes the ideal state. In this state law has no place; ideal rulers do not need to be bound by law in order to do justice, and governmental relationships need not be defined by law if they are by nature ideal. But later, in the *Statesman* and the *Laws*, Plato moves from the utopian and ideal to describing the best state practically obtainable – the second-best state, which because of the necessities of the human condition falls short of the ideal, the Utopia. Here law is readmitted, indeed is given high place; the second-best state, which is the best of earthly states, is in fact to be held together by the golden cord of the law.

There is a well-known utopian element in communist thought. It argues that in some final stage all social relations will be ideally just without the necessity of governmental intervention. Further, communist political thought, unlike Plato's, argues that its Utopia can in fact be attained. Ultimately, as class conflict disappears, the instruments and uses of political and governmental power will become unnecessary, and men will be truly free; the state will have withered away, in the endlessly familiar phrase.

But the communist Utopia of course has so far shown a tendency to recede as it is pursued, rather like a will-o'-the-wisp. This present a problem for communist political thought (laying aside the problems it also presents for communist political practice). What intellectual posture to adopt? Broadly

* Vol. 5, No. 1, Winter 1969–70.

speaking, there are three choices. One is to abandon, either explicitly or *sub silentio*, the goal and hope of the utopian end. But this would be almost fatally to strike the kingpost out of the whole structure of communist doctrine about society and socialism.

The second is to accept a long continuance of the phenomenon variously called the dictatorship of the proletariat, administrative rule by the party and its apparats, the temporary continuation of the strong state so as to cope with surviving class enemies and capitalist encirclement, and the like. Roughly, this second is the Soviet solution, exported also, more or less, to much of Eastern Europe.

The third choice is to attempt to devise some sort of Marxist constitutionalism, a rule of public law for the socialist commonwealth, a communist *Rechtsstaat*.[1] This is the Yugoslav choice and it entails new departures in communist political practice. The purpose of the present paper is to explore, in a brief and necessarily rather speculative way, some of the elements of this Yugoslav development and some of its implications. The literature on Eastern European and Yugoslav affairs[2] of course touches on the movement but there seems room for a more direct and analytic appraisal of the specially legal-political side of the movement than has so far been made, particularly since the movement, now approaching by one reckoning near to its 20th year,[3] seems both to be decisively broadening and deepening and also to be speeding up.[4]

THE CHANGE OF ROLE OF THE PARTY

The Yugoslav movement turns out to contain, surprisingly fully developed and flourishing, both of the elements to be found in

[1] See Brian Chapman, 'The Police-State', in *Government and Opposition*, 3, pp. 428–40 (1968), where the term and its companions, *Justizstaat* and *Polizeistaat*, are discussed and their relationships to public law and constitutionalism at least suggested.

[2] See, e.g., the basic study of East European politics by Ghiţa Ionescu, *The Politics of the European Communist States*, London, 1967.

[3] The Copernican turn can probably be put at about 1949–51, after Yugoslavia had broken with Russia and while it was beginning to grope for its 'own way'. Thus, for example, it was then that workers' self-management was begun, the courts were moved toward some power and independence, and the more extreme roles of the political police began to recede.

[4] The economic reforms of 1965 and thereafter, among other development, are profoundly important.

classic constitutionalism,[5] and thought of as the two parts of
the classic *Rechtsstaat*: the *garantiste* element, that of definition and
protection of rights, normally legal rights, for citizens, and the
institutional, or framework, or structural, element, the defining
and distributing (so to speak, institutionalising) of power
among agencies of government. We are here mainly concerned
with the latter of the two, partly because it is more prominent
in current Yugoslav government and politics and partly because
it is probably [6] more important, at least in the short run, in the
analysis of the political dynamics of a system in which it exists.

We need to open with some brief survey of a dominant
aspect of the politics of Yugoslavia. This is the near-revolution
in the role of the party. From the iron-fisted secret dictatorial
caste of the 1940s the party, now called the League, has
changed greatly. Briefly (in principle and proclamation at least;
there may be on occasion some legitimate doubts about practice) it has ceased to govern – has ceased, as the Yugoslavs say,
to be an 'instrument of power' and now strives to content itself
with being 'an ideological force'. Such a transmogrification
seems contrary to nature (at least contrary to the nature of
communism as usually seen from the West) and is often viewed
with doubt approaching disbelief. Yet it seems to be basically
genuine, at least in the ordinary daily run of things, even if the
strong hand may still exist behind the scene in crises, or in major
policy, or in various specific situations.

This withdrawal opened the way for constitutional developments of the structural sort (there can hardly be any when sole
rule is by a party, and government is merely a façade or tool).
And constitutional developments of this sort there have been,
in plenty. Of many four [7] may be mentioned. One of these is
that a general aura of legality, of law-determined relationships
and functions, has come to hang over nearly all of government

[5] See Giovanni Sartori, 'Constitutionalism: A Preliminary Discussion', *American
Political Science Review*, 56, pp. 853–64, December 1962, and the subsequent exchange between Sartori and Morris-Jones, ibid., 59, p. 439, June 1965. And today
any consideration of constitutionalism must take account of M. J. C. Vile, *Constitutionalism and the Separation of Powers*, Oxford, 1967.

[6] There may be some doubt if one gives the greatest possible weight to the
procedural view of democracy, under which all hangs upon the process of participation and so, perhaps, upon aspects of the *garantiste* element.

[7] A fifth, but one less closely and necessarily linked with constitutionalism, would
have to be added in any more comprehensive study: the special and highly interesting variations Yugoslavia has given to federalism and decentralisation.

and politics; the days of simple dictatorship, or even autocracy, are for the time at least gone. Yugoslavia is hardly a *Justizstaat* or a liberal parliamentary democracy but it is no longer a *Polizeistaat* in the traditional communist variant of that old form of rule. Another is that it is now possible to see several strong centres, or complexes, of governing activity and power in the official and governmental (as opposed to party) institutions of Yugoslavia that repay study much more than in the usual communist regimes.

A third, related to the first but more a matter of specific institutions than of general aura and tendency, is the emergence, and rise to very substantial power, of a strong, highly developed, influential and sophisticated legal-judicial culture; laws, lawyers, law courts, and legal things are very much in the forefront of Yugoslav public and governmental affairs. Finally, intangible but pervasive, there is the strong presence and influence of *political* culture and political life; Yugoslavia is now a country with a politics,[8] and a public politics of government and official government institutions and processes, not simply the secret palace politics of a totalitarian party.

Of these four the second and third, the institutionalisation (and governmentalisation) of power and the rise of a system of public law, are the concerns of the present paper. Some illumination of one and four will, it is hoped, emerge as byproducts, but these two are too slippery and pervasive for effective direct discussion in limited space.

DIS- AND RE-INSTITUTIONALISATION

The Yugoslavs have, at least in principle, not given up the ideal of the coming communist idyll when the state will have withered away and governmental and political power will have ceased to be necessary. For them this idyll is to come through 'social self-government', meaning workers' self-management in the economic enterprises and various forms of co-operative self-rule in all other social and political organisations. In fact, to their view, in their political thought, the idyll is already on the way because social self-government is extensively established and is developing further.

[8] A politics in the classic Western sense well expressed by Bernard Crick, *In Defense of Politics* rev. ed., Baltimore, Penguin Books, 1964.

But they recognise problems, including many they regard as not predicted by Marxist analysis. Indeed, some of their theoreticians now argue that conflicts and contradictions can exist even in socialist society and do in fact exist in theirs. So they expect that progress towards the idyll will be slow and bumpy, and, among other things, that social self-government needs to be protected against bureaucratism and a recurrence of dogmatic rule. An ingenious line of argument has appeared. Certainly by no means universally accepted, it has however become popular and influential, and other views can conveniently be ranged about it as a point of central reference. It is this:

Society has been developing instruments of power, devices for rule, for centuries, and the consequent potentialities for oppression and 'bureaucratism' (as the Yugoslavs call virtually any form of hypertrophied and misused official action) are correspondingly well developed. So for the present and for a substantial period into the future it is desirable to give attention to devices for restricting power as well as to the long-range goal of abolishing it. And the logical place to look for such devices is in the classic tradition, where the instruments of power themselves developed and where by a natural process the devices for restriction may reasonably be expected to be well grown also. Put the classic restrictive devices to work, *ad interim*, to prevent the classic instruments of power, surviving during the transitional period, from committing the classic abuses.

Under this broad argument a number of such devices of a structural sort, and of a rather Western cast, come in, some more easily than others: federalism; the general idea of 'socialist legality'; judicial controls of administrative action; rules about hierarchies of legislative competence and limitations on the right to legislate; even constitutional courts with the power of judicial review over legislative and executive acts; and certainly also, one *garantiste* device among many, a very modern and enlightened code of criminal procedure and of the accused's rights in criminal matters.[9] All these are in full bloom in Yugoslavia. But there is one which though it is coming into bloom is

---

[9] The new system, which went into effect beginning in 1967, is as regardful of legal constraints upon procedure and legal definition and protection of the accused's rights as any in Europe, and seems to be rather well observed in practice, even in cases with political aspects.

greeted with grave Marxist hesitations, even denials of its existence. That is the separation of powers.[10]

The separation of powers is of course frowned upon in ortho-dox Marxist-Leninist doctrine; in the capitalist state it is thought to be an obstacle to the proletarian seizure of power, and in the socialist state to be both unnecessary as a protection (there being nothing in workers' rule of themselves for it to protect against) and also inconsistent with the idea of unity of power, of all power, direct and unmediated, resting in the hands of the people and their representatives. So in the Euro-pean communist states one typically sees legislatures that are nominally omnipotent however much they may in fact be subservient to party and government. Further, the courts are excluded from any real share of power, on the two grounds that sharing would be inconsistent with direct workers' rule and that courts cannot properly have any control over the administra-tive-executive because they are two different things. (And of course there is the very practical ground that any different arrangement might interfere with party hegemony.)

Yugoslavia presents a radically different picture. There the legislature and the judiciary have much genuine power and are, in varying ways and degrees, independent of the political executive.

The development, and hence the internal dynamics, of this picture can be seen in different ways – the elements themselves are well known – but the following chain seems close to the heart of the matter of constitutionalism in the Yugoslav regime. The affair certainly began with the proclamation of social self-government (workers' self-management in industry first) shortly after the break in 1948–50 with the Soviet Union when the regime began to look around for bases of popular support. This was followed shortly thereafter by the fateful liberation of the courts; the Law on Administrative Disputes of 1952, which gave the courts real powers over the administration, is a con-venient landmark. In these same stormy years there began the rise of federalism, and, to some extent, of Yugoslavia's extra-ordinary decentralisation and de-etatisation. Also in the 1950s what the Yugoslavs call 'the assembly system' (a form of

---

[10] What is said here on this subject must be regarded as provisional. A more complete study by Dr Richard Kindersley of St Antony's College, Oxford, is forthcoming.

legislative supremacy under the sign of Marxist-Leninist 'unity of power') was proclaimed, and establishment of it was begun.

Then the epoch-making 1963 constitutions were adopted, proclaiming, among other things, a very sweeping and significant doctrine of 'constitutionalism and legality'.[11] In the next few years this doctrine was made real and was established among the bases of the state, so much so as to be able to withstand even the challenge of the powerful forces whose workings culminated in the Ranković affair of 1966. Meanwhile there had been the economic reforms of 1965 and following, which turned the economic system, and the whole society, decisively away from autarkic control and into the international economy and towards a more or less free and market-directed economy. And meanwhile also the real development of the assembly system had been going vigorously on, passing through the entailed ordeals and the elections of 1965, 1967, and 1969 and emerging in such a condition that it is today possible to speak, not perhaps of the 'assembly supremacy' which Yugoslavs sometimes speak of, but quite possibly of genuine assembly rule. With all this, and with the continued rise in the independence and governmental and political power and significance of the judiciary and the law, the question of the separation of powers must be confronted.

That it exists in substantial measure in Yugoslavia can hardly be much doubted. The courts are, as we have said, independent and potent. And power is genuinely divided between the assembly and the political executive, contrary both to the common Western supposition that all real decisions lie in the hands of off-stage party power-holders and the common Yugoslav assertion that the assembly is really supreme. As to the latter, we can say that the Yugoslavs have made, with social self-government, the assembly system, decentralisation, and de-etatisation, an extraordinary effort to reverse the common contemporary trend for power to drain towards the central executive. But we can further say that so far (the final issue may really be in doubt) they have not been able to do more than shift back the balance a little – in itself no small achievement for a regime bred in the tradition of communist centralist executive autocracy.

Sophisticated Yugoslav theoreticians recognise the presence

[11] 'Ustavnost i zakonitost'; see chapter 7 of the 1963 federal constitution.

of some separation of powers in their system. They further tend, though in some cases with varying degrees of reluctance, to recognise that liberty – particularly social self-government – must, as we have said, be protected against bureaucratic and centralistic and dogmatic tendencies until (*Deo volente*) it can produce the contradiction-free and hence power-free society. They differ sharply over the function separation can have in this task.

Some take the purist view; separation is unnecessary and undesirable in a socialist state, and such of it as exists in Yugoslavia is a degeneration. Others take views which although in no real sense Western in genesis or nature have their Western parallels: institutionalised distribution and limitation of power is vital and such institutionalisation must in some major degree depend upon use of the classic armoury of devices against autocracy; the separation of powers is at the least very important among these and may be the key to the real effectiveness of all of them.

The purists take their stand in part on the potentialities of social self-government as well as on general Marxist considerations; they argue that any institutionalisation, even for purposes of protection against abuses, cannot help but provide a foothold for the continuance of the 'instruments of power' and hence for their possible perversion, and that the only real hope is a full plunge – social self-government to the hilt, with no fatal stops at half-way houses, no corrupting reliances on temporary expedients. The separationists respond that this is utopian anarchism, that it is folly to think that any and all institutionalisation is necessarily a step backwards. At the level of theoretical and general political discussion the issue is delicately balanced. At the level of practical government and politics however the issue seems settled; Yugoslavia is going to move, barring some internal catastrophe or some drastic external event, towards more and more separation of powers: the executive in a modern state cannot, even by the Yugoslavs, be dislodged from its position; the Yugoslav legislatures will not give up, indeed will expand, their powers and competences, and the Yugoslav courts cannot possibly, in the normal course of things, be divested of their now deeply entrenched independence and widely expanded governmental-political authority.

As the the importance and function of our second topic, that

of the legal-judicial culture, the issue is not balanced at all; it
has been overwhelmingly settled – this culture, and the institutions which carry it, are put in very high place.

LEGISLATURE AND JUDICIARY

A most striking fact is the omnipresence of law in Yugoslavia;
it has truly been made into one of the country's central devices
of governing. Perhaps the most striking manifestation of this is
the constitutional judicature, the constitutional courts and
their vigorous programme of review of the constitutionality of
federal and republic legislation and of other official acts.

Another major manifestation is the energetic and vital
activity of the federal, republic, and commune assemblies in
legislation; legislation is truly a major industry in Yugoslavia.
Another is the very extensive work of the courts, both the regular courts and the interesting system of economic courts;[12] they
are all highly competent, now and for some years past unquestionedly independent, and extremely busy – and busy with
much litigation of genuine governmental and political importance, such as the extraordinary system of so-called 'administrative litigation'.[13]

Another is the general phenomenon of 'normative activity'.
Yugoslav federalism and decentralisation produce the abundance of legislative assemblies already mentioned. But this is not
the end of the matter. De-etatisation (the devolution of official
functions, and of the power of self-government, to innumerable
non-governmental associations and groups) generates literally
masses of further legislation.

And scholarly legal writing of high quality is copious. All in
all, Yugoslavia simply abounds in legal materials.

However, other communist countries on occasion have a
great deal of law. But the difficulty with it, we may deduce from
observers' reports,[14] is that it is either peripheral to the most

[12] These latter are genuine courts, much more independent and important than
the usual communist *Arbitrazh*.

[13] I.e., litigation by private citizens and independent organisations against
governmental and quasi-government agencies. It makes up about a quarter of
the business of the republic and federation supreme courts, and is an extremely
important influence for legality.

[14] See, e.g., the materials contained in the standard American studies of the
Soviet system, those by Berman and Hazard. Harold J. Berman, *Justice in the
U.S.S.R.*, rev. ed., Cambridge, 1963, and John N. Hazard, *The Soviet System of*

crucial issues of governing or else it is something of an empty form, or façade, with most real policy and decisions, even on matters of pure law (let alone those mixed questions of law and of governance and policy which are the domain of good public law) being made by the administrative machine and by the party and its apparats. Not so in Yugoslavia; there a very great deal of government and politics flows through the channels and the materials of public law.

Yet the proliferation of these materials and institutions in Yugoslavia would produce nothing but confusion, and they would certainly be unfit for the major roles they do play in government and politics, if they were not gripped, disciplined, and made rational by a genuine science of law, doing to them what the logic of the common law does to their counterparts in the Anglo-American countries. And Yugoslavia now has such a science, rapidly developing and largely new although in some measure based on classic foundations.

Yugoslavia grew to modernity in the continental tradition of law, the civil law system. This great tradition has its great virtues, but there can be great vices as well. One of these, a heritage of the French Revolution, is that in it the law (ideally) must be passive, positivist, and formalist, the simple technical mouthpiece of the law-giver – assembly or tyrant, it makes no difference. This view, virtue and vice, harmonises with the communist ideal of a beneficent people's dictatorship but it does not generate creative law and an autonomous and imaginative legal system.

The Yugoslavs however had in fact a creative element in their own legal tradition. They also have a capacity for innovation. So, built on this tradition they have, and innovated they have, so that today the style of their public law is indeed creative and independent. Three factors may be mentioned.

One is the weight which is coming to be given to legal scholarship – scholarship by the bench, the bar, and the university faculties. It is now expected that the infusions generated by Yugoslavia's tumultuous history of war, revolution, and development, and by the outpourings of 'normative activity', will be brought into order by vigorous scholarly legal thought.

Government, 4th ed., Chicago. 1968. See also those contained in Vladimir Gsovski and Kasimierz Grzybowski, *Government, Law and Courts in the Soviet Union and Eastern Europe*, 2 vols., New York, 1959.

A second is that there should be a creative legislative contribution. Codification, for example, is a lively subject in Yugoslavia. But it is not codification in the sense of sterile, abstract and axiomatic law-giving by a final authority speaking in a vacuum – the worst side of the continental style. Rather, it is regarded as, in its best and proper state, obliged to be artful and perceptive, epitomising and interpreting, by an astute eye, of the best that the whole of the legal process has produced. The Yugoslav legal system is growing, both by the work of many hands and by the projects of legislative intervention. The process of growth through both forces is a lively and dramatically independent one. We may expect, with some measure of confidence, the steady further development of a genuine system of public law as time goes on.

A third factor is that of the work of the courts themselves. There is a touch, a light but palpable touch, of the common law style here. It is expected in Yugoslavia that the current of 'judicial practice' (by which is meant something roughly, though only roughly, akin to the common law system of case precedent) will make a major contribution, as it certainly does.

Further, what is called the 'active role' of the courts is very strongly emphasised. They are expected to do far more than passively, even albeit creatively, decide cases as these come to them. They are expected to take the lead, through public discussion and their own work and through recommendations to the assemblies, in the growth and development of the law. This they do with increasing vigour, so that today one finds a really considerable amount of Yugoslav law, including public law, emerging from the judicial precincts. Indeed, there is a movement afoot, so far not fully adopted, urging upon the courts that they should feel bound to seek affirmatively for imaginative solutions to social problems rather than feel themselves limited to the traditional continental judicial role of simply formalistically and mechanically applying legislation. There has been some judicial response,[15] and more is already forthcoming.

Conjoined with all of this is what is at least the beginnings of a new attitude towards law and legal thought and institutions generally. The customary attitude in progressive circles in

---

[15] Often quite enthusiastic; some courts have relished the new role and most have been at least willing to play it.

Yugoslavia has, generally speaking, been that law is all very well and a very good thing, and that law and the courts have always been one of the most creditable aspects of the various regimes which have held sway at different times and places in the country; but that, though able, honourable, and devoted, they have tended to err somewhat in the direction of positivism and formalism, though not of bureaucratism, and hardly to be the voice of humanism, liberation, and creative thought in the social sciences and the realm of governing.

In some small but, one suspects, highly significant measure, the facts underlying this view are dying away. The good traditions of legitimacy, intellectual honesty and logical precision are surviving. New ones of responsible activism, intellectual creativity, and public concern are emerging. And the not-so-good traditions clustering around the ideas of formalism and positivism are fading. *Mutatis mutandis*, the warm and extraordinary renaissance which swept through American public law in the 1920s and 1930s under the banner of socio-realism seems to be being reproduced in Yugoslavia. The present contains much of high value and the future holds forth great though uncertain promise.

TOWARDS THE *RECHTSSTAAT*

Our two topics, Yugoslav governmental institutions and the use the Yugoslav polity makes of public law, nowhere come more dramatically and tellingly together than in the work of the constitutional judicature, the six constitutional courts of the republics and the very important constitutional court of the federation, all wielding the power of judicial review (the power to declare unconstitutional, and so invalid, legislation and all other official or quasi-official acts falling within their jurisdictions).

It is here that the interim struggle for the co-operative Utopia towards which Yugoslavia looks is most clearly based on constitutionalism, the third communist choice we spoke of at the beginning. It is to be grounded upon, and to function through, a constitutional system and a *Rechtsstaat*, legally and judicially defined and enforced, rather than on a wan hope that some day, magically, conflict, power, and oppression will all come to an end.

If Ionescu[16] is right (and competent observers find many small, and large, pieces of evidence that he is), that an irreversible political trend in Eastern Europe, now also driven by the economic reforms, is towards the pluralisation and institutionalisation of power, then here in the constitutional judicature is perhaps the very edge of the vanguard of the movement, a sensitive place where subtle shifts in the winds of growth and change can first be read. It is certainly premature to expect immediately a multi-party state, with recognised oppositions, and perhaps, though not certainly, it is a mistake to expect this at all. But a constitutionalised *Rechtsstaat* – that is certainly in the cards, and is a near at hand possibility, if things go on as they are, and indeed is even realised in more than small part already. And after constitutionalisation, and constitutional *controls*, we may yet see constitutional *oppositions*.[17]

The constitutional court of the federation was established with the specific mission, supported by broad powers, of seeing to it that order be attained in the storm of confused governing generated by 'normative activity', social self-government, assembly rule, decentralisation and federalism, and de-etatisation. That this prodigious and crucial political task should be so largely entrusted to a *court* is most revealing of the nature of the Yugoslav commitment to constitutionalism and legality.

The court is exercising, and has been both formally and informally encouraged to exercise, its broad powers in this vast area with steadily increasing vigour and with high independence. We witness the extraordinary scene of much of the most basic political and governmental ordering of a communist regime being done by a court, and *via* what is really a quite largely legitimate and legal mode and style. The court is also performing increasingly a *garantiste* function, looking out for the protection of individual rights and liberties as against official action, but from the standpoint of the political dynamics of the regime its function of dealing with the very frame of government is of unique and overwhelming importance.

---

[16] Ghiţa Ionescu, *The Politics of the European Communist States.*
[17] See Giovanni Sartori, 'Opposition and Control: Problems and Prospects', *Government and Opposition*, Vol. 1, pp. 149–54, 1965–6.

CONCLUSIONS

The conclusions of this paper can be stated with brevity. For some years we have known that we are witnessing in Yugoslavia a remarkable experiment in liberal communism. This paper has attempted further to explore two facets of this experiment, the institutionalisation of politics and the use of public law. These explorations must inevitably address themselves in the end to the permanent general question: is the Yugoslav system a viable possible alternative to the traditional repressive system, a workable self-contained alternative scheme of governing, and, if so, what are its prospects?

The second aspect of the question turns in part upon the first. To the first the study on which this paper is based returns two partial answers. First, as a practical political and governmental arrangement the parts of the system studied herein work. Investigation so far on the spot [18] suggests not only that they function pretty much as advertised but that they function well. Second, as intellectual constructs they are well developed and tenable. They depart widely in many respects from traditional Marxism, particularly of the Soviet variety, and certainly they are eclectic and experimental. But they do hang together, and they are able to provide reasoned answers out of their own resources to the questions of the organisation and conduct of government and politics that a modern polity must confront.

[18] The present study is based upon very numerous interviews ,and much discussion and observation, in Yugoslavia since September 1965, and the writer records here his heavy debt of gratitude to the many people who have helped him.

David Holloway

Scientific Truth and Political Authority in the Soviet Union*

Case Study

IN RECENT YEARS POLITICAL SCIENTISTS HAVE SHOWN increasing interest in the 'continuous process of cooperation and compromise' between natural scientists 'who work to discover or develop abstract and precise systems of knowledge' and politicians 'who make use of such knowledge to further human purposes'.[1] This interest embraces both the institutional arrangements through which politicians and administrators seek to direct scientific knowledge and expertise to desired ends, and the way in which the interaction between scientists and politicians is realised in terms of the political values of a given society. The relationship between science and politics has been especially close in the Soviet Union as the CPSU has endeavoured to achieve the sometimes conflicting aims of harnessing science to its own purposes as efficiently as possible, and ensuring the political loyalty of the scientific community. The attainment of these goals has been complicated by the party's claim to legitimate authority on the basis of its scientific understanding of the laws of social development. Marx and Engels claimed that their social theory was scientific and based this claim on the dialectic which was, in Marx's words, both 'critical and revolutionary'.[2] Lenin asserted in 1894 that the

---

[1] Don K. Price, *The Scientific Estate*, 1965, p. 118. Cf. also R. Gilpin and C. Wright (eds.), *Scientists and National Policy-Making*, 1964; Sanford A. Lakoff, *Knowledge and Power*, 1966.

[2] K. Marx, *Capital*, 1, 1915, Chicago, p. 26.

* Earlier drafts of this paper were read at the staff-graduate seminar of the Department of Politics, University of Lancaster, and the Sociology of Science seminar of the University of Salford. I am grateful for the helpful comments received. It also appears in *Government and Opposition*, Vol. 5, No. 3, Summer 1970.

main attraction of Marxism lay in the fact that it 'unites a rigorous and most lofty scientific nature . . . with revolutionary nature and unites them not by chance. . . . but unites them in the theory itself intrinsically and inseparably'.[3] The Soviet leadership has prided itself on being guided in policy-making by a scientific ideology.

The relationship between science and politics in the Soviet Union ranges from the ideological problems of interpreting new scientific discoveries within the framework of dialectical materialism to the organisational problems of ensuring the rapid introduction of new technology into industrial processes. This article, however, focuses on the relationship between political authority and fundamental research. The Academy of Sciences has been regarded as the leading centre of research in the natural sciences and the humanities since its foundation in 1725. The present charter declares in its first paragraph that the Academy is the 'highest scientific institution of the USSR, uniting in its membership the most outstanding scholars of the country'.[4] Not all its members, the academicians and corresponding members, who now number about six hundred, work in the Academy's institutes; there is an overlap, in terms of personnel and organisation, with the other establishments – particularly the specialised Academies, the Republican Academies, and the $VUZy$ – where fundamental research is carried on. Besides being the chief centre of fundamental research, the Academy also helps to exploit scientific knowledge for economic and military purposes, and provides the higher government organs with scientific expertise and advice.[5] The Academy is directly subordinate to the USSR Council of Ministers, to whom it presents an annual report, and from whom it receives over 90 per cent of its funds.[6] Inasmuch as the USSR Academy of Sciences in particular, and the Academy system in general, are both the institutional embodiment of the scientific community and party- and government-controlled agencies serving the interests of the Soviet state, they provide the best arena for

[3] In 'What the "Friends of the People" are', V. I. Lenin, *Sochineniya*, 4th ed., vol. 1, 1941, p. 308.
[4] *Vestnik Akademii Nauk*, 1959, No. 5, p. 7.
[5] Loc. cit. articles 2 and 4.
[6] On the annual report cf. the charter, article 1; on expenditure cf. E. Zaleski, J. P. Kozlowski, H. Wienert, R. W. Davies, M. J. Berry, R. Amann, *Science Policy in the U.S.S.R.*, OECD, 1969, p. 263.

examining the relationship between political authority and fundamental scientific research.

SOME FEATURES OF STALINIST SCIENCE

Before 1917 Russian Marxists were preoccupied with establishing the precise nature of the unity of scientific analysis and political action in Marxism. In the immediate post-revolutionary years, however, the bolsheviks were concerned with science exclusively as an instrument of economic recovery: it was now that Lenin coined the famous slogan, 'Communism=Soviet power+the electrification of the whole country'. But when the bolsheviks sought to enlist Russia's scientific and technical skills in the service of the new Soviet republic, they found that their own attraction to scientific ideology was not matched by a desire on the part of scientists to become revolutionary Marxists. Lenin, however, saw to it that high salaries and good working conditions were granted to scientists and technologists in order to obtain their collaboration. Political commitment was not required, for it was generally felt that scientists would be drawn, through their own work, to an appreciation and understanding of dialectical materialism, and thence to bolshevism. Until the late 1920s the scientific community enjoyed complete intellectual freedom in all but central political matters; the Academy of Sciences retained its intellectual autonomy and, although financed by the state, was not subject to censorship or political control.

By the late 1920s, however, the initial satisfaction with the results of the collaboration of the bourgeois specialists had worn off. There was growing disillusionment with the failure to convert scientists and technologists in large numbers to Marxism; and the new generation of 'red' scientists and technologists was not sufficiently numerous to meet the demands of the industrialisation drive, or to ensure the success of the Soviet aim, declared in 1928, of 'catching up and overtaking the advanced capitalist countries in both a technological and economic respect'.[7] What one writer called the 'contradiction between the ever-growing role of the scientific worker in socialist construction and his ideological and socio-political backwardness'[8] gave increasing

[7] Cf. *KPSS v Rezolyutsiyakh*, 1954, Vol. 2, p. 256.
[8] Quoted in D. Joravsky, *Soviet Marxism and Natural Science, 1917–32*, 1961, p. 223.

anxiety to the political authorities. The 'great break' affected science in two ways. First, the Academy of Sciences was bolshevised and lost its intellectual and organisational autonomy; it was converted from an independent research centre into a Soviet institution, designed to meet the demands of industrialisation. The so-called 'ideology of pure science' was defeated and science, now seen as part of the social superstructure, was to develop in response to the demands of the economy. Second, scientists were pressed into declaring their allegiance to Marxism-Leninism, and lest their professions of loyalty be mere hypocrisy, militant philosophers (and all philosophers had now to be militant) pursued them into their disciplines to root out what philosophical or political deviations their work might betray. There were sporadic attempts to reconstruct various disciplines on the basis of dialectical materialism – after all, if science were part of society's superstructure, socialist science must be different from bourgeois science.[9]

These reforms established the main features of Stalinist science. First, scientific work was directed towards the immediate economic and military ends of the Soviet state. Second, the debate about the philosophy of science which had flourished in the 1920s was ended, and the final source of philosophical authority was located in the Central Committee. Philosophers were reduced to interpreting Stalin's theoretical pronouncements and policy-decisions, and ensuring their observance in Soviet intellectual life. Third, scientific authority – the right to say what constitutes scientific truth – was politicised. Dialectical materialism, it was claimed, would lead the scientist to new discoveries and even to the reconstruction of science. Thus scientific problems were open to argument by philosophical authority, and hence ultimately subject to the authority of Stalin and the Central Committee. Moreover, a one-to-one relationship was postulated between philosophical and political deviation. Fourth, in order to ensure that research and development were undertaken as directed, and that scientists served the state loyally, a complex system of centralised administrative and political controls was imposed on the scientific

[9] On Soviet debates about science and philosophy during this period cf. Joravsky, op. cit.; on the reform of the Academy cf. Loren R. Graham, *The Soviet Academy of Sciences and the Communist Party 1927–32*, 1967; for a recent Soviet view of the relationship between the party and scientists cf. V. A. Ul'yanovskaya, *Formirovaniye Nauchnoy Intellientsii v SSSR 1917–37gg.*, 1966.

community.[10] Thus was the intrinsic and inseparable unity of science and politics assured.

The fate of individual disciplines under Stalin cannot be deduced from these features of the relationship between political purposes and scientific knowledge. The treatment accorded a branch of science depended on many factors, including perceived practical needs, the implications for the Stalinist worldview, and the stage of development of the science itself. Nor can one infer a consistent attitude on the part of the political authorities towards the scientific community as a whole: anxiety and mistrust were most marked in the years 1930–2, 1936–8, 1947–52. Nevertheless, some important features of the behaviour of Soviet scientists can be explained in terms of the principles underlying the Stalinist view of science and politics.[11] The most interesting of these, for present purposes, are those relating to the way in which scientific debate was conducted. Among the techniques of argument used were: quotation-mongering – appealing to the classics of Marxism-Leninism-Stalinism in support of one's arguments; and label-sticking – the attempt to defeat an opponent's argument by associating it with a philosophical or political deviation. These were symptomatic of the politicisation of scientific authority, and indicated an appeal to the political leadership, rather than to scientific colleagues, for recognition and approval. The use of 'administrative methods' to defeat one's opponents by removing them from their posts was symptomatic of the bureaucratisation of science and the association of scientific authority with position in the administrative hierarchy. These techniques involved attacks by individuals on individuals which, because of the penalties for losing an argument (abandonment of one's research, imprisonment or even death), naturally embittered personal relationships. Scientific schools, holding different views about a particular theory or paradigm, were no longer certain of being able to resolve their differences by reasoned discussion or new discoveries, but were transformed into cliques seeking to destroy their opponents by political means. It is not suggested that these

[10] An analysis of the organisation of the Academy of Sciences and the ethos of science during the last years of Stalin's rule can be found in A. Vucinich, *The Soviet Academy of Sciences*, 1956.

[11] Z. A. Medvedev, *The Rise and Fall of T. D. Lysenko*, 1969, provides fascinating insight into some aspects of the politics of Soviet science. An earlier draft of the same work is to be found in *Grani*, No. 70, pp. 127–66, and No. 71, pp. 78–161, 1969.

techniques were employed in all disciplines to an equal extent, or by all scientists in the same way. The acceptance of such norms of behaviour as legitimate, however, opened the way for attacks by unscrupulous or fanatical individuals and groups and compelled other scientists to take up the same weapons in their own defence. Moreover, Soviet scientists were denied the right to justify their own work in terms of research done abroad, because of the distinction between bourgeois and socialist science. Under Stalin the scientific community, in spite of the resistance of many of its members, was often compelled to conduct scientific debate in the same terms as political debate.

The clearest examples of the exercise of political authority in deciding what was to be accepted as scientific truth came in the last years of Stalin's life. In 1948 Stalin gave his full support to Lysenko and his followers, and in 1950 the Central Committee endorsed Pavlovian teaching in physiology.[12] Both these interventions were followed by the removal of large numbers of scientists from their academic and administrative posts.[13] Encouraged perhaps by Lysenko's success, and responding to Zhdanov's call upon the 'land of victorious Marxism and its philosophers' to lead the 'struggle against corrupt and base bourgeois ideology'[14] militant philosophers in the following years launched attacks against the theory of relativity, quantum mechanics, mathematical logic and cybernetics. While these onslaughts were probably viewed with sympathy by the Central Committee, and scientific work retarded, there appears to have been no specific intervention to stop or redirect research in these fields.

It is sometimes suggested that Stalin's *Marxism in Linguistics*, published in 1950, betrays some doubts about the advisability of resolving scientific debates by political intervention. In this work Stalin attacked the linguistic theories of N. Y. Marr, who had claimed that language was a class phenomenon and part of the social superstructure. Stalin also criticised the way in which Marr's disciples had imposed their views on all Soviet students of linguistics. 'It is generally recognized', he wrote,

---

[12] Cf. *The Situation in Biological Science*, Proceedings of the Lenin Academy of Agricultural Sciences of the USSR, Session, July 31–August 7, 1948; 1949. Cf. *Scientific Session on the Physiological Teachings of Academician I. P. Pavlov*, 1951.

[13] Cf. Vucinich, op. cit., ch. 6 and pp. 103–6; Medvedev, op. cit., pp. 117–31.

[14] A. Zhdanov, 'Vystuplenie na diskussii po knige G. F. Aleksandrova "Istoriya Zapdano-yevropeyskoy Filosofii",' 1951, p. 44. The speech was made in 1947.

'that no science can develop and flourish without a struggle of opinions, without freedom of criticism. But this generally recognised rule was ignored and flouted in the most unceremonious fashion. There arose a close group of infallible leaders, who having secured themselves against any possible criticism, became a law unto themselves and did whatever they pleased.'[15] Although this comment may be seen as a penetrating criticism of Stalin's own rule, it led to no immediate change in the relationship between science and politics. The view which Stalin is sometimes thought to have implied, that science was no longer to be seen as part of the social superstructure, could have been very significant for Soviet science, but the implications were not drawn out until after Stalin's death.

The terms on which scientists were being urged to engage in debate were not conducive to an open exchange of views and opinions. One month after the last of Stalin's contributions to linguistics had appeared, an unsigned article entitled 'For free, creative, scientific criticism' was published in *Vestnik Akademii Nauk*. This stressed the importance of Stalin's pronouncements on linguistics for the natural sciences, and noted that 'in recent years there was not one occasion when the initiative for posing and discussing the acute open questions of science came from the pages of the Academy's journals';[16] it complained that 'creative, business-like criticism has difficulty in forcing its way into the Academy's institutions'.[17] In the same article a distinction was drawn between criticism of scientific mistakes and criticism of the bourgeois world-view. Moreover it declared that 'Soviet scholars do not discuss, but unmask and smash to smithereens the anti-scientific fabrications of the scholarly lackeys of the aggressive bourgeoisie'.[18] Soviet scientists found themselves in an intolerable position: they were urged to engage in discussion when the expression of 'incorrect views' might lead to expulsion from scientific work. The line between science and philosophy was so vague that scientists could not be sure when they were liable to be unmasked rather than merely criticised.

Academician I. I. Meshchaninov, the leading Marrist, criticised for being too dogmatic in his views, was given no opportunity to initiate a 'struggle of opinions' between Marr's

[15] I. V. Stalin, *Concerning Marxism in Linguistics*, Moscow, 1950, p. 22.
[16] 'Za svobodnuyu, tvorcheskuyu, nauchnuyu kritiku,' *Vestnik Akademii Nauk*, 1950, No. 8, p. 13.   [17] Loc cit.   [18] Ibid., p. 12.

theories and Stalin's. All energy was now devoted to applying Stalin's new theories in linguistics. The Council on the Problem of the Physiological Teaching of Academician I. P. Pavlov which had been set up to ensure that the resolutions of the 1950 conference were being enforced, continued to meet until 1953.[19] More problematical are the attacks on Lysenko's theories which appeared in *Botanicheskiy Zhurnal* at the end of 1952.[20] These opened the way for genuine scientific criticism of Lysenko's views, but the initial attacks were based on the authority of Stalin, Engels, Darwin and Michurin. This would suggest that while they signified some erosion of Lysenko's position, they did not mark any change in the basic principles underlying the relationship between scientific truth and political authority.

THE DE-STALINISATION OF SCIENCE

There is perhaps a curious parallel between the attempt to reconstruct the natural sciences on the basis of dialectical materialism, and the search of the logical positivists in the West for strict criteria of scientific truth. The latter did not of course lead to action to force transformations in the natural sciences, but both have now been superseded by the rather paradoxical, and in many ways intellectually unsatisfying, notion that 'scientific truth is defined as that which scientists affirm and believe to be true'.[21] Such a view is implicitly rather than explicitly held in the Soviet Union inasmuch as philosophers and politicians are no longer willing, or able, to push the logic of their claims to scientific understanding to the extent of active intervention in fundamental research.

This situation has been reached by a gradual and uneven process of change which was initiated by Stalin's death. In the last months of 1953 and early in 1954 there were signs of a changing policy towards science. There was a revival of debate

---

[19] Cf. for example, what appears to have been the final meeting of the council: 'O resheniyakh IX sessii Nauchnogo Soveta po problemam fiziologicheskogo ucheniya I. P. Pavlova,' *Vestnik Akademii Nauk*, 1953, No. 6, pp. 61–2.

[20] Cf. N. V. Turbin, 'Darvinizm i Novoye Ucheniye o Vide'; N. D. Ivanov, 'O Novom Uchenii T. D. Lysenko o Vide', in *Botanicheskiy Zhurnal*, No. 6, 1952, pp. 798–818, 819–42.

[21] Michael Polanyi, 'The Growth of Science in Society,' *Minerva*, Vol. 5, No. 4, Summer 1967, p. 533.

in biology, physics and cybernetics; the ethnocentrism of Stalin's last years began to disappear; contacts with the international scientific community were revived; and there was a relaxation of the control exercised by militant philosophers and vigilant administrators. A leading article in *Kommunist* criticised interest groups and monopolies in science and attempts by individual scientists to stifle criticism and substitute 'administrative methods' for creative discussion.[22] Lysenko in particular was censured, but there were no immediate purges. In 1955 Einstein was rehabilitated, and A. A. Maksimov, the chief opponent of relativity theory, was removed from influence.[23] In the same year N. I. Vavilov, the great Soviet geneticist whose school had been destroyed by Lysenko and his followers, was rehabilitated, and in the following year Lysenko lost his post as president of the Lenin All-Union Academy of Agricultural Sciences.[24]

The new freedom in scientific debate was the result not only of ideological and administrative relaxation by the collective leadership, but also of considerable pressure from the scientists themselves. The whole tone of scientific discussion had changed: attacks on individual scholars had ceased to be common, and the scientific community began to assert its own authority more confidently. The removal of Lysenko from the presidency of the Academy of Agricultural Sciences, and of Academician A. I. Oparin, one of his protectors, from the secretaryship of the Biological Department of the Academy of Sciences, had been effected in response to a petition from three hundred scientists at the end of 1955.[25] More general demands were voiced at the meetings of the Academy of Sciences' *aktiv* in the months after the 20th Party Congress. Considerable dissatisfaction was expressed at the way in which the Academy was run, and proposals for reform were put forward. The resolution adopted at

[22] 'Nauka i Zhizn'', *Kommunist*, 1954, No. 5, p. 10.
[23] G. Wetter, *Dialectical Materialism*, 1958, p. 420. Maksimov was criticised for his 'nihilistic views about one of the most important theories in modern science (relativity theory)' and removed from the editorial board of *Voprosy Filosofi*.
[24] Medvedev, op. cit., pp. 137–8.
[25] Ibid. The reasons for Lysenko's resignation are probably much more complex than this in view of his relationship with Malenkov, and opposition to Khrushchev. Cf. Sidney I. Ploss: *Conflict and Decision-Making in Soviet Russia. A Case Study of Agricultural Policy, 1953–1963*, 1965, passim. It is clear, however, that from about 1957 on Lysenko enjoyed Khrushchev's support because Khrushchev was able to use him as a pliant supporter in arguments with other experts.

the Moscow meeting urged the 'overcoming of dogmatism and quotation-mongering and also the liquidation of the consequences of the personality cult which is alien to Marxism'.[26] It went on: 'The *aktiv* called on all Soviet scholars to struggle decisively with manifestations of the personality cult in science, condemned the sometimes encountered substitution of a genuine struggle of scientific opinions between different schools and directions by unprincipled and unobjective attacks on the basis of hostile personal relationships, and by the use of the authority of a great scholar to stifle other opinions and suppress criticism. It is necessary to develop more widely criticism and the creative free discussion of scientific problems, to eliminate more boldly the defects which are retarding the development of science, and to raise significantly the role of the scientific community.' By the mid-1950s scientific authority was being returned to the scientists. The meshing of political and scientific authority, and the consequent use of political arguments in scientific debate were criticised. In February 1956 the President of the Academy of Sciences declared that biologists should be allowed to 'work and conduct scientific discussions and arguments without label-sticking or using in scientific discussion unscientific arguments'.[27]

Philosophers, whose role under Stalin had been at once subservient and despotic, now came under severe criticism from scientists for their dogmatism and incompetence in scientific matters. Their hegemony was being undermined by the pressure from scientists for intellectual independence and by the absence of a clear final source of authority in Marxism-Leninism. There was a generally acknowledged 'weakening of the alliance between scientists and philosophers', which was judged so serious that in June 1956 it was decided to convene an All-Union Conference on the Philosophical Problems of Contemporary Science.[28] The Conference met in October 1958 after a delay caused by certain unspecified 'difficulties',[29] one of which may have been the revival of Lysenko's fortunes. The conference did not discuss genetics and officially, though in a half-hearted fashion, endorsed Lysenkoist theories. In other fields of science,

[26] *Vestnik Akademii Nauk*, 1956, No. 6, p. 49.
[27] *Vestnik Akademii Nauk*, 1956, No. 3, p. 14.
[28] Cf. M. E. Omyel'yanovsky, 'Zadachi Razrabotki Problemy "Dialekticheskogo Materializma i sovremennogo yestyestvoznaniya",' *Vestnik Akademii Nauk*, 1956, No. 10; *Filosofskiye Problemy Sovremennogo Yestyestvoznaniya*, 1959, p. 650.
[29] Cf. *Filosofskiye Problemy Sovremennogo Yestyestvoznaniya*, p. 589.

however, the demarcation dispute between science and philosophy was solved in favour of the scientists. Philosophers and
scientists were urged to work more closely together, and philosophers were enjoined to take more account of developments in
modern science.[30] The view that the philosopher should lead
the scientist to new discoveries was abandoned.

Nevertheless, the weight of past decisions pressed heavily upon
the scientific community. In physiology the official commitment
to Pavlovian theories presented an obstacle to scientists who
wished to introduce new ideas. The extent of external influence
is difficult to gauge, and the official constraints appear to have
dropped away by the early 1960s.[31] More spectacular was the
resurgence of Lysenko in 1957 and 1958, which coincided with
the emergence of Khrushchev as the dominant figure in the
political leadership.[32] Lysenko was once more able to use
political influence to control appointments and hamper research in genetics, but his domination of Soviet biology was by
no means as extensive as it had been during 1948–52. Soon after
Khrushchev's fall, Lysenko too was removed from influence.[33]
Early in 1965 the President of the Academy of Sciences censured
'the scholars headed by Lysenko', who had 'ignored a number
of the most important theoretical orientations in modern biology'.[34] Academician N. N. Semenov commented that 'Lysenko
and such of his supporters as, for example, I. I. Prezent, by
using the conditions of the personality cult, have transferred
the struggle against those with different ideas from the level of
scientific discussion to the level of demagogy and political accusations'.[35] In September 1965 a joint session of the presidia of
the Academy of Sciences and the Academy of Agricultural
Sciences and the collegium of the Ministry of Agriculture condemned Lysenko's work at the agricultural research station
Gorki Leninskiye, not so much on scientific grounds, as on the un-
economic and inefficient nature of his agricultural proposals.[36]

[30] The proceedings are published in *Filosofskiye Problemy*.
[31] Cf. P. N. Fedoseyev's opening speech at a conference on physiology and
psychology in 1962, in which he criticised the effect of the personality cult on
physiology and psychology: *Filosofskiye voprosy fiziologii vysshey nervnoy deyatel'nosti
i psikhologii*, 1963.
[32] Cf. Medvedev, op. cit. pp. 138–9; Wetter, op. cit. p. 464.
[33] Cf. Medvedev, op. cit. pp. 221–43.
[34] *Vestnik Akademii Nauk*, 1965, No. 3, p. 111.
[35] *Nauka i Zhizn'*, 1965, No. 4, p. 43.
[36] Cf. the report and discussion in *Vestnik Akademii Nauk*, 1965, No. 11

Lysenko was allowed to continue his research, but his influence was effectively destroyed.

The fall of Lysenko and his school completed the process of restoring scientific authority to the scientists. The manner of his downfall is significant. Lysenko's authority and power had been derived from the support of the political leadership. The disappearance of that support left him vulnerable, but, as Medvedev points out, the decision to remove Lysenko and his followers from leading posts 'had to be made independently since there were no special party or government directives on these issues'.[37] This fact accounts in part for the mildness of the treatment accorded to Lysenko and his school. This treatment is also a reflection of what Medvedev calls 'the general democratization of scientific and social life. The constant struggle over many years, by scientists, against repressions and administration by injunction in science makes a new, radical clean-up of scientific establishments difficult now, when truth has triumphed. A clean-up is going on, but by legal means of competition and recertification. It is a *gradual* selective process.'[38]

The Soviet scientific community appears to have moved closer to the model described by W. O. Hagstrom: 'social control in science is exercised in an exchange system, a system wherein gifts of information are exchanged for recognition of scientific colleagues. Because scientists desire recognition, they conform to the goals and norms of the scientific community. . . . The very denial by scientists of the importance of recognition as an incentive can be seen to involve commitments to higher norms, including an orientation to a scientific community extending beyond any particular collection of contemporaries.'[39] Thus the source of recognition is also the source of control. In so far as the Central Committee in the time of Stalin exercised the right to say what was a contribution to science, and what merely bourgeois fabrication, it controlled the course of fundamental research: inasmuch as the source of recognition has returned to the scientists themselves, control over the development of science is now located in the scientific community.

[37] Medvedev, op. cit., p. 234.   [38] Medvedev, op. cit., p. 241.
[39] W. O. Hagstrom, *The Scientific Community*, 1965, p. 52. It is clear that in terms of such a model secrecy will introduce distortions into the behaviour of the scientific community, both by restricting communication between scientists, and by making it difficult for scientists engaged on secret research to obtain the recognition of the community.

Moreover, the loosening of the ties between science and philosophy has meant that the concern with orthodoxy in Marxism–Leninism no longer constrains to the same extent the shifts of focus effected by scientific revolutions. If, as was claimed by the mid-1950s, the natural sciences developed not only in response to external demands but in accordance with their internal possibilities, of which scientists were the best judge,[40] the canonisation of scientific theories with the symbols of communist legitimacy would serve merely to hamper the logic of internal development. Thus the scientific community has come to be regarded as a self-regulating system with its own internal control mechanisms, the functioning of which might be impeded by excessive interference from outside. In his book, *The Science of Science*, G. M. Dobrov writes that 'the approach of the French cybernetician Louis Couffignal allows us to view science as a whole as a special kind of enterprise, consisting of self-organising units. The essence of such an "enterprise" consists in the fact that it is "an association of people whose basic contribution to the enterprise is the information they present".' [41]

THE SCIENTIFIC-TECHNICAL REVOLUTION

It would be wrong to infer from the foregoing argument that the scientists' gain was necessarily the politicians' loss. The conditions of collective leadership and the fragmentation of political authority undoubtedly facilitated the scientists' emergence as an autonomous community. But an equally important factor in the development of the relationship between science and politics since 1953 has been the scientific-technical revolution. By this is meant the unprecedented growth of science which has taken place since the war, and the increasing importance of its socio-economic role. The rate of this revolution is indicated by the growth of the number of people engaged in R & D in the Soviet Union from about 800,000 in 1957 to almost two million in 1966, and by the increase in R & D expenditure from about 1·5 per cent of the GNP in the mid-1950s to over 3 per cent in the mid-1960s.[42] All industrial societies have experienced a

[40] Cf. A. N. Nesmeyanov, 'Nauka i Proizvodstvo', *Kommunist*, 1956, No. 2, p. 39; also M. V. Keldysh, *Vestnik Akademii Nauk*, 1961, No. 7, p. 22.

[41] G. M. Dobrov, *Nauka o Nauke*, 1966, p. 26.

[42] Cf. Zaleski *et al.*, op. cit., p. 534; R. W. Davies, *Science and the Soviet Economy*, 1967, p. 14.

research revolution over the last twenty years. The rate of the Soviet revolution has been accentuated, however, by the fact that it has coincided with a stage in Soviet scientific and technological development where she can no longer borrow from the West to the same degree as before, but must now rely to an ever-increasing extent on her own R & D for technological progress.

The increased emphasis on the need for basic research has resulted not merely from catching up with the West in certain fields of applied science, but also from the realisation that fundamental research in its own right can provide the stimulus for new technologies and new industries. It was clear by the mid-1950s that Engels's dictum that 'if society has a technical need, that helps science forward more than ten universities' was outmoded.[43] It was realised that the analysis of science as part of the superstructure of society was no longer valid. What Stalin had hinted at in 1950 now became widely accepted. In 1959 the the authoritative textbook, *Fundamentals of Marxist–Leninism*, declared that 'the time which Marx foresaw is coming – the time when science will be transformed into a direct productive force'.[44] The 1961 Party Programme stated that 'science will itself in full measure become a direct productive force'.[45]

The rapid increase in the scale of scientific research and technological development reflects a belief, widespread in all advanced industrial societies, that modern science can make a substantial contribution to economic growth, national security and public welfare. The Soviet political leadership has been well aware of the importance of science to its own political goals. At the All-Union Conference of Scientific Workers in June 1961, the letter of greeting from the Central Committee and the Council of Ministers declared that 'the successes of science to a great degree determine the rate of our progress to communism'.[46] Moreover, they were conscious of the military and political benefits which Soviet military and space science had already brought. In his speech to the conference A. N. Kosygin stated that 'we are living at a time of unprecedented flowering of science and technology. Outstanding successes have

[43] Marx and Engels, *Selected Correspondence*, n.d., Moscow, p. 548.
[44] *Osnovy Marksizma-Leninizma*, 1959, p. 689.
[45] Programme of the CPSU, 1961, part two, section 1.
[46] *Vestnik Akademii Nauk*, 1961, No. 7, p. 4.

been achieved by [our] native science. The Central Committee
of the party, the government and N. S. Khrushchev personally,
value highly the selfless labour of our scholars. The Soviet
people takes great pride in the achievements of our science and
sees in these achievements the guarantee of the victory of
socialism in peaceful competition with capitalism.'[47] The attitude of the political authorities towards the scientific community had changed from hostile suspicion in the late 1940s and
early 1950s to confident anticipation in the latter half of the
decade.

The new science-politics symbiosis has presented the political
leadership with a dual problem of organisation: first, how to
harness scientific research and development to political goals in
the most effective and efficient way; secondly, how to ensure
that the institutional arrangements designed to achieve this aim
do not impede the scientists in their pursuit of knowledge. The
organisational problem is of acute political significance. It is no
longer claimed that socialist science is inherently better than
bourgeois science, but it is claimed that the Soviet Union can
progress more rapidly in the pursuit of knowledge than Western
societies, and apply that knowledge more effectively to human
purposes. The Party Programme declares: 'Mankind is entering
the period of a scientific and technical revolution bound up with
the conquest of nuclear energy, space exploration, the development of chemistry, automation and other major achievements
of science and engineering. But the relations of production under
capitalism are much too narrow for a scientific and technical
revolution. Socialism alone is capable of effecting it and of
applying its fruits in the interests of society.'[48]

Reforms in the institutional arrangements for Soviet science
since 1953 can be divided, for present purposes, roughly into
two groups: changes in the internal organisation of the Academy of Sciences, and changes affecting the relationship between the Academy and other research bodies. It is significant
that the initiative for internal reforms seems to have come
largely from within the Academy, whereas the proposals for
changing the role of the Academy in Soviet science have
originated in the political leadership, though the shape these
reforms took may have been influenced by discussion within the

[47] *Vestnik Akademii Nauk*, 1961, No. 7, p. 96.
[48] Programme of the CPSU, 1961, part one, section 4.

scientific community. These distinctions are of course extremely difficult to establish, especially as the role of the Presidium of the Academy is to represent the government's interests to the scientists, and, perhaps to a somewhat lesser extent, the scientists' interests to the government.

The reforms in the Academy's structure have been designed to improve the administration of an increasingly complex organisation, and to eradicate some of the worst features of the rigid system of bureaucratic controls through which Stalin had sought to direct science. In 1954 and 1955 the degree of centralised decision-making was reduced. The scholarly secretariat which had been set up in 1949 was disbanded, and the Chief Scholarly Secretary was given five deputies with restricted rights of supervision over scientific work.[49] Since the Chief Scholarly Secretary is generally regarded as the most important administrator, and the main focus of party control in the Academy (though the balance of authority seems to have changed since Keldysh became President in 1961), this signified some lessening of party vigilance in the Academy.[50] It is notable that the Chief Scholarly Secretary's report to the Academy in 1955 was the first since 1946 to contain no attacks on individual scholars.[51] In 1955, after representations by the Academy, the government decided to reduce the size of the Presidium's apparatus and give the departments direct control over the scientific institutes.[52]

These reforms did not, however, satisfy the Academy's scientists. During the months after the 20th Party Congress the Presidium of the Academy was severely criticised at the meetings of the *aktiv*. Among the demands made were: more emphasis on theoretical research, greater attention to central problems of theoretical and practical significance, democratisation of the running of the Academy, increased decentralisation of control with greater autonomy for the departments and institutes.[53] A more remarkable manifestation of dissatisfaction was the proposal by the Department of Physico-Mathematical Sciences that the re-election of Academician A. N. Nesmeyanov as President be postponed for several months to allow him to present an account of his work and set forth plans for the future.[54]

[49] *Vestnik Akademii Nauk*, 1954, No. 11, p. 88.
[50] Cf. Vucinich, op. cit., pp. 33–5.   [51] Cf. *Vestnik Akademii Nauk*, 1955, No. 3.
[52] G. I. Fed'kin: *Pravovyye Voprosy Organisatsii Nauchnoy Raboty v SSSR*, 1958, p. 49.
[53] *Vestnik Akademii Nauk*, 1956, No. 6, pp. 3–50.
[54] *Vestnik Akademii Nauk*, 1956, No. 11, p. 7.

Urging the postponement, Academician I. E. Tamm called for greater democracy in running the Academy and for more consultation of the members before taking decisions; he complained that meetings of the general assembly had become little more than ceremonial parades. The proposal was taken seriously, but Nesmeyanov was re-elected immediately.

In September 1956 a commission was set up to draft a new charter for the Academy. This was adopted in 1959 and was designed to meet many of the earlier criticisms.[55] The Academy as a whole was given greater autonomy in conducting its own affairs. The Presidium was to be responsible in all its activity to the general assembly, which was to be convened at least twice a year with greater freedom to discuss questions of science and the organisation of science. The powers of the departments and institutes were increased. In order to bring more of the scientific community into the resolution of questions of scientific development the annual reports by the members of the Academy were to be subject to scrutiny not only by the Presidium, but also by the scholarly councils of the institutes. The rapid growth in the number of the Academy's science councils in particular fields of research has been intended in part to facilitate the coordination of work being conducted in more than one institution.[56] In 1963 the number of departments in the Academy was increased from nine to fifteen in order to ensure that all the members of a given departmental bureau were in fields closely enough related for them to be able to understand one another, and that all the major directions of science were properly represented.[57] There has been a great increase in the number of scientific conferences, drawing together scientists from the Academy and other research institutions. It will be seen that these reforms are related to the scientific community's search for intellectual autonomy: they were designed to make freer the flow of information across the different organisational divisions and facilitate the community's processes of discussion and evaluation. They appear to be the institutional reflection of more important informal developments.

The second group of reforms – those affecting the Academy's

55 Cf. *Vestnik Akademii Nauk*, 1959, No. 5.
56 Cf. Zaleski *et al.*, op. cit., pp. 227–31.
57 *Vestnik Akademii Nauk*, 1963, No. 6, p. 17.

functions – was designed to achieve two objects: the rational division of scientific labour, and the rapid introduction of new knowledge into industrial production. At the Central Committee Plenum of June 1959 Khrushchev complained that neither of these objectives was being attained, and that reform of the Academy would have to be undertaken.[58] His speech sparked off an intensive debate amongst scientists and technologists about what functions the Academy should perform. This issue was becoming increasingly acute in view of the rapid growth of the Academy and the increasing importance of fundamental research. Various schools of opinion emerged, but the 1961 reforms embodied the proposals of the 'pure' scientists that the Academy concentrate on fundamental research, and that the institutes engaged in applied research and development be transferred to the jurisdiction of the appropriate state organs.[59] The Academy was henceforth to focus its attention on major theoretical and fundamental technological problems. A new administrative body, the State Committee for the Coordination of Scientific Research, was set up to ensure the rational use of scientific manpower and to 'guide and control the work of scientific institutes' in accordance with the directives of the party and government, 'ensuring continuity of research up to the introduction and assimilation of its findings into the national economy'.[60] The State Committee was given a wide range of responsibilities and powers, and the Academy's role in the administration of science was diminished. The creation of a powerful state committee was probably essential if the Academy was to avoid becoming a Ministry of Science and Technology. In Keldysh's words, the Academy was neither a ministry nor 'a monastery'.[61] Concentration upon fundamental research was not to be allowed to degenerate into the pursuit of knowledge for its own sake. The Academy, according to the 1961 decree, was to conduct its activity 'with the aim of utilising the results of completed scientific research for the development of the national economy and culture'.[62] It is evident that there have

[58] Cf. Loren R. Graham, 'Reorganization of the USSR Academy of Sciences', in P. H. Juviler and H. W. Morton (eds.), *Soviet Policy-Making*, 1967, pp. 133–61.

[59] Cf. Graham: 'Reorganization . . .'; and Zaleski *et al.*, op. cit., pp. 202–3.

[60] *Pravda*, 12 April 1961, p. 1; translation in A. G. Korol, *Soviet Research and Development*, 1965, pp. 325–9.

[61] A. Vucinich, 'Science', in A. Kassof (ed.), *Prospects for Soviet Society*, 1967, p. 337.

[62] Cf. Korol, loc. cit.

been difficulties in deciding upon the division of responsibilities
between the various organs concerned with planning and administering R & D. The 1963 reform of the Academy extended
its role in Soviet science by giving it greater responsibilities in
planning and coordinating fundamental research.[63] One of the
important features of these reforms was that they distinguished
between fundamental and applied research, and by institutionalising the distinction reversed the main thrust of the 1929–31
reform of the Academy of Sciences. Fundamental research is
now recognised as a distinct activity, the direction of which is
defined by scientists. Although such research is increasingly
conducted on a mission-oriented basis, it is generally agreed, by
scientists and administrators alike, that it is not open to evaluation on economic criteria.[64]

Further changes in institutional arrangements and continuing
discussion in the press indicate that the problems of organising
science are very far from being solved. It is true, of course, that
serious conceptual obstacles (e.g. the choice of criteria for allo-
cating resources between fundamental and applied research
projects) stand in the way. Furthermore, there are difficult
problems of organisation and communication involved in
ensuring the rapid application of new knowledge in production.
The current trend of reform is to provide incentives to both
enterprises and R & D establishments, and to set up direct and
feedback links between the two, so that technical innovation
may be effected without the exercise of administrative pressure.
The general view amongst scientists and administrators seems
to be that increased functional efficiency requires greater
structural flexibility.

POLITICAL IMPLICATIONS

The new relationship between fundamental research and political authority has its origins in the years 1953–6, in the death of
Stalin and the heightened realisation of the need for, and the
possibilities of, research and development in economic progress.[65] With the de-Stalinisation of Soviet science, scientific
authority has returned to the scientific community, the rela-

---

[63] Cf. Zaleski *et al.*, op. cit., pp. 202–3.   [64] Cf. ibid., pp. 570–2.
[65] Cf. ibid., p. 394; also Decisions of the Plenum of the Central Committee,
CPSU, held in July 1955, Moscow, 1955.

tionship between scientist and philosopher has been redefined to ensure that philosophers no longer impede scientific progress (though they may perhaps help it), Soviet links with the international scientific community have become much stronger, and the system of administrative controls imposed by Stalin has been loosened. The aim of applying scientific knowledge to national purposes still remains, however, and with the advent of 'big science' has presented organisational problems of a new magnitude. At the same time, the contribution of science to these purposes has grown enormously, and the authority of the scientist has been consequently enhanced. De Solla Price points out that 'with everything said to be depending on him, from freedom from attack to freedom from disease, the scientist now holds the purse-strings of the entire state'.[66]

The political influence of scientists appears to reflect the new political importance of science. The political role of Soviet scientists is complex and requires detailed examination, but some points about it may be made here. Their influence appears to be greatest in the formation of science policy, which is becoming an increasingly important aspect of overall government policy. The exercise of this influence within government organs is probably enhanced by the democratisation of scientific life. Freedom of scientific discussion, and the return of scientific authority to the scientists, is perhaps likely to make politicians and administrators feel that the science they are paying for is valid and likely to produce results.

Although the scientists have won considerable independence in the activity of fundamental research, it would be wrong to assume that they are completely free of the legacies of Stalinist rule. It is by no means clear, for example, that the bureaucratisation of science has been sufficiently relaxed to ensure the free flow of scientific information across institutional boundaries, or to remove all obstacles to the processes of discussion and evaluation which are said to be necessary to scientific progress.[67] Other more intangible brakes on scientific progress may also exist. In trying to account for the relative lack of Soviet success in formulating new fundamental theories, as distinct from

[66] D. J. de Solla Price, *Little Science, Big Science*, 1963, p. 111.
[67] For a description by a Soviet writer of the difficulties he faced in trying to form an 'invisible college' cf. V. V. Nalimov, 'Kolichestvennyye Metody Issledovaniya Protsessa Razvitiya Nauki', *Voprosy Filosofii*, 1966, No. 12, pp. 43–5.

applying or developing them, G. N. Volkov writes of the need to 'create in scientific life such an atmosphere as would make it impossible to use authority and power in personal, institutional or group interests'.[68]

Just as the desire to harness science to political purposes as effectively as possible has led to widespread discussion of the organisational and economic problems of science, so the desire to make the work of the scientific community as productive as possible has been reflected in the emergence, since the mid-1960s, of the sociology of science and the science of science. The former is concerned generally with the optimum size of research laboratories, the division of scientific labour, the selection of specialists, the training of research workers, the physical and social conditions of work, and the patterns of formal and informal communication amongst scientists.[69] The latter is essentially interested in the quantitative study of the processes of scientific development, the interaction between various branches of science, and the constraints upon the development of science. These disciplines, although still largely derived from Western studies, seem now to be firmly established, and may produce theoretical and empirical findings of interest to both administrators of science and students of Soviet society.[70]

It is clear, however, that the success of the scientific-technical revolution depends upon the efficient organisation not only of science but of the whole education-science-economy-defence nexus. As the political importance of science has grown, so the role of scientists in advising on policy in these areas has increased.[71] We know very little about the involvement of scientists in the making of specific decisions; nor do we know much about the kind of authority they enjoy in the corridors of power, e.g. whether their authority is based upon an apolitical stance.[72]

[68] G. N. Volkov, *Sotsiologiya Nauki*, 1968, p. 234.

[69] Cf., for example, Volkov, op. cit., for a very general discussion of the field, also A. I. Shcherbakov: *Puti sovershenstvovaniya organizatsii truda nauchnykh sotrudnikov*, 1966. Ye. Z. Mirskaya, 'Kommunikatsii v nauke', *Voprosy Filosofii*, 1969, No. 8, pp. 107–15.

[70] Dobrov, op. cit., is probably the best general Soviet discussion of the science of science.

[71] 'In recent times, the number of scientists called on to participate in the work of the governmental apparatus, even at the highest levels, has increased.' Quoted in Zaleski *et al.*, op. cit., p. 205.

[72] Cf. Robert C. Wood, 'The Rise of an Apolitical Elite', in Gilpin and Wright (eds.), op. cit., pp. 41–72. The technological education received by the great

We do know, however, that scientists have shown increasing concern about the way in which institutional arrangements and planning methods in education and the economy provide for the complex needs, and exploit the enormous opportunities, of the scientific-technical revolution. In the public discussion of economic planning, for example, computer engineers and mathematicians were instrumental in creating the new school of economic cybernetics. The various conferences on mathematical economics in the early 1960s showed a clear division between economists and mathematicians both in style of argument and their views on the ideological implications of new theories such as linear programming.[73] The institutionalisation of this school in the Central Economic-Mathematical Institute of the Academy of Sciences does not of course guarantee that their policy proposals will be implemented or, if implemented, successful; but it does mean that the discussion of problems of planning and administering the economy can be conducted in an atmosphere relatively free from political intervention and in language that is not ideologically contaminated. The same process may be observed in embryonic form in the creation of a new sociological theory employing concepts drawn from systems theory and cybernetics and supported by as yet highly selective empirical research.[74] The Soviet authorities have encouraged (or permitted) the development of social and economic cybernetics in the hope that it will enable them to cope with the increasing complexity of Soviet society and to improve their control over social and economic processes. There are indications that a new science of society, originating amongst the scientific community, and leading to the formation of a new social-scientific intelligentsia, is emerging. This may represent not merely a striving for improved management and administration but also, at least potentially, an attempt to take a critical look at Soviet society.

majority of the political leadership presumably makes it easier for scientists and technologists to communicate their demands and priorities to the politicians and administrators; conversely, it may make the politicians less likely to attribute superior powers of insight and wisdom to the scientists.

[73] Cf., for example, 'Matematicheskiye Metody v Ekonomike', *Voprosy Ekonomiki*, No. 8, 1960, pp. 100–20; 'Ekonomisty i Matematiki za "kruglym stolom"', *Voprosy Ekonomiki*, 1964, No. 9, pp. 63–110.

[74] Cf. for example, Yu. A. Levada, 'Kiberneticheskiye metody v sotsiologii', *Kommunist*, 1965, No. 14; I. V. Blauberg, E. G. Yudin, 'Sistemnyi podkhod v sotsial'nykh issledovaniyakh', *Voprosy Filosofii*, 1967, No. 9.

The use of concepts and techniques drawn from the natural sciences, in particular from cybernetics, in the analysis of social and economic organisation represents a new stage in the relationship between science and politics. The implication of many of the contributions to these discussions has been that the Soviet economic and administrative (and hence political) systems are organised on highly inefficient lines, and that decisions are based on unscientific criteria; the application of cybernetic concepts in analysis and the implementation of proposals based on such analysis would make a truly scientific control of society possible.[75]

Besides this technocratic tendency, there appears to exist another broad current of political belief in the scientific community. This is derived not from the concepts and techniques of a particular branch of science, but from the principles which scientists believe to underlie the behaviour of the scientific community. This current of thought has emerged from the scientists' struggle for intellectual independence in the post-Stalin years. One of the most interesting features of that struggle was the way in which the words 'political' and 'philosophical' became terms of condemnation in the mouths of scientists. This implied that the scientific mode of argument was incompatible with philosophy and politics as then conducted – a conclusion that is itself incompatible with the claim of the leadership to be guided by a scientific ideology. Academician A. D. Sakharov opens his 'Reflections on progress, peaceful coexistence and intellectual freedom' by stating that

the views of the author have been formed in the milieu of the scientific-technical intelligentsia, which shows great anxiety about the questions of principle and the concrete questions of mankind's future. In particular, this concern feeds upon consciousness of the

[75] An ex-Soviet science journalist has described this current of belief. According to him, Soviet scientists 'regard the political and economic systems as working, in cybernetic terms, without feedback and with an enormously high level of noise. To continue the analogy, this means that the system must be destroyed and another one built up. . . . They still hope for some change at the top, in some way similar perhaps to those that have occurred in Yugoslavia or Czechoslovakia. . . . Today they think this kind of change is inevitable. They are thinking in terms of a technocracy – rule by technologists and scientists – as a transition stage before some more democratic system can be installed. Although this talk sounded rather strange to me, I found it to be quite widespread among scientists, except for those that are cynics and sceptics, and there are many of them.' Leonid Vladimirov, 'Soviet Science – a Native's Opinion', *New Scientist*, 28 November 1968, p. 490.

fact that the scientific method of directing politics, economics, art, education, and military affairs has not yet become a reality. We consider 'scientific' that method which is based on a profound study of the facts, theories, and views, presupposing unprejudiced and open discussion, dispassionate in its conclusions. At the same time, the complexity and many-faceted nature of all the phenomena of contemporary life, the enormous opportunities and dangers connected with the scientific-technical revolution and with several public and social tendencies, urgently demand just such an approach, as is acknowledged even in several official utterances.[76]

Under Stalin the structure of authority and the norms of behaviour in the scientific community mirrored those in society at large; now it seems that some scientists wish to see their own newly-regained norms of behaviour reflected more widely in social and political life.

It is not suggested that one can speak of scientists in politics as a group in the same way that one can speak of scientists engaged in research as forming a community. There is clearly a much greater difference between, say, Academicians and junior scientific workers in terms of political activity than in terms of scientific work. No doubt there are many scientists who are apolitical, or firmly conformist communists. Besides, scientists exist as political beings outside their professional roles, and the beliefs and actions of individual scientists are evidenced in the petitions and letters of protest about the lack of observance of the civil rights guaranteed in the constitution. It appears that scientists, having won intellectual independence in their research, and conscious of their contribution to national purposes, have become more concerned about political life in general. Moreover, their political beliefs arise, to some extent at least, out of their perception of what science is and what it can do. The two main currents of belief that appear to exist – the technocratic and the democratic – represent, each in its own way, a new conception of scientific politics. The breakdown of the Stalinist relationship between science and politics has not, it seems, undermined the belief that politics ought to be scientific.

It is difficult to assess the significance of these currents of belief. The scientific-technical revolution and the democratisation

[76] A. D. Sakharov, *Razmyshleniya o progresse, mirnom sosushchestvovanii i intellektual'noy svobode*, 1968.

of science have involved scientists more closely in the making of science policy and in advisory roles in a wide range of policy areas. If one assumes that scientists are more rational and tolerant than other men, their recruitment may have some impact on the style of political life and on the way in which decisions are reached. Perhaps the important point here, however, is not that scientists are more admirable than other men, but that their involvement in government indicates a new, and increasingly important, source from which to recruit administrators and officials, who may have skills and values different from those of the party *apparatchiki* and state bureaucrats. In a more general way the influence of scientists in politics has been felt in the introduction of new concepts into the discussion of social and economic problems. The greatest influence, however, may have been felt in ways that are most difficult to discern: in the changing of social values through technological progress, and in the erosion of the party's legitimacy as a result of the disjunction between political authority and scientific truth.

Although considerable problems remain, the Soviet leadership has had considerable success in exploiting the scientific technical revolution for its own ends. The party has allowed, indeed encouraged, scientists to manifest in public their concern about various areas of government policy. Over the last two years, however, the party has shown increasing anxiety about the social and political attitudes of scientists, who seem to exercise their social consciousness by entering into debate and controversy rather than by lending their authority to party decisions. The last number of *Kommunist* in 1968 published an article entitled 'The party's concern for the education of the scientific-technical intelligentsia', which stressed the need to improve the level of political work among scientists. Soviet scientists, it declared, 'want to know in detail how industry and agriculture are developing, how our workers and collective farmers are working. They raise a multitude of questions, to which, unfortunately, they do not always receive exhaustive answers. Thus, possessing inadequate information, some of them attempt to supplement it with casual news and on this shaky basis make sometimes far-reaching conclusions.'[77] Moreover, the writer declares that when scientists interest themselves in

[77] N. Svidorov, 'Partiinaya Zabota o Vospitanii Nauchno-Tekhnicheskoy Intelligentsii', *Kommunist*, 1968, No. 18, p. 40.

social and political problems they are far from scientific: 'It's curious, but it's a fact. A man who works in the natural sciences, dealing with physical phenomena, will never build an analysis on the basis of deliberately unauthenticated data, but he often judges social phenomena only on what he somehow or somewhere hears.' [78] The remedy suggested by the author is to make the information at the disposal of political workers more 'operative'. He notes that the party has worked out ways of dealing with writers, artists, and journalists, but that political work amongst scientists has been neglected. A more militant tone is to be found in a speech given by the President of the Academy of Sciences in April 1968. [79] Keldysh declared that an effort would have to be made 'to explain the true state of affairs' to scientists who had sent letters of protest to the political authorities, and copies of these letters abroad. He warned scientists against believing that their status as scientists would protect them from reprisals: 'These individuals ... must remember that it is not they who define our science. The development of science will proceed in any event.'

This raises the question of whether or not heightened political control over scientists, and sanctions against individuals, would recreate the distortions evident during Stalin's rule and thus diminish science's contribution to national purposes. The Stalinist attempt to ensure the political loyalty of scientists and harness their work to national goals is now seen to have impeded the development of Soviet science. The restoration of the old relationship would be even more destructive now inasmuch as the role of science in society has increased greatly. If, as de Solla Price suggests, science is reaching saturation point in terms both of the number of able men it can attract and of the proportion of the GNP it can consume, political reprisals against able scientists might well hamper the growth of Soviet science. The idea that the exponential rate of growth of science is developing into a logistic curve is, however, unpopular in the Soviet Union. If Academician Kapitsa's vision of a society in which one half of mankind engages in scientific research, while the other half supervises automatic factories, begins to be realised, it may prove increasingly difficult to educate Soviet scientists in communist values. It seems clear that the problems faced by the Soviet

---

[78] Ibid., pp. 40–1.
[79] *Pravda*, 1 April 1968, p. 2.

leadership in relating science to national purposes and values will require more than the current intensive debate on the organisation and planning of science for ther solution. A new theory of the relationship between the authority of the scientist and the authority of the politician is needed.

Julian Birch

The Albanian Political Experience[*]

Case Study

IN THE GENERAL FLURRY OF ARTICLES AND BOOKS
on Albania's role in international communist politics and on her
relations with Russia and China,[1] it is all too often overlooked
or forgotten that she has an internal political life of her own.
Nor is this fault by omission too surprising, in view of the relative inaccessibility of the country to both the traveller and the
researcher, the obvious linguistic barrier,[2] and the familiar
problems of dealing almost exclusively with official publications[3] of a type long bemoaned by and pored over by Krem-
linologists and Sinologists alike.

[1] See particularly, A. Logoreci, 'Albania: A Chinese Satellite in the Making',
The World Today, London, Vol. 17, No. 5, May 1961, pp. 197–205; W. E. Griffiths,
Albania and the Sino-Soviet Rift, MIT, Boston, Mass., 1962; S. Skendi, 'Albania and
the Sino-Soviet Conflict', *Foreign Affairs*, Boston, Mass., Vol. 40, No. 3, April
1962, pp. 471–8; H. Hamm, *Albania, China's Beachhead in Europe*, F. A. Praeger,
New York, 1963; 'Mao's Mayfly on the Rise in Europe', *The Irish Times*, 24 June
1969; *Sino-Soviet Contacts Arouse Hoxha's Suspicions*, Radio Free Europe Research Paper,
15 October 1969; and A. Fontaine, 'L'Etoile Rouge sans les Russes', *Le Monde*,
15 November 1969. Even A. Logoreci's, 'Albania: The Anabaptists of European
Communism', in *Problems of Communism*, Washington, Vol. XVI, No. 3, May–June
1967,p p. 22–8, is largely concerned with her international affairs. See also P.
Katona and L. Jotishcky, 'New Patterns in Inter-Communist Relations', *The
Year Book of World Affairs*, 1963, pp. 63–4 and 74–5.

[2] The provision of an official, unified orthography, resulting from the fusion of
elements of the Geg and Tosk dialects, spoken respectively in the North and the
South of the country, may encourage more Western researchers to enter the field –
see J. Gjinari, 'The Dialectical Demarcation of the Albanian Language', *Albanian
Life*, London, No. 1, January 1969, pp. 29–33.

[3] Principally *Zeri i Popullit* (the party daily), *Rruga e Partise* (the party theoretical monthly), *Bashkimi* (organ of the Democratic Front), *Gazeta Zyrtare* (the
Official Gazette), *Zeri i Rinise* (organ of the Albanian League of Working Youth),
Drita (organ of the writers and artists) and the organs of the Ministry of Agriculture and the Economic Ministries, *Bujqesia Socialiste* and *Ekonomia Popullore*.
Among the very few unofficial or *émigré* materials are *The Albanian Resistance* (news
bulletin of the National Democratic Committee for a Free Albania, Paris) – containing much dubious material; *Flamuri*, Rome – the more informative organ of

[*] Vol. 6, No. 3, Summer 1971.

Notwithstanding these problems, it seems worthwhile here to contribute a few notes on the nature of the internal politics of the regime, now that it has celebrated its 25th anniversary (29 November 1969), including observations on conflict and opposition in a state which has given the impression of being probably the most rigid, dictatorially controlled system in Europe.

The first significant point about the communist regime in Albania concerns its very considerable debt to its past and particularly to the clan structure of its society.[4] Unlike most revolutionary communist regimes, breaking with the past, emphasising the break, and throwing up a new cast of leaders to replace the old ruling class, there remains in Albania a strong element of the clan factor, particularly among the northern Gegs, with a number of the small leadership group either related through their clan connections or through intermarriage.

This striking example of continuity as opposed to change is reflected in the person of and background to the Party First Secretary Enver Hoxha himself and the apparently widespread practice of nepotism, not unlike that of Khrushchev – this in spite of the open letter from the Central Committee to the people in March 1966, which, among other matters, called for an end to nepotism.[5] Although unable to confirm this, the present author was told that Hoxha, a Tosk, was the offspring of a powerful clan, having been born in the family stronghold.[6] His wife, Nexhmije Hoxha, moreover, currently holds a most prestigious post as director of the Institute of Marxist-Leninist Studies and is also a member of the Central Committee.[7]

A second feature, reminiscent of practices one has come to accept from the other East European regimes, is the self-

the Albanian Agrarian-Democratic Party; the American-Albanian weekly, *Liria*; and the various sympathetic publications of the Albanian Society, London – particularly *Albanian Life* (formerly Albanian Notes).

[4] On the clan structure see particularly *Naval Intelligence Division, Albania, Geographical Handbook*, London, series BR542 and *Historical Section, Foreign Office, Albania – Handbook*, London, 1920.

[5] *Zeri i Popullit*, 4 March 1966.

[6] For biographical details of Hoxha see *Current Biography*, New York, Vol. 11, No. 1, January 1950, pp. 27–9; *Bolshaya Sovetskaya Entsiklopediya*, Moscow, 1951; D. Ingber, 'Enver Hoxha: Albanian Dictator', *Contemporary Review*, 176, August 1949, pp. 86–93; 'Hoxha, Strong Man of Albania', *World Report*, 3 December 1946, pp. 34–5; J. Gunther, *Behind the Curtain*, Harper, New York, 1949, pp. 127–8; and *The Times*, London, 10 February 1961.

[7] See report by her, in her capacity as director of the Institute, in *Rruga e Partise*, March 1969.

imposed seclusion and isolation of the political elite from the mass of the people, particularly with respect to their private lives. Many of them live in blocks of flats in a walled compound directly connected with the government offices on the New Albania Boulevard in central Tirana. Similarly, at least in the seaport resort of Durres, a rest home, along with its frontal stretch of coastline, constitutes a preserve for the senior leadership, when in residence, with beach patrols diverting the unwary on to the coast road. The author also caught a glimpse of a veritable feast, involving a number of Chinese, in a private dining room of one hotel.

Hoxha himself, nevertheless, continues to make frequent public appearances, addressing crowds up and down the country – clearly a medium in which he takes some personal pleasure and in which he excels, with his dignified and relatively immaculate appearance – while Fontaine has provided an interesting description of ministers leaving a reception on foot and mingling into the crowds, as the privileged elite depart in the few available cars.[8]

Again, one is struck by the pivotal role and dominating position exercised by Hoxha. Twenty-six years after attaining power, he appears as firmly in control as ever, in spite of giving up his status as virtual one-man government in the early, formative years of the regime, when skills were at a premium. At that time, Hoxha was able, from the age of 35 in 1946, simultaneously to hold until 1953, the posts of Secretary-General of the Communist Party, Chairman of the Council of Ministers (or Prime Minister) and Supreme Commander of the Armed Forces, Minister of Foreign Affairs and Member of the Presidium of the People's Assembly.

Equally striking is the apparent degree of control exercised over the country as a whole. Small as it is, Albania is extremely rugged, with poorly developed communications[9] and few tarmacked roads – a situation matched by the paucity of vehicles. And yet, as far as it was possible to ascertain, party control and influence extends to the most obscure and backward villages,[10]

[8] A. Fontaine, 'Vingt-Cinq Ans de Socialisme en Albanie', *Le Monde*, 30 November 1969.
[9] The newly constructed Fieri-Rrogozhina railway will not assist in providing ready access to the hinterland.
[10] In terms of coverage, Hoxha revealed that even in 1966 few villages lacked a party organisation – see E. Hoxha, *Report on the Activity of the Central Committee of*

where portraits of Hoxha, and even Mao, as well as the routine
Marxist slogans, are to be seen in abundance.[11] It was not
however possible to discover anything of the underlying attitudes in, for instance, the Mati region, a former stronghold of
support for ex-King Zog.

Another significant aspect of the political culture was the
almost total lack of access to outside information and the rather
naïve ignorance of the world shown by students. Newspapers and
'decadent' magazines are almost invariably confiscated from
the visitor at the border, while the foreign news datelines in the
press are very largely limited to Tirana or Peking, except for
occasional items from such outposts of Albanian diplomatic
activity as Paris and Rome. The celebrated *Peking Review* was
viewed as a primary source of foreign news and comment by
those students spoken to. In the circumstances of this extremely
rarefied atmosphere and restricted flow of information and
viewpoints, one is able to comprehend the conformist attitudes,
and the lack of questioning of regime policies and of the regime
itself, exhibited by otherwise well-trained specialists, quite
apart from the masses – a situation left unaltered by the largely
itinerant trickle of foreign visitors, and hardly contributed to by
the cessation of BBC broadcasts to Albania (however limited
their audience).[12] Access to alien ideas thus remains extremely
limited,[13] although, doubtless, some small pockets or 'islands of
separateness'[14] continue to exist, even with the abolition of one
such area – religion.[15] The physical destruction of mosques and
the turning over of many church buildings, to other uses,

---

the *Party of Labour of Albania*, Naim Frashëri Publishing House, Tirana, 1966,
p. 113.

[11] Considerable effort seemed to be put into the slogans, those on the side of an
embankment of the railway near Fieri keeping fully abreast, in huge letters, with
the construction of the embankment itself.

[12] See *The Guardian*, London, 11 January 1967.

[13] This direct aspect of thought conditioning is supported by a second range of
indirect methods such as the Chinese produced tapes used by foreign language
students of English in the language laboratory.

[14] C. J. Friedrich and Z. Brzezinski, *Totalitarian Dictatorship and Autocracy*,
Cambridge, Mass., 1956, pp. 239ff.

[15] Albania was officially declared an atheist state in November 1967 on the
grounds that churches were used for opposition caches of arms and were no longer
attended by the populace at large – see *The Times*, London, 3 November 1967 and
Radio Free Europe Research Paper, *Albania Claims: First Atheist State in the World*,
9 October 1967 – it having been reported in September of that year that 2,169
religious establishments had been closed in the previous six months.

is unlikely to eradicate long ingrained beliefs over-night.[16]

The Chinese presence, though clearly visible, appears to be limited to economic[17] and military involvement,[18] while in the political sphere the thoughts of Mao are stressed in strict conjunction with, and usually subordination to those of Hoxha himself – thoughts declared to be suited to the specifically Albanian experience.[19] The mini 'cultural revolution', consisting essentially of sending mainly low-level officials to work in the provinces and the fields, and the mobilisation of youth and intellectuals, particularly students, to assist in bringing new life to old and outmoded methods in agriculture in the more mountainous areas (it also resulted in the abolition, in March 1966, of military ranks and the establishment of a full system of political commissars in the forces; reduction of wage differentials; and attempts to limit excessive bureaucracy, in line with a Party Central Committee resolution of 24 December 1965), was never allowed to get out of control, and was tempered by a marked degree of moderation to this end.[20] Considerable use of 'volunteer' labour groups of young people, containing as many as several thousand persons, is still widespread; some obvious enthusiasm for the contribution they were making to build up the economy being apparent.

Something must now be said of the current internal policy concerns of the regime. In a year (1969) notable for the celebration of its 25th anniversary,[21] a year marred only by the April

[16] A factor recognised by Hoxha in his speech to the congress of the Democratic Front in September 1967 and brought home by the post-abolition article 'Let us carry on the uninterrupted struggle against the influences of religious ideology' in *Zeri i Popullit*, 6 February 1969.

[17] See Radio Free Europe Research Papers, *Sino-Albanian Economic Relations*, 15 November 1968; *Forging Tighter Sino-Albanian Political, Economic and Military Ties*, Pts. 1 and 2, 4 and 6 December 1968; and also *The Economist*, 1 February 1969.

[18] See *The Observer*, London, 8 December 1968; *The Guardian*, London, 9 December 1968; *Le Monde*, Paris, 10 December 1968; *The Observer*, 2 February 1969; and *The Daily Telegraph*, London, 21 August 1969.

[19] Ideologically, the year also witnessed a celebration of the 90th anniversary of Stalin, with a major exhibition devoted to him in Tirana, Radio Tirana report 12 December 1969.

[20] See Radio Free Europe Research Paper, *Albania Institutes Radically New Measures*, 2 March 1966; *The Times*, London, 27 October 1966; 19 January 1967; 8 March 1967; and 14 March 1967. Also P. R. Prifti, *Albania's Cultural Revolution*, Center for International Studies, MIT, C/68–9, September 1968.

[21] For Hoxha's report on the state of the nation on this occasion, see *Zeri i Popullit*, 29 November 1969. See also A. Fontaine, 'Vingt-Cinq Ans de Socialisme en Albanie', *Le Monde*, 29 and 31 November 1969.

earthquake, the principal policy themes and campaigns have taken something of a second place, and, for the most part, have been continuations of policies already under way, including the economic tasks of the 4th Five Year Plan (1966–70).

Agriculture, largely as a result of its backwardness in this predominantly agrarian society [22] retains a prominent position in the scale of priorities, with much attention devoted to land reclamation in an effort to increase the area under cultivation. [23] Indeed, the annual production growth rate appears to have slumped to a disastrous 2·1 per cent in 1968, [24] while in 1969 a 10 per cent growth was recorded instead of the planned 22·1. [25] A 17 per cent growth is envisaged for 1970 [26] but may well not be attained. Meanwhile, the collective farms continue to be amalgamated [27] and the private plots reduced. [28]

Not surprisingly, the annual growth of industrial production (an average of 14 per cent for the three years 1966–8, and a planned 12·4 per cent for 1969) [29] is the highest in Eastern Europe – indicative merely of the currently low level of industrial development rather than of any exceptional performance. However, with a 1969 actual attainment of only 11 per cent, the 1970 planned target dropped to a more realistic 7·5 per cent. [30] Rather more surprising, although in line with a general regime tendency towards control of all productive forces, has been the abolition of the 28,000 member artisan co-operatives and their re-establishment as state enterprises [31] – a feature found nowhere else in Eastern Europe.

Electrification is another important issue, projected in the form of a major campaign, with attendant publicity. Coverage

[22] The population in 1965 was 66·8 per cent rural as against 33·2 per cent urban (*Vjetari Statistikor i Republikës Popullore të Shqipërisë*, Tirana, 1966), although industry accounts for approximately 50 per cent of the national product (*The Financial Times*, 12 December 1969).

[23] Some 19,700 hectares were to be reclaimed in the spring of 1970 – see *Bashkimi*, 7 January 1970.

[24] See Radio Free Europe Research Paper, *Albania's 1968 Plan Fulfilment and the 1969 Plan*, 28 January 1969.

[25] See the report of the Chairman of the State Planning Commission, Abdyl Kellezi, to the Peoples' Assembly, *Zeri i Popullit*, 17 February 1970.

[26] Ibid.

[27] See *Bujqesia Socialiste*, November 1969.

[28] See *Rruga e Partise*, January 1970.

[29] For discussions of the economic plan and the plan itself, see *Zeri i Popullit*, 14 and 15 January 1969.

[30] Report by Abdyl Kellezi, loc. cit.

[31] *Gazeta Zyrtare*, 24 March 1969.

of the entire country being planned for 1971, much emphasis in the campaign is placed upon completion and construction, respectively, of the Mao Tse-tung and Fierza hydro-electric power stations in the Drini valley.

Yet in spite of the strides being made by this well endowed country, particularly in industry, a striking feature, in comparison with surrounding Yugoslavia, is the continuing austerity and inefficiency. Cars are scarcely to be seen (in a country with indigenous oil supplies), and roads are generally in a poor condition; new blocks of flats are speedily and badly constructed; no single person may live alone; pitiful displays are to be seen in the shops; and ox and water-buffalo power is widespread in the countryside. Even sea fishing seems to be almost totally absent, though a fear of mass escapes may lie behind this. Nevertheless the solution of the basic problems of food and clothing at a uniform level for all appears to have been largely attained, though the poverty is considerably more noticeable in the rural areas.

In this general economic context, the questions of economic reform, which had become apparent in 1965, and decentralisation have continued to loom large on the political horizon, with the problem of avoiding the 'revisionist' traps of the other East European states undergoing a similar process. Various proposals are currently being aired in the press on the reform of the planning method [32] and ways of achieving better co-ordination of production and distribution of goods, [33] as well as measures to curb excessive centralism in line with the decisions of the Tenth Central Committee Plenum in June 1970.

Following Hoxha's report to the Politburo 'On the further revolutionisation of the school', [34] and a subsequent national conference on education, [35] much attention, and controlled public debate, has been devoted to educational policy [36] – a drive which had previously provided one of the keynotes of the cultural revolution. The conference called for a re-orientation to eradicate remaining undesirable features and a closer link

[32] E.g. *Ekonomia Popullore*, Vol. 2, March–April 1969; *Rruga e Partise*, August 1969 and October 1969.
[33] E.g. *Zeri i Popullit*, 31 May 1969.
[34] 7 March 1968.
[35] 11 April 1968.
[36] See J. Mako, 'To Further Revolutionize the School', *Albanian Life*, No. 1, January 1969, p. 34.

with extra-scholastic life, and measures to implement the reform were approved at the Eighth Plenum of the party in June
1969, for implementation last year.[37] The resultant educational
structure involves polytechnical instruction (with primary
emphasis on Marxist-Leninist ideology), production work and
military training, in which the formal academic work constitutes a little over a half – a move very much motivated by economic considerations quite apart from any ideological factor.

Another stiking feature, as well as a policy concern, is the
militarisation of the populace, and particularly the youth,
following the lines of the Chinese pattern. Every secondary
education pupil is now obliged to spend approximately one
month each year on military training.[38] Similarly, it was
announced, at the January 1969 session of the National Assembly, that the open defence budget for the year was to be
increased by 38 per cent, although it still remained quite small
at 419,680,000 leks (30 leks to the £) in a total budget of 4,750
million leks. The 1970 figure involved a further 12·2 per cent
increase over 1969, representing 9·2 per cent of the total budget
as opposed to the previous 9·1 per cent.[39]

It is hoped that these observations convey some of the essential character and reality of Albanian politics which are not
readily apparent from the formal, legalistic and constitutional
structure and developments as purveyed in the press.

The governmental system itself, established by the constitution of March 1946 and amended on 4 November 1950,
follows a strictly Stalinist pattern establishing a People's Assembly (elected for a four-year period by all citizens over 18 –
at present on the basis of one deputy to every 8,000 inhabitants,
a total of 240 in 1966), which, besides its five standing committees, is theoretically empowered to appoint a presidium and
council of ministers, while sitting itself usually only twice
yearly. At the local level, people's councils are elected for 3
years at the level of village, district, town and county,[40] and in
turn appoint executive committees (to supervise day-to-day
work), a presidium and a secretary (the servicing apparatus).

[37] See the report by Shehu in *Zeri i Popullit*, 29 June 1969.
[38] Radio Tirana report 12 March 1969. See also *Zeri i Popullit*, 5 March 1969.
[39] See the report by Abdyl Kellezi, loc. cit.
[40] On Albanian local government see J. A. Sabine, 'Local Government in
Tirana', *Albanian Notes*, No. 9, December 1967, pp. 5–7, and No. 10, July 1968,
pp. 42–9 – an article reproduced from the *Municipal Review*.

This formal structure itself probably plays even less of a role in Albania in the real process of policy formulation and basic decision-making than in most of the other European communist states, confining itself almost exclusively to elite supporting and justifying activity, and a participatory function in confirming and ratifying the outputs of the political system rather than significantly contributing to the inputs. In fulfilling its participatory or mobilising role with respect to the electorate,[41] the formal system appears supremely efficient, for, if one is to accept the official statistics, only four persons, from an electorate of 978,000, failed to register a vote in the 1966 national election to the People's Assembly. Statistics on the post-war elections at this level are as follows:

TABLE I

Election results for the Albanian National Assembly – 1945–66[42]

Election	Registered electors	Voters	Voters as % of electorate	Votes for candidates	% of votes for candidates
2.12.1945	603,566	542,400	89·81	505,304	93·16
28.5.1950	641,241	637,578	99·43	626,005	98·28
30.5.1954	702,476	701,942	99·92	700,983	99·86
1.6.1958	788,250	788,123	99·98	787,812	99·96
3.6.1962	889,875	889,868	99·99	889,828	99·99
10.7.1966	978,161	978,157	99·99	978,114	99·99

The constitutional provisions, however, give no guidance to and make virtually no mention of the motivating core of the system, the party and its leading organs. On these it remarks only, in a more or less direct plagiarism of the Soviet original, that, 'the more active and conscientious citizens of the working class and of the other working masses join the ranks of the Albanian Party of Labour, the vanguard organization of the working class and of all the working masses in their endeavours to build the bases of socialism and the leading nucleus of all the

[41] For a brief and rather predictable examination of voting practice, see T. Murray, 'Albanian Election Procedure', *Albanian Notes*, No. 6, December 1966, p. 7.

[42] Source: *Vjetari Statistikor i Republikës Popullore të Shqipërisë*, Tirana 1966. The 1970 elections took place on 20 September, providing few surprises.

organizations of the working masses, both social as well as of the State' (Article 21).

In fact, structurally, the party closely resembles its Soviet model, its current Congress even being similarly overdue. At its centre lies the 11 man Politburo dominated by Hoxha and his chief lieutenants Mehmet Shehu (who simultaneously heads the government as chairman of the council of ministers), Beqir Balluku (the Minister of Defence), Spiro Kolleka (chairman of the State Planning Commission) and Hsyni Kapo (a secretary of the Central Committee). The Politburo also has a second string of 5 candidate members.

A noticeable feature has been the very considerable degree of overlapping membership which has always existed between the Politburo and the uppermost state organs. For instance, in April 1969, the picture was as follows:

	Party Politburo	Secretariat	Council of Ministers	Presidium of the National Assembly
Members: Enver Hoxha	——→	——————————————————→		
Mehmet Shehu	——————————→			
Beqir Balluku	——————————→			
Haki Toska	——————————→			
Adil Çarçani	——————————→			
Hsyni Kapo	——————→			
Ramiz Aliya	——————→			
Spiro Koleka	————————————→			
Manush Myfti				
Gogo Nushi [43]	————————————————————————→			
Rita Marko	————————————————————————→			
Candidates Kadri Hazbiu	——————————→			
Koco Theodhosi				
Petrit Dume				
Abdyl Kellezi				
Pilo Peristeri	————————————————————————→			

This situation clearly facilitates overall control of the apparatus of government, remaining untouched by the 'cultural revolution' at lower levels.

The party as a whole retains a firmly elitist character embracing some 3·5 per cent of the population at present. The growth pattern of its membership is shown in Table 2.

[43] Nushi died in April 1970.

TABLE 2

Membership of the Albanian Party of Labour

1961 February		53,659[44]
1966 November		66,327[45]
1969 March	'approximately'	50,000[46]

The drastic drop in membership, if definite, appears to have been the result of the 'cultural-ideological revolution' of 1966–8, involving a cleansing of the party ranks.[47] This tendency, however, may well now be under reverse if one is to judge from an article by a member of the Party Control Commission, which, in effect, calls for a restriction of the widespread expulsions from the party and indicates that earlier cases of dismissal may be reviewed[48] – a move which probably received its initial impetus from a Central Committee instruction of May 1968, calling for an improvement in the field of party 'administrative measures'.[49]

The social composition of the 1966 membership figure provided the interesting picture of Table 3.

It is thus a party of labour with a shortage of proletarian labourers, and in which a large proportion of members are officials drawn from the party – state structure. The continued preponderance of this official stratum, by status if not origin, was ruefully remarked upon by Hoxha, in his 1966 report, as being 'in spite of the limitations that have been put for their

[44] E. Hoxha, *Report on the Activity of the Central Committee*, op. cit., p. 100.
[45] Ibid.
[46] *Rruga e Partise*, March 1969, p. 65; cf. figure of around 70,000, given to a *Guardian* correspondent, briefly visiting Albania, *The Guardian*, 17 June 1969. Confirmation of the latter has now been given by Hysni Kapo at the 10th CC Plenum, in reporting the January 1970 total as 75,673 (*Zeri i Popullit*, 28 June 1970).
[47] Hinted at in the March 1966 open letter from the Central Committee, which launched the cultural revolution (see *Zeri i Popullit*, 4 March 1966) and by Hoxha's claim, in his report to the 5th Party Congress (op. cit., p. 96, and in *Zeri i Popullit*, 2 November 1966), that there had taken place a reorganisation of the party and state machine in which 'nearly 15,000 cadres passed from office work to production' – although the timing of this latter is unclear. See also Radio Free Europe Research Papers, *Signs of an Impending Shake-up in Albania*, 14 July 1966, and *Signs of a Shake-up in Albanian Party Basic Organisations*, 27 July 1966.
[48] I. Sina in *Rruga e Partise*, June 1969.
[49] Ibid.

admission to the Party'.[50] Statistics in subsequent years may thus be expected to reveal a continued proletarianisation of the party, and a growth in the number of workers and peasants admitted.

TABLE 3

Social composition of the Albanian Party of Labour in 1966 as compared with 1961 [51]

Status	1966	cf. 1961
Workers:	32·9%	+3·24%
Members of agricalatural co-operatives:	25·81%	+2·19%
Individual peasants:	3·14%	−0·01%
State administrative employees, functionaries of the party and mass organisations and the military:	37·14%	−4·80%
Various (students and housewives)	0·98%	−0·64%
Of whom women comprised:	12·47%	+2·30%

The lack of women, also pointed to by Hoxha, is not unduly surprising in this formerly Moslem state. Purdah has departed, but old attitudes die hard.

In terms of coverage of the country, it was revealed that the party had a total of 2,852 primary organisations of which 1,586 were in towns.[52]

The membership itself is, moreover, predominantly urban (67·9 per cent as opposed to 32·1 per cent rural) in a largely rural population. In this respect, Hoxha called for a more rational policy on admissions, taking into account the needs of various areas, and avoiding favouritism or the selection of as many unsuitable candidates as had previously occurred.

A cadre reshuffle has in fact since been under way, probably aimed at a rejuvenation of the membership and local leaderships.[53]

[50] E. Hoxha, *Report*, op. cit., p. 101. In fact Kapo's June 1970 report (loc. cit.) showed the worker and white-collar proportions to have drawn almost level, at 35·22 and 35·81 per cent respectively, as of 1 January 1970.

[51] E. Hoxha, *Report*, op. cit., p. 101.   [52] Ibid., p. 113.

[53] See Radio Free Europe Research Papers, *Rejuvenation of the Party through Organisational Change*, 10 June 1968, and *Revolutionising of Party Life means Shake-up*, 23 October 1968, and *Seeking New Blood, East Europe*, Vol. 18, No. 1, January 1969, p. 37. This process was to be further stressed by Hoxha in his speech to the Tirana party organisation in December 1968 – *Zeri i Popullit*, 22 December 1968.

The question of conflict and opposition in Albanian politics is one more shrouded in secrecy than most, and available information is often incomplete or difficult to interpret. Although, thanks to the intervention of Kim Philby, the invasion forces of Albanian exiles (assembled by the British Intelligence Service and transported into Albania) had little opportunity of testing the degree of opposition to the regime within its early days,[54] a number of other oppositions had become and continued to become apparent at various times, contending both with the regime itself and with specific policies.

The first signs of the opposition at large appeared in revolts in the Kelmendi region in 1945, the Postripa region, and the attack on Shkodra in September 1946, part of a sporadic rebel guerilla resistance to the regime (partly aided from without and only finally eliminated in 1952). This involved wartime collaborators, monarchists, catholics, peasants opposed to collectivisation as well as social democrats. The British backed opposition movement got under way in 1946[55] and had soon resulted in trials, notably that which started on 29 June before the Tirana Supreme Military Court and brought about death sentences for nine of the thirty-seven accused, terms ranging from 30 years to life for others and two acquittals.[56] The charges, backed by confessions, which now appear to have had some considerable basis in fact, involved treason on behalf of nationalist leaders such as Fiqri Dine and Muharrem Bairakhtar, the preparation of a coup with foreign help, and plotting to assassinate political leaders, including Hoxha – the foreign help being members of the British military mission in Tirana, and principally Lieut. Col. Palmer and Maj. Arnold.[57] Similar trials took place in July[58] and September 1947,[59] again producing death sentences and charges concerning armed uprisings which were receiving support from Britain and the United States; while in January 1948, a further seven members of so-called 'secret' associations, including four former deputies

[54] See B. Page, D. Leitch and P. Knightley, *Philby – The Spy Who Betrayed a Generation*, London, 1968, pp. 193–8; H. A. R. Philby, *My Silent War*, London, 1968, pp. 117–99; and E. H. Cookridge, *The Third Man*, Barker, London, 1968, pp. 156–9.

[55] B. Page, ibid., p. 193.

[56] *The Times*, 9 July 1946.

[57] See H. Seton-Watson, *The East European Revolution*, London, 1956, p. 226.

[58] *The Times*, 14 and 29 July 1947.

[59] See H. Seton-Watson, op. cit., p. 227.

in the legislature, were sentenced to death on charges of seeking to restore the regime of ex-King Zog, with the same outside assistance.[60]

Alongside this outright military opposition, a post-war series of political purges had already been set in progress, resulting in the arrest, in May 1947, of supposedly government supporters from among the National Assembly deputies, and including the director of the State Bank and long-time party member Boshnjaku. Seyfulla Mallesheva was also removed from the Ministry of Education, and probably deported to the Soviet Union.[61] A climax to these purges was, however, reached in 1948, when, following the Russo-Yugoslav split and a pattern repeated in other East European states,[62] Koci Xoxe, Minister of the Interior, Deputy Premier and secretary of the department for party cadres, was, in the wake of two plenary sessions of the Central Committee, transferred to the Ministry of Industry. He was subsequently criticised, along with Pandi Christo (former head of the Party Control Commission), by Hoxha and trade union leader and Party Second Secretary Tuk Jakova, at the first Party Congress in November.[63] Arrested shortly after, along with Christo and supporters mainly from the Ministry of the Interior,[64] Xoxe was tried in May 1949,[65] and executed by firing squad on 11 June 1949.[66] Christo was sentenced to 20 years imprisonment.

Xoxe had in fact supported the Yugoslav line in opposition to the then Moscow oriented position of Party Secretary General Hoxha, and may also have engaged in a power struggle against the latter from his base in the organs of state security and party appointments. He was said, moreover, to have been supported by the political department of the armed forces, although not the general staff, and at the trial, confessed to forming an opposition group within the party, and of directly collaborating with the Yugoslavs. This so-called Trotskyist group, according to the charges against him, had hoped to

[60] *The Times*, 27 January 1948.
[61] H. Seton-Watson, op. cit., p. 227.
[62] For a brief general, but readily comparable, survey of the trials in Albania and East Europe see 'Les épurations dans les démocraties populaires', *Le Monde*, 20–1 July 1969.
[63] *The Times*, 10 December 1948.
[64] *The Times*, 11 December 1948. See also *Le Monde*, 20–1 July 1969.
[65] *Radio Tirana*, 10 June 1949.   [66] Ibid., 13 June 1949.

'create in the Balkans, with the aid of Tito and his band, a Great-Serb empire of an imperialist type, susceptible to becoming an aggressive base against the Soviet Union'. Any attempt to rehabilitate him, in the more liberal climate of the Russo-Yugoslav detente in 1956, was, however, refused.[67]

Shortly thereafter, a renewed challenge emerged from without with the now celebrated landings of an Albanian opposition in exile, the British-American backed Committee of Free Albanians.[68] Following Hoxha's announcement, at a rally of party workers on 29 April 1950, that rebel invaders had been engaged and killed, captured or driven out, death sentences were passed in June on agents apparently parachuted in from Italy,[69] and a larger infiltration by parachute and submarine was reported by the Ministry of the Interior in January 1951,[70] of which 29 were killed. Some further 14 infiltrators, apparently trained in West Germany, were brought to trial in Tirana in October 1951,[71] charged with an attempt to overthrow the government by force – resulting in the execution of 2, and various prison terms for the remainder. That same month, two other groups of 20 agents, parachuted in, were all declared to have been killed, save one, upon resisting arrest, while 33 others were apparently 'rendered harmless' by death in battle or capture.[72] A further trial of 7 infiltrators, supporting the cause of ex-King Zog, and, in large measure, drawn from his retinue, took place at Easter, in 1952, among the accused being Captain Zenel Shehu and Captain Nalil Sufa. All were exectuted,[73] and with this the visible opposition from the supporters of the *ancien régime* largely came to an end, along with the widespread use or planned use of force to dislodge the regime altogether.[74]

A bomb explosion at the Soviet legation office in Tirana in February 1957, had also led to the arrest of a considerable

---

[67] *The Times*, 19 May 1956. See also A. Logoreci, op. cit., p. 23.

[68] Founded 1949 – see *The Times*, 27 August 1949. See also statement by its president, ibid., 10 September 1949.

[69] *The Times*, 7 June 1950.

[70] *The Times*, 2 January 1951. A death sentence and various prison terms were also passed on a group of agents on 29 November 1950 but it is not clear whether these were involved in the same movement – see *The Times*, 1 January 1951.

[71] *The Times*, 17 October 1951.

[72] Ibid., 29 October 1951.

[73] B. Page *et al.*, op. cit., p. 197.

[74] Some trials of spies and saboteurs nevertheless continued to occur – see *The Times*, 27 February 1953 and 23 June 1953.

group of people, including Sabiha Kasimati, a professor of biology, and Manush Peshkepia, a writer. Members of this group were subsequently executed.[75]

At this time too, a widespread purge was taking place within the party itself, the removal of 5 out of 21 Central Committee members (elected at the first Party Congress in 1948) being revealed at the second Congress in 1952. In this report at the same Congress, Hoxha declared that 12,000 party members, a quarter of the total membership, had been removed in the period November 1948–December 1951.

Reports of purges of opponents or declared opponents continued in 1953[76] and the remaining elements in the leadership group, particularly Central Committee members Tuk Jakova (the former accusor of Xoxe) and Bedri Spahiu, were purged and expelled from the party in 1955. This left the way more clear for facing up to subsequent pressures on Hoxha, which appear to have emerged the following year, with the healing of the Russo-Yugoslav split, Khrushchev's denunciation of Stalinist methods, and the Soviet invasion of Hungary.

In early 1956 there was reported one of the most interesting cases of opposition to the leadership group, not by a faction but by the National Assembly itself.[77] While no mention of this unique matter appeared in the Albanian or other Soviet bloc countries, a Yugoslav correspondent for a Skopje newspaper, who had been in Albania at the time, reported that a government bill on the social services had been voted down in spite of the attempts of Prime Minister Shehu to force its acceptance. At the first count, a mere six had voted in favour, whereupon an indignant Shehu took the floor, challenged the counting, called for a second vote in public and failed again by a similar margin. Shehu was then reported to have angrily reminded the house of the necessity of the bill, expressed surprise at the action of the deputies and demanded a further vote, at which point the chairman (in a seemingly unlikely gesture) informed Shehu that, as just another deputy, he possessed no such rights. While it is impossible to determine the veracity of this account, and particularly the details, it is possible that the broad outlines had at least a basis in fact – the more so in such a tempestuous year.

[75] A. Gegai and R. Krasniqi, *Albania*, *ACEN*, New York, 1964, p. 29.
[76] *The Times*, 20 October 1953.   [77] Ibid., 19 May 1956.

The Third Party Congress may also have witnessed opposition to Hoxha (of which more will be said below), and the Albanian legation in Rome was constrained to issue denials of rumours of anti-Soviet demonstrations in Albanian factories.[78] The year 1956, moreover, drew to a close with the execution, in Tirana on 23 November, of three former associates of Xoxe – Andreu Dali (a former Politburo member and wartime partisan commander), his wife Liri Gega (also a former Politburo member), and Petar Bulatovich (a Yugoslav citizen and former leader of a wartime Albanian partisan brigade). The charge against them was of espionage for an unnamed country,[79] but it is likely that they were critics of Hoxha's rule.

Opposition to the pro-Soviet policies of Hoxha was in fact revealed high in the apparatus of government, and specifically in the Ministry of Defence, by the defection to Yugoslavia, in May 1957, of the deputy Minister of Defence, General Panajot Pljaku.[80] His defection resulted in the arrest not only of his family but also of a supporter in the ministry, deputy Chief of Staff, Miyslin Peza,[81] who was, furthermore, charged with aiding Pljaku's act of voting with his feet. Pljaku had already been purged in the 1948 crisis, only returning to the political scene in 1955, whereupon he had openly made accusations against the dominance of Russian specialists, his departure following almost immediately after a dispute with a senior Soviet official.[82] He was later to be implicated, by assertion, in the 1961 Sejku trial.

A further, and, to this date, the last major shake-up of the political leadership, took place in September 1960, when two leading figures in the party were purged.[83] Mrs Liri Belishova, a member of the Politburo was expelled from the Central Committee, being charged, at a joint meeting of the Politburo and

[78] Ibid., 27 October 1956.

[79] *Keesing's Contemporary Archives*, Bristol, 16396, 1956. Hoxha in fact later referred to them as Titoist agents caught trying to flee to Yugoslavia, in his speech to the Moscow Communist Conference in 1960 (first published in full in Vëllimi i 3-të, PPSh–Dokumente Kryesore (*Principal Documents of the Albanian Workers' Party*, Vol. 3), Institute of Marxist-Leninist Studies, Tirana, 1970.

[80] *The Times*, 21 May 1957.

[81] Ibid., 4 June 1957.

[82] Ibid. He was, however, accused by Hoxha, in the latter's 1960 Moscow Conference speech (loc. cit.), of having also sought Khrushchev's support in 'liquidating' the 'anti-Marxist and Stalinist' Albanian leadership, and of having been offered asylum in the Soviet Union.

[83] *The Times*, 10 September 1960.

the committee, with having committed 'grave mistakes against the party line'; while Koco Tasko, the chairman of the party's Revision Commission, was expelled from both the Central Committee and the party, standing condemned for 'hostile activity'.[84] Moqo Chomo, Minister of Agriculture and Belishova's husband, was also subsequently removed from his post, and was not re-elected to the central committee at the February 1961 Congress. Belishova, it seems clear, had opposed the anti-Khrushchev line then emerging before the split with the Soviet Union in Moscow on 16 November 1960, said of her that she had 'capitulated to the dishonest threats of the Soviet Union'.

With her departure, the Politburo regained a good measure of stability, although a verbal attack by Hoxha on Yugoslavia, at the 4th Congress in 1961, evoked an illuminating response from the Yugoslav paper *Borba*. In this (after perceptively declaring that Hoxha resorted to terror and the raising of an external enemy whenever internal difficulties became acute and he was threatened by opposition to his policies), it was pointed out that of the 14 Central Committee members elected at the foundation of the party in 1941, Hoxha was the only one still alive; that 14 of the 31 Central Committee members elected in 1944 had been liquidated and only 9 remained in office; and that of the original 109 members of the National Assembly, 17 had been shot, 15 imprisoned, 2 had committed suicide and only 29 were still politically active.[85]

Indications of a new purge of opponents at lower levels of the party began to emerge very shortly after,[86] followed by more substantial reports of the disappearance of a number of politicians and military officers.[87] What emerged eventually was an apparently more widespread opposition to the split with Russia than had at first been indicated by the Belishova case, commencing with the arrest on 1 March and execution on 3 May 1961, after a secret trial, of two officials of the Ministry of Foreign Affairs, Jakov and Mehani. The two were accused of espionage – specifically, of supplying to an attaché of the Soviet embassy in Tirana, confidential information on the recent party Congress.[88]

[84] *Keesing's Contemporary Archives*, 18042A.
[85] *Keesing's Contemporary Archives*, 18042A.
[86] *The Times*, 21 February 1961.
[87] Ibid., 22 March 1961.
[88] Ibid., 19 May 1961 and *Keesing's Contemporary Archives*, 18302A.

The indications, in the early reports of this case, that a number of army and navy officers were somehow implicated in the opposition, were borne out shortly after when the trial opened in the capital on 15 May 1961, of Rear-Admiral and former C-in-C of the Albanian Navy, Teme Sejku; former chairman of the Elbasan district party committee and Albanian representative at Comecon, Tahir Demi; ex-officer, Hajri Mane; an official Avdul Resuli; Jonuz Puriz and five others.[89] Sejku, who had been trained in the Soviet Union and, like Demi, thus had close ties with that country, was charged with having worked to overthrow the regime in Albania since 1951, with having set up a spy network in the main towns and cities, and, after unsuccessfully attempting to remove Hoxha at the 1956 Congress, with plotting an armed insurrection for August and September 1960, in which aid was to be forthcoming from Albanian exiles, Yugoslav and Greek troops, as well as, inevitably, the US 6th Fleet. General Pljaku, the 1957 defector,[90] was referred to, in Puriz's confession, as one of the conspirators in meetings which had taken place on Greek territory.

Although many of the charges were of a rather routine show-trial nature, it seems clear that the accused were in some way opposed to the Stalinist rule of Hoxha, following Khrushchev's denunciation of those methods in 1956 (and thus may have involved a measure of revenge seeking by Hoxha for opposition which had taken place then), and/or opposed to the split with Russia in the international communist movement. In any event, Sejku, Demi, Mane and Resuli were sentenced to death on 28 May and shot three days later. The others received prison terms from 15 to 25 years.

The defection to Czechoslovakia of the commercial counsellor at the Albanian embassy in Prague[91] did nothing to hide the significance of the elements opposing the split with the Soviet camp.

With the elimination of the Sejku group, the major trials of internal opponents came to an end for the present, and although a group of 'American and Yugoslav spies', who had infiltrated by parachute, were condemned in June 1963, the evidence of subsequent opposition is slim and has not yet resulted

---

[89] *The Times*, 6 October 1961 and *Keesing's Contemporary Archives*, 18302A.
[90] He died in Belgrade on 13 July 1966, aged 47.
[91] *Le Monde*, 9 June 1961.

in major trials. The cadre reshuffles involved in the 'cultural revolution' may have been used by Hoxha to remove conservative, ex-partisan, elements,[92] doubtless including those who had retained old (and presumably pro-Soviet) attitudes and failed to keep abreast of ideological demands.[93]

Organised religion, as an opposition, or potential opposition force, received a further blow, after repeated physical assaults against the leaders in the past,[94] with the reported disappearance of the Archbishop of Durres and the detention of some 20 priests,[95] probably to join others similarly said to be engaged in forced labour.

The expulsion of 30 students from Tirana University for 'pursuit of a revisionist line outside the confines of Marxism-Leninism', was reported in the Italian communist press in July 1969,[96] which also claimed a degree of more general unrest among the emerging intelligentsia, motivated by a desire for a more humanist approach in the fields of culture and politics, and a new role for both technologists and the intellectuals.

That the educational reform had provoked 'fiery debates' and the criticism of those with 'different viewpoints' was admitted by Shehu[97] – criticism probably from among the educators, if the similar case of Khrushchev's 1958 educational reforms in the Soviet Union is any guide.[98]

The existence of opposition today is, however, largely an unknown quantity. While Albania had an estimated 4,000 political prisoners in 1965[99] the security police, the Segurimi, of the Ministry of the Interior (presided over since the mid-1950s

[92] As was indicated by the attack on conservatives in his speech on 6 February 1967.

[93] See article by I. Sina, *Rruga e Partise*, June 1969.

[94] See *The Times*, 21 February 1948; 15 May 1948; 31 July 1950; and 16 October 1950.

[95] *Avvenire*, Rome, 25 February 1969, which claimed that the Pope had received, in May 1968, a document from 8 Albanian Catholics giving details of the persecution of Catholics.

[96] *L'Unitá*, 21 July 1969.

[97] *Zeri i Popullit*, 29 June 1969.

[98] See R. Schlesinger, 'The Educational Reform', *Soviet Studies*, Vol. X, April 1959; and J. J. Schwartz and W. R. Keech, 'Group Influence on the Policy Process in the Soviet Union', *American Political Science Review*, Vol. LXII, September 1968, pp. 840–51.

[99] Council of Europe report, *The Times*, 28 January 1965. This figure does not include wartime collaborators, many of whom were amnestied in January 1956 – see J. Sabine, 'Some Notes on Albanian Law and Legal Administration', *Albanian Notes*, No. 7, March 1967, pp. 1–7, particularly pp. 6–7.

by the minister, Kadri Hazbiu),[100] have an apparently wide brief, backed by an effectively harsh penal code (in spite of appearances to the contrary).[101] and have shown themselves eminently capable of fulfilling their task.[102]

Detailed study of the Albanian case nevertheless reveals a rather surprising amount of oppositional activity, but activity carried out in a state marked by a very firmly contained diversity of views. The opposition has essentially polarised into that against the regime and that against specific policies, being generated to a large extent in the latter case by each turnabout or major shift in policy line by Hoxha and his immovable close associates. Most important among these shifts have been those associated with the breaks with Yugoslavia in 1948 and with the Soviet Union in 1961. While violence by opponents of the regime largely disappeared in the early 1950s, violence by the Albanian regime to its opponents of both varieties has not noticeably slackened.

The picture which emerges from these internecine conflicts and manifestations of opposition is thus not one of monolithic unity within the Albanian body politic. Opposition has clearly gone beyond the albeit limited bounds of pre-decision making debate permissible in accordance with the Leninist principles of democratic-centralism. It has, in fact, entered the more serious and hazardous stage of challenging established policy, thereby drawing attention to a problem area the Albanian system shares with other communist systems – that of permitting discussion and/or criticism of a policy after implementation and of initiating change, particularly if the policy is proving less successful than anticipated.

How then is the Albanian regime to be interpreted? Perhaps it may be viewed as a totalitarian system in the Friedrich and Brzezinski tradition. But the degree of control is far from total in so far as it has failed to stem opposition for once and for all And yet it is probably as near as any regime can come to this ideal type. It remains in all essentials Stalinist (the intrusion of

[100] Hazbiu has recently been in Peking, where he met the former head of the Chinese security police (Kang Sheng) on 16 June 1970.
[101] See e.g. for an official view of the penal code, I. Elezi, 'The Penal Law of the Peoples' Republic of Albania', *Albanian Notes*, No. 10, July 1968, pp. 49–54. Cf. Sabine, ibid., No. 7, March 1967, p. 607.
[102] An electrified fence on the border effectively limits the possibilities of departure for dissenters.

Maoism appearing rather limited), and is, moreover, a system marked by a very personalised pattern of power centering still on the person of Hoxha and a few key colleagues entrenched since the establishment of the regime. Cultural revolutions may come and go, particularly at the lower levels of the administration, but these leaders, it seems, will remain unto death or honourable retirement. Looming large in the not so distant future is the problem of succession as the ex-partisans almost simultaneously begin to reach the end of their political lives.

How much the overtures to Belgrade and the extension of the as yet largely one-way contacts with Kosovo, along with the furtherance of other selected diplomatic and trade contacts [103] will bring about change, remains to be seen (and the recent stipulation that West German tourists will be tolerated on condition that they carry out four hours of farm labouring a day [104] does little to enhance the prospects). Albania, meanwhile rests secure and politically stable, for the moment, in her self-imposed isolation from the mainstreams and turbulence of European political affairs.

[103] Besides the now celebrated trade agreement with the Greek colonels, ambassadorial-level relations have recently been established with Switzerland – see *The Daily Telegraph*, 21 July 1970.
[104] *The Times Educational Supplement*, London, 17 July 1970.

David E. Powell

Controlling Dissent in the Soviet Union*

Case study

> After the Uprising on June 17th
> The Secretary of the Writers' Union
> Had leaflets distributed in the Stalinallee
> Which said that the people
> Had lost the confidence of the government
> And could win it back only
> By redoubled labour. Wouldn't it
> Be simpler in that case if the government
> Dissolved the people and
> Elected another?
>
> > (Bertold Brecht, writing about the 1953 Berlin
> > uprising against the East German regime)

POLITICS INEVITABLY PRODUCES DISSENT. WHERE men must choose among various public policies, some will inevitably differ and dissent from official decisions. What distinguishes one political system from another is the extent to which majorities tolerate, protect, or even encourage minorities to express their views.[1]

Soviet leaders have never been receptive to non-conformists

[1] This paper will follow Leonard Schapiro's distinction between 'dissent' and 'opposition'. The former involves an effort 'merely to criticize, to exhort, to persuade, and to be listened to', while the latter refers to 'an organized political group, or groups, of which the aim is to oust the government in power and to replace it by one of its own choosing'. Leonard Schapiro, ' "Putting the Lid on Leninism"; Opposition and Dissent in the Communist One-Party State' (pp. 33–58 above). See also Frederick C. Barghoorn, 'Soviet Political Doctrine and the Problem of Opposition', *Bucknell Review*, Vol. XII, No. 2, May 1964, pp. 1–29.

* Vol. 7, No. 1, Winter 1972.

or dissenters. However, political dissent in the USSR has become an increasingly urgent concern for the Soviet leadership. The expectations generated during the relatively permissive period of Khrushchev's rule have been frustrated by the more restrictive policies of Brezhnev and Kosygin. This has brought about a volatile situation. In the past few years, outspoken members of the intelligentsia, religious organisations, representatives of national minorities, and opponents of various Soviet foreign and domestic policies have expressed open, vigorous and frequent dissent. The authorities appear to have had little difficulty thus far in coping with manifestations of dissent; they have punished the dissenters and threatened their families and friends. Nonetheless, for the first time in many years, the elaborate network of constitutional, legal and ideological restraints is being subjected to far-reaching pressures. Indeed, the harshness with which the party is dealing with dissenters may, instead of solving the problem, only serve to alienate other sectors of the Soviet population.

The imprisonment of Andrei Sinyavsky and Yuli Daniel in the spring of 1966 – the two writers were found guilty of 'anti-Soviet agitation and propaganda' after having smuggled abroad satirical works – has been followed by the sentencing of many lesser figures. Their names are not important; few people either in the West or the USSR are likely to recognise the names of Pyotr Grigorenko, Alexander Ginzburg, Pavel Litvinov, Larisa Bogoraz-Daniel, Vyacheslav Chornovil, or Yuri Galanskov. What they have done, however, is extraordinary. They have publicly manifested their disagreement with policies of the party and government, rendering themselves vulnerable to almost certain arrest. Some were seized for having protested against Soviet policy towards the Dubček reform movement, while others demonstrated against the invasion of Czechoslovakia in August 1968. Still others submitted petitions to leading Soviet officials, Western newsmen or the United Nations, decrying violations of the Soviet constitution, 'the repression of basic civil rights in the Soviet Union', 'a rebirth of Stalinist methods', and illegal arrests and trial procedures. [2] Most have been sent to labour camps, others have gone to prison, and a

[2] See, for example, the two special issues of *Problems of Communism*, Vol. XVII, No. 4, July–August 1968, pp. 31–114, and Vol. XVII, No. 5, September–October 1968, pp. 66–112. See also *Survey*, No. 69, October 1968, pp. 107–21.

few have been incarcerated in mental institutions.[3] While this policy of punishment and harassment is less harsh than Stalin's practices, it is still shocking by Western standards.

The Soviet government has, of course, always been intolerant of dissent. From the very beginning of Soviet rule, the party moved against those who did not support the aims of the revolution. Far from disguising their 'dictatorship of the proletariat', the bolsheviks openly suppressed dissenters. 'The arms and legs of the enemy must be shackled', an early Soviet legal theoretician declared, ' and its mouth must be muzzled with the revolutionary dictatorship.'[4] According to Mikhail Latsis, a prominent Cheka official:

We are no longer waging war against separate individuals; we are exterminating the bourgeoisie as a class. Do not seek in the dossier of the accused for proof as to whether or not he opposed the Soviet government by word or deed. The first question that should be put is to what class he belongs, of what extraction, what education and profession. These questions should decide the fate of the accused. Herein lies the meaning and the essence of the Red Terror.[5]

A 1917 decree authorised the closing down of opposition newspapers as an 'emergency measure'.[6] This decree has never been

[3] According to Bertram Wolfe, 'there are now two lunatic asylums, one on the outskirts of Moscow and another near Leningrad, given over to "political lunatics", and a third of increasingly political character'. The practice of incarcerating political dissidents was foreshadowed a decade ago when Nikita Khrushchev declared: 'We have no more political criminals in the USSR. The only ones who oppose our system today are madmen.' See Bertram Wolfe, *An Ideology in Power*, New York, 1969, pp. 393–4, footnote 23.

[4] F. Ksenofontov, 'Revolution, Dictatorship and Civil Freedom', in Michael Jaworskyj (ed.), *Soviet Political Thought*, Baltimore, 1967, p. 198. According to Nikolay Bukharin, 'In the hands of the working class, the state power is an axe that is being held ready against the bourgeoisie.' Quoted in A. Ya. Vyshinsky, 'Proletarian Justice', in Jaworskyj, op. cit., p. 201.

[5] Quoted in 'Information on Russia', Senate Document 50, 67th Congress, 1st session, Washington, D.C., 1921, p. 64. Cited in Merle Fainsod, *How Russia Is Ruled*, revised edition, Cambridge, Mass., 1963, p. 426. To this, Lenin added that courtroom trials 'must not supersede the terror. To promise that they would do so would be self-deception or deceit; it [the terror] should be put on a definite basis and legalized as a matter of principle, clearly, without hypocrisy or embellishments'. Quoted in N. V. Krylenko, 'Changes and Additions in the Codes of the RSFSR', in William Rappard *et al.*, *Source Book on European Governments*, Princeton, 1937, part 5, p. 173.

[6] The decree, promulgated on 10 November, authorised the closing down of newspapers which 'call for open opposition' to the government or 'sow sedition by a frankly slanderous perversion of facts'. It added that, 'As soon as the new order

revoked. The 1918 constitution specifically denied freedom of speech, association and assembly to those who did not support the new order.[7] Mensheviks, socialist revolutionaries, 'right-wing and left-wing renegades' were, it was said, demanding freedom only 'to harm Soviet rule, to sow confusion in a society that was actually in the position of a besieged fortess'.[8] As late as 1922, after the civil war had ended and bolshevik rule was relatively secure, Lenin demanded capital punishment for 'public advocacy of Menshevism'.[9]

These directives and practices have been supplemented over the past half-century by the development of a comprehensive censorship system,[10] an official style of artistic expression (social-ist realism), and a set of laws and administrative procedures designed to punish those who deviate from prescribed norms. Thus, in 1922, the Soviet government resuscitated the old tsarist censorship agency Glavlit (Main Administration for Literary Affairs and Publishing). Provision was made for both pre-publication and post-publication censorship, to guarantee that only those materials deemed acceptable would reach the public. Over the years, Glavlit has been authorised to forbid the printing and distribution of books, plays, films, broadcasts, lectures, ballets, musical works and even circus acts. Glavlit's powers are enormous. Works may be forbidden if they: (1) contain agitation and propaganda against Soviet authority and

---

will be consolidated, all adminstrative measures against the press will be sus-pended', 'Suppression of Hostile Newspapers', *Izvestiya*, 10 November 1917, in James H. Meisel and Edward S. Kozera (ed.), *Materials for the Study of the Soviet System*, Ann Arbor, Michigan, 1953, pp. 23–4.

[7] See Article 65, in *Sovetskiye konstitutsii*, Moscow, 1963, pp. 148–9.

[8] D. Kraminov, 'Krokodilovy slezy', *Pravda*, 3 March 1968, p. 4.

[9] V. I. Lenin, 'Politicheskiy otchet tsentral'nogo komiteta RKP (b)', 27 March 1922, in V. I. Lenin, *Sochineniya*, fourth edition, vol. 33, p. 253.

[10] Soviet officials are reluctant to acknowledge the existence of a censorship system. Thus, for example, in a 1957 interview with Turner Catledge of *The New York Times*, Nikita Khrushchev resorted to the following casuistry: 'I don't know about this censorship or check on the flow of news. We apply it only in case of libel . . . I believe some restrictions should be applied if people call for the dis-ruption of normal society. . . . We take measures only in the case of correspondents who distort conditions and the real life of our country. I would not call that censorship, but the rational use of the means at the disposal of society, in order not to waste means such as ink, paper and paint on information that only creates harm.' *The New York Times*, 11 May 1957, p. 3. According to *Izvestiya*, 3 September 1957, '. . . everyone is entitled to write what he likes and how he likes. But must everything that is written be published . . .?' Cited in Maurice Friedberg, 'Keeping Up with the Censor', *Problems of Communism*, Vol. XIII, No. 6, November–December 1964, p. 27.

the dictatorship of the proletariat; (2) reveal state secrets; (3) stir up ethnic and religious fanaticism; (4) have a pornographic character; or (5) are characterised by 'ideological weakness', 'mysticism', or have an 'anti-artistic character'.[11] They must all conform to the requirements of socialist realism.

The party, because it needs the intelligentsia's services, provides them with status and some measure of autonomy. But, as Barrington Moore has pointed out, such autonomy is distinctly limited; the regime is determined 'to prevent intellectual autonomy from endangering its overall political control, and to reserve for itself matters of ultimate political truth...'[12] Just how slight this autonomy is can be seen in a 1963 remark by Nikita Khrushchev.

We favour autonomy in art and professional associations, provided they help to develop art in the right direction. But if anyone expects to use those associations to combat the party line in art, he is sorely mistaken... We concede no association a leading role in society except the association known as the Communist Party... All other associations would inevitably clash with the party and the people should they try to direct their activities against the policy of the party. I am saying this by way of a warning. It is better to serve a timely warning than to wait until matters go too far for a warning to be effective. We had better agree on that.[13]

For those who violate the boundaries laid down by the party, a variety of sanctions is available. The most threatening of these, and those with which we are most concerned, are legal measures.

The use of police, courts and legal codes to control or punish dissent began long before 1966. George Bernard Shaw once

[11] Maurice Friedberg, 'Soviet Books, Censors and Readers', in Max Hayward and Leopold Labedz (eds.), *Literature and Revolution in Soviet Russia, 1917–1962*, London, 1963, p. 199. Censors are to review performances at least ten days before the official *première*. The management must reserve for the censors two seats at every performance, no farther from the stage than the fourth row. Ibid.

[12] Barrington Moore, Jr., *Terror and Progress, USSR*, Cambridge, Mass., 1954, p. 153.

[13] N. S. Khrushchev, 'Marxism–Leninism Is Our Banner and Our Fighting Weapon' (speech at a plenary session of the Central Committee of the CPSU, 21 June 1963), in *The Great Mission of Literature and Art*, Moscow, 1964, p. 219. In 1905, Lenin wrote: 'Every artist... has the right to create freely, according to his ideal and independently of everything else. But we are communists, of course. We must not stand with folded arms and let chaos develop as it will. We must guide this process according to a systematic plan and mould its results.' V. I. Lenin, in M. Lifshits (ed.), *Lenin o kulture i isskustvo*, Moscow, 1938, p. 112.

remarked that, 'Assassination is the extreme form of censorship.'[14] Soviet legal practices, in this sense, for many years constituted an extreme form of censorship;[15] they perform this same function today, though in somewhat more muted form. A central purpose of the Soviet legal system has always been to contain and/or punish dissent, not to protect it. The courts were, from the beginning, seen as instruments of party control. In 1923, N. V. Krylenko, who was later to become People's Commissar for Justice, wrote: 'We look at the court as a class institution, as an organ of government power . . . Our judge is above all a politician, a worker in the political field.' According to Krylenko, 'a club is a primitive weapon, a rifle a more efficient one, the most efficient is the court'.[16] All were seen as instruments of compulsion; all have been used to deter manifestations of dissent or to punish dissenters.

The present Soviet constitution – described by Stalin when it was promulgated in 1936 as 'the only thoroughly democratic constitution in the world'[17] – guarantees all the familiar rights and freedoms. But it stipulates that these rights are to be exercised only in the interest of socialism. The guarantees are secured, in the constitution's words, 'in conformity with the interests of the working people, and in order to strengthen the socialist system'.[18] In elucidating the meaning of the various constitutional guarantees, Andrey Vyshinsky, Stalin's principal spokesman on legal affairs, made it clear that they were limited to those who supported the goals and methods of the party. 'In our state', he declared, 'naturally there is and can be no place for freedom of speech, press, and so on for the foes of

[14] Quoted in Robert Conquest, *The Politics of Ideas in the USSR*, New York, 1967, p. 43.

[15] According to Andrey Vyshinsky, 'when it is a question of annihilating an enemy, we can do it without a trial as well'. N. V. Zhogin, 'Ob izvrashcheniyakh Vyshinskogo v teorii sovetskogo prava i praktike', *Sovetskoye Gosudarstvo i Pravo*, No. 3, 1965, p. 27. Vyshinsky and Stalin seem to have viewed dissenters as counterrevolutionaries. 'Peremptorily silencing the dissenter, labelling him an anti-Marxist and sometimes an out-and-out saboteur, and then applying measures of criminal repression – this is what characterized the "scientific leadership" provided by Vyshinsky.' Editorial, 'Do kontsa likvidirovat' vrednyye posledstviya kul'ta lichnosti v sovetskoy yurisprudentsii', *Sovetskoye Gosudarstvo i Pravo*, No. 4, 1962, p. 15.

[16] Quoted in Harold J. Berman, *Justice in the USSR*, revised edition, Cambridge, Mass., 1963, p. 36.

[17] J. V. Stalin, 'On the Draft Constitution of the USSR', *Problems of Leninism*, 11th English edition, Moscow, 1953, p. 700.

[18] Article 125.

socialism. Every sort of attempt on their part to utilise to the detriment of the state . . . those freedoms granted to the toilers must be classified as a counter-revolutionary crime.'[19] More recently, a Soviet professor of law echoed Vyshinsky's remark. In the USSR, N. Farberov argued, 'very extensive democratic freedoms are implemented exclusively in the interests of the people and cannot be taken advantage of for actions hostile to the socialist state'. The Soviet interpretation of individual freedom, he suggested, 'differs radically from the interpretation that the apologists for some kind of generalized, "pure" democracy are trying to give to it . . .'[20] Thus, the party has guaranteed the various freedoms only within severly circumscribed boundaries. Indeed, the party can arbitrarily set boundaries, alter them or interpret them, and it has often done this in such a way as to further restrict the operational meaning of the guarantees.

To control dissent, the authorities rely on a variety of legal measures; they range from the application of 'anti-parasite' statutes and refusal to grant residence permits to the use of criminal sanctions. The principal statutes used to discourage dissent are Articles 70, 190 (1) and 190 (3) of the RSFSR Criminal Code (plus analogous sections of the criminal codes of the other republics). These laws prohibit:

. . . agitation or propaganda carried on for the purpose of subverting or weakening Soviet authority or circulating for the same purpose slanderous fabrications which defame the Soviet state and social system, or circulating or preparing or keeping, for the same purpose, literature of such content . . .[21]
. . . the systematic dissemination in oral form of recognizably false fabrications defaming the Soviet state and social order, as well as the preparation or dissemination in written, printed or other form of works having such a content . . .

[19] Andrey Vyshinsky, *The Law of the Soviet State*, New York, 1948, p. 617.
[20] N. Farberov, 'Socialist Democracy', *Trud*, 28 January 1969, pp. 2–3. Translated in *Current Digest of the Soviet Press* (hereafter CDSP), Vol. XXI, No. 5, pp. 17–18. Another legal scholar has remarked that the Soviet regime 'long ago left behind the decrepit attributes of bourgeois political freedoms, which are thoroughly saturated with the mutual antagonisms of bourgeois parties and with class and national animosities'. A. Lukyanov, 'Sotsializm i politicheskiye svobody', *Pravda*, 4 December 1968, p. 3.
[21] 'Criminal Code of the RSFSR', in Harold J. Berman (ed.), *Soviet Criminal Law and Procedure*, Cambridge, Mass., 1966, p. 180.

... the organization of, as well as active participation in, group activities which grossly disturb public order, are coupled with manifest disobedience of lawful demands by the authorities, or involve disturbance of the functioning of transport or state or public institutions or enterprises . . . [22]

The scope of these prohibitions is broad indeed; each is susceptible of very far-reaching interpretation. The provisions of Article 70, for example, were the legal basis for the trial and conviction of Sinyavsky and Daniel. [23] Article 190 (1), passed in the aftermath of the Sinyavsky–Daniel affair, avoids the difficulty of proving a deliberate attempt to weaken or slander the regime. [24] And, since it leaves the interpretation of what constitutes a 'fabrication' in the hands of the state and its judicial authorities, its value in inhibiting and controlling dissent is very great. Article 190 (3) has been employed against persons participating in unauthorised demonstrations. [25] It has been applied in much the same way that some American police officials have used 'disturbing the peace' or 'loitering' ordinances to intimidate civil rights and Vietnam protesters. Vladimir Bukovsky, who was arrested in 1967 for taking part in one such demonstration (protesting at the arrest of the editors of an underground literary journal), argued in court that rights guaranteed by the Soviet constitution were being denied to him. (The constitution guarantees 'the right of street processions and demonstrations'.) 'It is not necessary', Bukovsky declared, 'to include such an article for demonstrations that the government

[22] 'Decree of Presidium of Russian Republic Supreme Soviet: On Additions to the Russian Republic Criminal Code', *Vedomosti Verkhovnogo Soveta RSFSR*, No. 38, 22 September 1966, p. 819. In *CDSP*, Vol. XVIII, No. 41, p. 3.

[23] Until 1956, the practice had been to interpret Article 70 rather strictly. Oral or written attacks, no matter how false, on any individual Soviet leader, were not covered by Article 70. Nor was criticism of particular programmes of the party or government, such as the virgin lands scheme or some foreign policy measure. Personal diaries with an anti-Soviet content were said to be not covered by the Article. However, Article 70 was applied against persons who supported the 1956 Hungarian uprising and who openly opposed Soviet intervention to put down the revolt. Harold J. Berman, 'The Writer and Soviet Law', *The New Leader*, Vol. XLIX, No. 4, 14 February 1966, pp. 14–15.

[24] Sinyavsky and Daniel denied having deliberately attempted to weaken or slander the regime. Indeed, the presiding judge at their trial acknowledged on one occasion that the authors' views and words spoken by their characters were not necessarily the same. See Max Hayward (ed.), *On Trial*, revised edition, New York, 1967, p. 56.

[25] Paul A. Smith, Jr., 'Protest in Moscow', *Foreign Affairs*, Vol. 47, No. 1, October 1968, p. 154.

organizes – it is clear that no one will disperse those demonstrations. We do not need freedom "pro" if there is no freedom "anti" . . . Freedom of speech and of the press is, first of all, freedom for criticism. Nobody has ever forbidden praise of the government.'[26] Bukovsky's arguments did not sway the court; his views were summarily dismissed. Dissenters cannot fall back on freedoms allegedly guaranteed by the constitution, for the party and government categorically refuse to permit criticism of their policies.

More broadly, the legal system always functions in such a way as to protect the state's interests, rather than those of a dissenter. Despite the objections of a number of legal scholars, the situation has not changed materially from 1935, when Vyshinsky said:

The formal law is subordinate to the law of the Revolution. There might be collisions and discrepancies between the formal commands of laws and those of the proletarian revolution . . . This collision must be solved only by the subordination of the formal commands of law to those of party policy.[27]

To this day, *raison d'état* remains a higher value than 'the rule of law'. The constitutional requirement that judges are 'independent and subject only to the law' is interpreted in practice to mean the exact opposite. A Soviet legal textbook comes closer to the truth when it notes that, 'The court does not and cannot stand beyond politics . . . beyond the direction of the party.'[28] The party is responsible for the appointment and removal of legal officials; it supervises and criticises their work at all levels. Indeed, a Soviet professor has described

. . . reproaches levelled against judges who . . . refuse to bend to the demand of the local administrator to discuss this or that criminal case or not to sentence such and such a defendant. Such a judge is termed a formalist, and it is said that he has set himself against public opinion, does not understand 'the line', etc.[29]

[26] 'Final Trial Statement of V. Bukovsky', 1 September 1967, *Problems of Communism*, Vol. XVII, No. 4, July–August 1968, pp. 32–3, 35.

[27] Andrey Vyshinsky, *Sudoustroistvo v SSSR*, Moscow, 1935, p. 32. Cited in Berman, *Justice in the USSR*, op. cit., pp. 42–3.

[28] Cited in George Feifer, *Justice in Moscow*, New York, 1964, p. 251.

[29] I. Perlov, 'Pravosudiye i obshchestvennoye mneniye', *Izvestiya*, 30 June 1966, p. 6.

Virtually all judges are members of the party, and they must be 'politically mature', i.e., politically reliable.[30] They are responsible for supporting the established order, not its critics.[31]

Dissent is further inhibited by three striking features of the Soviet legal system: (1) the impressive status and authority of the Procuracy, (2) the correspondingly low status and virtual impotence of defence counsel, and (3) the distinctive Soviet practice of encouraging press attacks against defendants in certain criminal cases. While some in the USSR have raised their voices to criticise these features, the system remains weighted in favour of the state.

Soviet procurators are entrusted with two very different – some would say incompatible – responsibilities. They are public prosecutors, and at the same time, they are responsible for guaranteeing that the accused's rights are protected.[32] Both Soviet and American commentators have remarked that, in practice, the former responsibility is given priority. Indeed, it is said that Soviet judges listen intently to the prosecution and then appear bored, disdainful or even contemptuous when the defence argues.[33] According to A. F. Gorkin, Chairman of the USSR Supreme Court, court sessions 'often betray an accusatory bias, legitimate petitions of the defendant or his defence counsel are rejected without grounds, and the testimony of witnesses in favour of the defendant is left out of consideration'.[34] Prosecutors apparently suffer from an inflated view of their own

[30] In 1964, some 3,120 of the 3,413 people's judges elected in the RSFSR were party members or candidate members; in 1966, the 'overwhelming majority' of all people's judges were said to be communists. At the same time, 44 per cent of all people's assessors are party members or candidate members. Robert Conquest, *Justice and the Legal System in the USSR*, New York, 1968, p. 111. Morevoer, according to a Central Committee official, 'The political and ideological tempering of the personnel of courts . . . is a most important task before party organizations . . . [Personnel must be] morally stable, totally devoted and politically mature'. N. Mironov, 'Ukrepleniye sotsialisticheskoy zakonnosti i pravoporyadka', *Partiinaya Zhizn'*, No. 5, 1962, p. 14.

[31] The prosecutor in 'The Trial Begins', a short story by Abram Tertz (Andrei Sinyavsky), declares at one point: 'Let scores, let hundreds of innocents be condemned rather than allow one enemy to go free.' Abram Tertz, *The Trial Begins*, New York, 1960, p. 56.

[32] See Glenn G. Morgan, *Soviet Administrative Legality*, Stanford, California, 1962.

[33] Yury Idashkin, 'Reflections on Legal Defense', *Oktyabr*, No. 5, 1967, pp. 172–7. In *CDSP*, Vol. XIX, No. 26, pp. 23–6; Feifer, op. cit., p. 245. According to Frederick C. Barghoorn, the best legal minds in the Soviet Union work in the Procuracy. The courts and the bar are staffed with persons of more modest talents. See Frederick C. Barghoorn, *Politics in the USSR*, Boston, 1966, p. 329.

[34] A. Gorkin, 'O sotsialisticheskom pravosudii', *Izvestiya*, 2 December 1964, p. 3.

skills, denying even the possibility that they can err. One out-
raged prosecutor, responding to criticism of the Procuracy,
declared: '... according to your theory ... the prosecutor's
office brings innocent people to trial! The prosecutor accuses an
innocent person in court! Is this conceivable? No, it is nonsense!'
The law, he went on,

... gives the investigatory agencies the right to bring charges
against someone and to interrogate him as the accused, and hence
to recognise him as guilty. And the prosecutor brings to trial and,
in criminal proceedings, accuses a person who is already guilty in
the eyes of the authorities. And the court merely verifies to what
extent the individual brought to trial and accused by the prosecutor
is guilty and whether or not this offender deserves criminal punishment ... Criminal guilt is proved to begin with by the investigatory
agencies, after which the court verifies the objectivity of the conclusions of the investigatory agencies and hands down its decision
in the form of a sentence.[35]

The defendant's position is further compromised by the fact
that his attorney is permitted to represent him only after the
completion of a preliminary investigation.[36] As Professor M. S.
Strogovich has pointed out, it is precisely in the investigation of
a case that errors most frequently arise.[37] And, in fact, judges

[35] 'Letters: Replies, Comment, Discussion: On the functions of the Court and
the Investigatory Agencies, *Literaturnaya Gazeta*, 18 August 1964, p. 2. In *CDSP*,
Vol. XVI, No. 39, p. 24. Similarly, a Soviet professor of law has argued: 'In
criminal cases a great deal is said and written about guarantees for the individual.
What individual is this? A criminal! We are afraid that the investigator, the
militiaman or the court might "offend" the criminal and we worry about the
criminal's rights and guarantees and thus impede the struggle against crime.'
Quoted in A. Bovin, 'Istina v pravosudii', *Izvestiya*, 9 February 1962, p. 4. The
prosecutor's position, in addition to being disturbing, has no basis in law. When a
criminal case is sent to a court with the prosecutor's office concurring in the findings of the indictment, the judges issue an order to bring the accused to trial
'without deciding the question of guilt beforehand'. 'Letters: Replies, Comment ...', op. cit., p. 24. Moreover, Article 7 of the Principles of Criminal Procedure of the USSR and of the Union Republics states that 'no person may be
considered guilty of a crime and subjected to criminal punishment except by
sentence of a court'. Gorkin, op. cit., p. 3.
[36] For suggestions that the role of defence counsel be enlarged by permitting
him to participate in the preliminary investigation, see M. Strogovich, 'O
pravovykh garantiyakh v ugolovnom sudoproizvodstve', *Izvestiya*, 23 August 1957,
p. 2, and O. Chaikovskaya, 'Opasnoye nevezhestvo', *Izvestiya*, 10 September
1964, p. 3. See also Stephen Weiner, 'Socialist Legality on Trial', *Problems of
Communism*, Vol. XVII, No. 4, July–August 1968, pp. 11–12.
[37] M. S. Strogovich, 'Law, Morality and the Individual: Judicial Error',
Literaturnaya Gazeta, 23 May 1964, p. 2. In *CDSP*, Vol. XVII, No. 39, p. 23.

sometimes *do* send back cases for a new hearing or even acquit defendants.[38]

Although the regime remains implacably opposed to any expression of dissent, advocates of due process continue to seek guarantees of defendants' rights. A Moscow prosecutor, for example, has publicly criticised the excesses of his colleagues. He cites, in particular, their

... tendentiousness, lack of objectivity [and] prejudicial inclination to produce a criminal charge in the examination of criminal cases ... such activities of the inquisatorial, procuratorial and judicial authorities ... lead to unfounded accusations or illegal imposition of harsher penalties.[39]

Given these circumstances of bias and even outright conniv-ance, it is not surprising that defence attorneys are accorded a relatively minor role. Not only are they prohibited from repre-senting clients in the police and investigatory stages of a case, but their courtroom influence has been reduced to a minimum. Defence attorneys have, in the main, confined themselves to explanations of mitigating circumstances and pleas for mercy.[40] Some lawyers, a Supreme Soviet deputy pointed out in 1957, fear entering into 'a genuine debate of principles with repre-sentatives of the prosecution'. They thereby nourish 'the strange sort of attitude towards lawyers as people who interfere with, rather than contribute to, the exercise of justice'.[41]

The dominant view of defence counsel in the USSR is that he is an 'aide of the court', rather than counsel for the defence. Prevailing practice is to reject the so-called 'bourgeois' concep-tion of the defence attorney in favour of a 'socialist' conception. For example, one writer argues:

[38] Chaikovskaya, op. cit., p. 3.

[39] S. O. Urakov, 'Povisit kulture sledstva', *Sotsialisticheskaya Zakonnost'*, No. 7, 1960, pp. 12–16. Cited in Kazimierz Grzybowski, 'Soviet Criminal Law', *Problems of Communism*, Vol. XIV, No. 2, March–April 1965, p. 58.

[40] Indeed, as late as 1956, a Soviet commentator acknowledged that, 'Fre-quently defence counsel assume the role in court of public accusers and virtually become second accusers.' *Pravda Vostoka*, 27 July 1956. Quoted in Robert Conquest, *The Soviet Police System*, New York, 1968, p. 76, footnote 19.

[41] Cited in Feifer, op. cit., p. 233. Another commentator has added: 'An attorney has no right to harm his client under any circumstances, no matter how he feels about the case. . . . [If] he fails in this, he ceases to be the counsel for the defence, and thereby breaks the law.' Ya. Kiselev, 'Speeches for the Defense', *Zvezda*, No. 12, 1955, pp. 69–98. In *CDSP*, Vol. XIX, No. 10, p. 29.

The Soviet defence attorney cannot convert himself into the servant of his client, blindly following him in the defence of his interests, even though these interests are not legal and detract from, rather than contribute to, the interests of social justice. In defending the rights and legal interests of his client, the Soviet defence attorney must stop short at the brink where truth ends and falsehood begins, where the interest of the state and society are damaged by the counterposing to them of the illegal interests of his client . . .

[Defence counsel must protect] not only the personal interests of the accused but also the interests of society and, therefore, of the state. [A defence lawyer] must not defend at all costs . . . Defence of the criminal must not transform itself into defence of the crime.[42]

The familiar adversary proceeding is almost completely absent in the Soviet Union. A conspiracy of silence and/or connivance renders the defendant in a criminal case – particularly one involving political dissent – almost surely guilty.

Recent years have witnessed the publication of a number of articles calling for greater initiative and latitude for defence counsel. Current practices, it is said, have led to frequent instances of violation of the accused's procedural rights, on the pretext of effective prosecution of criminals. Perhaps the most persuasive argument has been made by O. Chaikovskaya:

No matter how fine the investigator is, he is working alone at his job and does not have – at the outset – an adversary; no one argues with him, no one presents him with ideas contrary to his own. Needless to say, he can be mistaken . . . The defence lawyer will call your every conclusion into question . . . [If] the structure erected by the investigator is infirm at its foundations, it will collapse under the onslaught of the defence and, later, of the court.[43]

Clearly, one cannot insist with confidence on a person's guilt if only the evidence that tends to convict him is gathered, if his

[42] I. D. Perlov, *Sudebnoye sledstviye v sovetskom ugolovnom protsesse*, Moscow, 1955, pp. 124–5. Quoted in Robert Conquest, *Justice and the Legal System in the USSR*, New York, 1968, pp. 37–8.

[43] Chaikovskaya, op. cit., p. 3. Similarly A. Gorkin has argued that: 'A competent prosecution and a vigorous defence of the defendant are equally necessary to administer justice correctly . . . the defence counsel helps the court in examining the contradictory and often confused materials of the case. . . . [Justice will be achieved only when each party] renounces claim to infallibility, bias and subjectivism.' Gorkin, op. cit., p. 3. See also N. Chetunova, 'The Right to Defend', *Literaturnaya Gazeta*, 20 September 1966, p. 2. In *CDSP*, Vol. XVIII, No. 38, pp. 18–19. For a more comprehensive treatment of the proper role of defence counsel, see A. L. Tsypkin, 'Aktual'nyye voprosy teorii i praktiki sovetskoy zashchity', in A. A. Kruglov (ed.), *Sovetskaya advokatura*, Moscow, 1968, pp. 48–54.

explanation is not heard, and if no effort is made to explore evidence favouring him.[44] The implications of such an attitude for political nonconformists are vast indeed.

Similarly, the widespread practice of encouraging newspaper attacks on defendants in political (and other) cases compromises any dissenter. The press often criticises defendants before and during a trial; the Soviets acknowledge that this exerts a definite influence on the trial's outcome.[45] In the weeks before the Sinayavsky–Daniel trial, for example, newspaper articles condemned the writers and called for harsh punishment. The writers were said to be 'anti-Soviet' and guilty of 'malicious slander'; they were 'renegades' and 'traitors' who should be severely punished'.[46] Attacks of this sort would in an American court clearly be grounds for a mistrial. As the Sheppard case (1966) made clear, the constitutional guarantee of freedom of the press does not permit interference with a man's right to a fair trial.[47] In the Soviet context, where the press has an official character, newspaper attacks on accused persons cannot help but deprive the accused of a fair trial. Witnesses will be afraid (or not permitted) to give evidence for the defendant, experts may close their eyes to circumstances which make their findings dubious, defence attorneys will be able to provide only marginal aid, and judges will respond more to outside pressure than to the requirements of law.[48]

Some Soviet judges have begun to question the practice of permitting and encouraging such prejudicial publicity. A. F. Gorkin, for example, pointed out in 1964 that:

... the press sometimes publishes articles that, before the hearing of a case in court, pronounce various persons guilty and prejudge the question of punishment, mostly in favour of maximum punish-

---

[44] M. S. Strogovich, op. cit., pp. 23–4.

[45] See, e.g., Yu. Korenevsky and K. Sukhodolets, 'Otchevo byvayut oshibki', *Izvestiya*, 15 March 1966, p. 6.

[46] Dm. Yeremin, 'Perevertyshi', *Izvestiya*, 13 January 1966, p. 6, and 'Klevetniki – perevertyshi', *Izvestiya*, 18 January 1966, p. 3.

[47] Sheppard v. Maxwell, 384 U.S. 333 (1966). It is perhaps appropriate to recall Alexander Hamilton's remarks in Federalist No. 84: 'What is liberty of the press? Who can give it any definition which would not leave the utmost latitude for evasion? I hold it to be impracticable; and from this I infer, that its security, whatever fine declarations may be inserted in any constitution respecting it, must altogether depend on public opinion, and on the general spirit of the people and of the government.' *The Federalist*, Modern Library edition, New York, n.d., p. 560.

[48] Korenevsky and Sukhodolets, op. cit., p. 6.

ment . . . [To] prejudge the sentence of the court and thereby exert pressure on the court means, instead of combating mistakes in the work of the courts, contributing to the commission of these mistakes.[49]

The argument, it would seem, is compelling: a judge cannot decide a case 'on the merits' if pressure is being exerted on him by his political superiors. But that is precisely the point. In political matters, the party has indicated no inclination whatsoever to renounce its guiding, dominant role. The practice of outside interference with judicial decision-making has continued, and the fact that this has a 'chilling effect' on freedom and dissenters is a mark of its success.

One wonders if repressive practices such as censorship and legal pressure, which prevent 'undesirable' sentiments from being expressed in public, simultaneously produce alienation and dissent. The system clearly has generated problems. For example, certain writers have sent abroad for publication works which have not been – and perhaps could not be – accepted for publication in the USSR. To send a manuscript abroad for publication without permission is not itself a criminal offence. It is, however, likely to produce a hostile response from Soviet authorities when they learn of it. A number of prominent authors have been involved in such difficulties, including Boris Pasternak, Yevgeni Yevtushenko and Alexander Solzhenitsyn. Until the Sinyavsky–Daniel affair in 1966, none of these writers was jailed. Since then, however, many have been sent to labour camps.

In the 1920s, Boris Pilnyak and Yevgeni Zamyatin were charged with having sent abroad works that had not been passed by the Soviet censorship. When it became apparent that neither had deliberately violated Soviet law, they were merely expelled from the Writers' Union.[50] (While this was hardly a trivial punishment, it was very different from imprisonment.) One recanted and the other was granted permission to emigrate. More recently, Yevtushenko's *A Precocious Autobiography* was

[49] Gorkin, op cit., p. 3. See also Yu. Feofanov, 'Angely, demony i istina', *Izvestiya*, 5 January 1966, p. 4. Korenevsky and Sukhodolets, op. cit., p. 6; Perlov, op. cit., p. 6; and G. Anashkin, 'A Word to Our Readers: Reading Courtroom Reporting', in *Literaturnaya Gazeta*, No. 14, 26 March 1966, p. 10, in *CDSP*, Vol. XXI, No. 14, p. 10. For the opposite view, see I. Galkin, 'Sud i obshchestvennyye strasti', *Izvestiya*, 17 April 1969, p. 3.

[50] Max Hayward, 'Introduction', in Hayward and Labedz, op. cit., p. 13.

published abroad without the permission of Soviet authorities. Yevtushenko was publicly reprimanded, but there was no suggestion of bringing criminal charges against him.[51] In Solzhenitsyn's case, it is unclear whether he himself deliberately sent *The Cancer Ward* and *The First Circle* out of the country. He has disclaimed any responsibility for sending the manuscript abroad, and it may well be that the KGB (the security police) did this for him, in a deliberate effort to discredit him and his works.[52]

Perhaps two conclusions emerge from this survey of constitutional and legal restraints on dissent in the USSR. First, the party has erected a rather formidable barrier to inhibit and/or punish those who would dissent from officially prescribed policies. The list of intruments is imposing: the dominant role of the Communist Party in political, legal and cultural matters; the network of laws prohibiting 'anti-Soviet' agitation and propaganda; the censorship network; the doctrine of socialist realism; the political use of mental institutions, and so on.

But a second conclusion seems equally inescapable. That is, neither the criminal law, nor the macabre procedure of institutionalising deviant intellectuals, nor any other procedure seems to have inhibited dissent. These measures certainly make it more difficult for dissenters to circulate their views, but they cannot prevent dissent from forming or developing. As the dissident writer Alexander Yesenin-Volpin says in the introduction to his collection of poems and essays (published abroad): 'There is no freedom of the press in Russia, but who can say there is no freedom of thought?'[53]

[51] See Berman, 'The Writer and Soviet Law', op. cit., p. 13.
[52] See the editorial, 'The Ideological Struggle: The Writer's Responsibility', *Literaturnaya Gazeta*, No. 26, 26 June 1968, p. 5. In *CDSP*, Vol. XX, No. 6, p. 4.
[53] Alexander Yesenin-Volpin, *A Leaf of Spring*, New York, 1961, p. 7.

Zygmunt Bauman

The Second Generation Socialism[*]

A review of socio-cultural trends in contemporary Polish Society

HAVING FOCUSED HIS ATTENTION ON THE INTERNAL struggles of elite caucuses, the 'pecking order' of those invited to official ceremonies, the secret missions of Kremlin emissaries and the like, many a Western scholar pursues his efforts to understand what is going on in the socialist East only to find himself led astray in the vast but barren fields of Kremlinological 'conspiracy'. The worst difficulty with this approach is that it pushes the investigator's mind into the realm of rather secondary and irrelevant facts.

Another cluster of popular fallacies in dealing with the socialist East may be traced to the otherwise understandable premise, that *the* problem of socialist societies is 'just how close' they are to their Western, pluralistic-democratic-multiparty-freemarket counterparts. The 'how close' problem, according to its two different versions, means either 'just to what extent have they matured enough to be dealt with as responsible and predictable partners' or 'just how unlike us are they still (or how like us are they already)'. This double methodological

* This paper was prepared for one of the conferences held in connection with the project on 'Social and Political Processes in Eastern Europe'. The author is very grateful to Professor Ghiţa Ionescu, on whose initiative the paper was written, to the Centre for International Studies, LSE, which created favourable conditions for the discussion and the elaboration of the preliminary draft, and to Mr David Stafford who helped the author to prepare the paper for publication. New developments which have taken place since then have not been, obviously, taken into account. They do not however seem to invalidate most of the hypotheses put forward in this article. They bear at the same time eloquent testimony to the changing social role of the second-generation working class – who, unlike their fathers, are literate, well-educated, open-minded and tend to treat seriously the ideological legitimation of their state.

assumption is attractive in two respects. First, it liberates the scholar from the rather irksome need to apprehend certain peculiar and unfamiliar problems the socialist regimes are striving to solve or forced to respond to. Secondly, it supplies him with a comforting belief that the 'end of the affair' is already known and can even be investigated empirically in the student's immediate neighbourhood.

One underlying, though usually unconscious assumption is, that the only people who could possibly develop their vested interests in a reverse trend (away from the Western patterns) are the professional party functionaries. It is by no means an accident that most Western writers stubbornly refuse any attempt to find an English equivalent for the Russian word 'apparatchiki'. The idea that somebody entitled to bear a respectable Western name could deliberately support such a strange system on his own initiative is perhapsy psychologically unbearable to many; if however we allow our psychological fears to interfere with methodological considerations the final effect may be most unfortunate.

The present article in contrast is based on the two following assumptions:

(a) The social system initiated by the socialist upheaval constitutes an autonomous whole, differing by many significant variables from the systems which have not been through the socialist reshuffle. As such, it has developed its own frame of reference within which one ought to assess the rationality of accepted and dismissed structural solutions. It would be utterly misleading to assume that the 'different' must be synonymous with the 'irrational' and so ascribed to intrigues of the wicked. It would be equally misleading to try to allocate the systems under consideration on a uni-linear evolutionary scale based upon the Western historical experience and Western political values.

(b) The proper framework for the analysis of political developments in the societies in question is provided by specific conflicts and tensions whose solution is pressed upon and thus sought for by the ruling elite. These conflicts and tensions are rooted in the structural dynamics of the system itself and determine the range of freedom of any ruling group actually or potentially in power. Only a limited number of political responses can fit the given set of socio-cultural stimuli. Instead of providing us with the universal explanation of internal developments in the communist East the 'personal side' of the story becomes itself meaningful only if projected analytically on the screen of the socio-cultural dynamics.

The notion of 'structural dynamics' is interpreted here in a somewhat broader sense than the one usually ascribed to it in the analysis of the current history of communist systems. Much too often its meaning is reduced to a common-sense equation: standard of living low (workers) + censorship harsh (intellectuals) = dissatisfaction; enjoyment of material goods rising (some groups of workers and – second rank by definition – intellectuals) = satisfaction. Instead of this rather simplified interpretation we propose to extend our concept in two main directions:

(a) We assume that behavioural effects of apparently identical parameters may be radically different if allocated in a different time series; it is thus assumed that the genuine function of any variable at any point of the system's development becomes fully comprehensible only when seen against the background of the system's dynamics.

(b) Even inside the limits imposed by the above assumption the causal link between the basic socio-cultural variables of the system and its behavioural responses is by no means direct. The structural dynamics of the system are indeed responsible in large measure for its long-range trends. This however is hardly the case when short-term trends are concerned. To put it in more general terms – the structural dynamics of the system delineate solely the range of possible behavioural responses. The actual choice depends on many additional factors which cannot be treated is internal variables of the system without risking that the analytical model should become unworkable.

It should be apparent from the above remarks that the present survey does not pretend to explain why Polish government policy in 1969 was what it was or why it was not what it could have been, had Gomulka's faction been less successful in doing away temporarily with its rivals. Even less does it pretend to explain why other Eastern European regimes operating in apparently similar socio-cultural settings have chosen different political solutions to similar socio-cultural problems. Neither does it offer a secure basis for predicting the future turn of political events and the fate of dissenting factions. But this survey does pursue the goal of enumerating the basic socio-cultural problems, with which any kind of a ruling group – be it Gomulka, or any 'stop-gap' leader – will have to cope in the foreseeable future.

EMERGING CLASS STRUCTURE

Twenty years or so constitute a critical period in the history of any post-revolutionary regime, particularly in the case of millenarian and egalitarian revolutions, which promise to up-root social inequities and challenge the very principle of dividing human beings into deprived and privileged. That the few who made the revolution and dedicated their lives to its victory are rewarded and enjoy preferential access to power and some economic advantages – is not necessarily looked upon as a violation of revolutionary ideals of equality. Most egalitarian ideologies only challenge 'unmerited' privileges (if measured by standards they accept). But in twenty years the second generation grows up and the privileged eagerly extend the splendour of revolutionary sacrifice to their children. This time however a major revision of ideological principles is necessary. After twenty years the post-revolutionary regime faces its first, though decisive, test: just how class-immune is it really? As inheritance of differential social positions constitutes the focal institution of any class structure – what is at stake is in the last instance the class or class-less structure of the allegedly equali-tarian society.

The ownership of capital means no longer implies special access to vital goods. This crucial function is however taken over by another institutional set – a cumulative power hierarchy ruled by bureaucratic norms. The traditional capitalist patterns of inheritance are obviously inapplicable in the new setting. Thus the growing pressure towards inter-generational continuity of privileges must inevitably, elevate another institution to the role of the class-allocating mechanism. Only an institution relatively easy to manipulate by the factors harboured in the families of ascription can be chosen to accomplish this role. The skill complex, defined by the length of formal education and testified to by a theoretically un-limited number of official certificates, fits the role-prerequisites well. The alternative institutional sets serving basically similar ends can be shown schematically in the following way:

MODEL 1

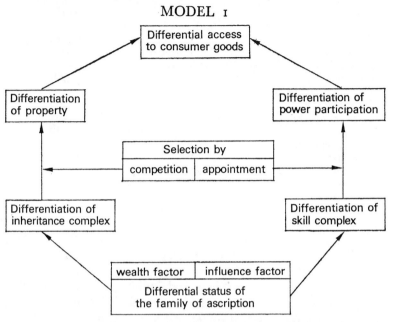

Now, as the formalised educational system assumes the role of the single factor operative in the realm of skill-distribution, it is only natural to expect that the indices of the new emerging class structure will be most clearly seen in the competition for educational opportunities. Both the figures illustrating the social composition of different types of schools and the nature of social forces struggling for or against extension of educational opportunities assume a crucial relevance in any analysis of the dynamics of the class structure.

The fact that the statistics containing this kind of information belong to the carefully guarded secrets is indicative both of the guilty conscience of the ruling elites and of their extraordinary significance. Despite the partial nature of the available evidence the general picture is however unambiguous. The following table compiled on the basis of the official 1966 Polish Statistical Yearbook, contains data only partly comparable and thus offers only a general survey of the situation which crystallised in Poland around 1965.

TABLE I

	Peasants' children	Manual workers (or their children)	Non-manual workers (or their children)
	(Figures quoted in thousands)		
Employed (total)		5,388	2,560
Schoolboys (students):			
Primary schools	2,700		2,500
Sec. comprehensive	129		297
Elem. vocational	108	181	46
Sec. vocational	124	196	150
Sec. art	2·5	9	18
University & college	26	41·5	76·7

The broad lines of the picture are sufficiently clear. Still what ought to be borne in mind is the unsatisfactory character of these statistics in so far as a quantitative estimation of the actual differentiation is concerned; by grouping together in one category of 'non-manual' workers (i.e. salaried) such distinct groups as white collar workers and highly paid professionals and managers, the data blur the genuine dividing lines. Moreover, the schools classified under one heading, because of their differential allocation (quality of teaching staff, vocational profile and established social status), in fact offer to their graduates highly differentiated opportunities of further achievement. Some of them function simply as 'sewage pumps' eliminating their graduates from more sophisticated educational careers – others resemble rather the broad and smooth avenues leading to the summits of cumulative power hierarchy. If these variations were quantifiable the trends indicated by our table would undoubtedly become more pronounced, even if they did not acquire a new qualitiative dimension.

The two most rigorous filters screening the upward flow of educational status seekers are located respectively at two strategic points of the Polish educational system: between primary schools and secondary comprehensive and secondary vocational schools (elementary vocational schools being the blind alley designed for the failures); and between the secondary level and universities. In the year under analysis, 661,000 pupils left primary schools, but only 117,000 were accepted in secondary comprehensive schools and 101,000 in secondary vocational schools; 290,000 entered elementary vocational schools. From among roughly 80,000 pupils leaving all types of secondary schools, only 45,300 found places in universities and equivalent educational institutions, including university evening courses, a theoretically, but even more practically, inferior type of higher education.

The more effective the institutionalised filters, the more pronounced are their class-generating capacities and the more contradictory the class-type vested interests accumulating around them. The severe competition focused around entrance procedures produces two distinct pressures which shape the framework of the *first* of several conflicts the Polish ruling elite has to face, i.e. the conflict between:

(a) The pressure exerted by those placed in the strategically privileged positions, aimed at two goals: (i) the undermining of all 'artificial' protective measures for the 'underdogs', and (ii) the obstruction of the expansion of educational opportunities which could threaten their present status-allocating capacity. The present size of secondary 'general' schools and universities is made to the measure (though certainly not consciously) of the hereditary needs of the privileged, and any increase could only jeopardise their relatively satisfactory position. The motto of this group could be taken as 'God save us from our friends (= state intervention), we will deal with our foes ourselves'. This group is in fact able to dispose of not-so-well-armed competitors through the functioning of two factors: (i) the natural advantage in competitive examinations granted to their children by their privileged background, providing opportunities for general cultural development; (ii) the time-honoured possibilities for parents to transform their own assets into preferential treatment of their children. (This is by no means confined to socialist societies.) The wider the gap between the absorptive capacity of two successive rungs of the occupational ladder, the tougher the entrance examinations, and therefore the greater the dependence of final success on auxiliary factors, both marketable (e.g. additional courses, private tuition) and non-pecuniary (family connections).

(b) The pressure exerted by those handicapped in their bargaining powers. Almost inescapably condemned to lose out in a straightforward competitive fight with the privileged, they can count only on the elimination of the competitive situation itself. Hence their 'vested interests' in the radical expansion of educational institutions. This demand too can hardly be regarded as peculiar to socialist societies. In Eastern Europe, however, those raising the banner of educational revolt are supported by the dominating egalitarian ideology. The new regime transformed equality of opportunities into the basic dimension of cultural expectancies. This factor alone cannot be over-estimated.

THE CLASS STRUCTURE IN SEARCH OF SELF-EXPRESSION

The value of goods, particularly beyond the mere subsistence level, cannot be simply reduced to the satisfaction of primary needs. There is something which is not so much inherent in the goods themselves, but arises from the fact that they are unevenly and differentially distributed and acquired. By being offered to one group of people and refused to another they assume an additional role as signs. What they signify is the social structure, e.g. the unequal position allocated to the given groups in the web of mutual dependencies and opportunities. Thus some goods may be craved for merely as 'signs', with but little sense of any organic need they can simultaneously satisfy. The farther removed a society is from a subsistence level economy the greater the role which should be ascribed to the signifying (semiotic) role of goods whenever an explanation of their distributional dynamics is sought.

In Poland, during the period of post-war reconstruction and the hardships of over-accumulation, the distribution of scarce commodities was carried out on an inequitable basis. Their semiotic role was negligible, anyway, as far as the great majority of the nation was concerned. Goods were almost entirely derivative – ascribed to social/political position and so secondary to it. Blatant inequality was not expressed semiotically. It was concealed both on the level of sign differentiation and, more important, on the level of social differentiation itself. The social divisions created by the revolution were as yet too feebly-rooted to confirm the sceptics' suspicions of the class structure as an inert, underlying 'social reality' in itself capable of producing its phenomenal expressions in the form of dress, dwelling and cuisine differentiation. It was more plausible and also more easily defensible to take the empirically tangible phenomena for the social differentiation as such, devoid of any deeper, firmer, or latent reality. Both those who were already developing at a high speed their class-like vested interests in the new regime, and those who were going to suffer from it, could easily cherish the illusion that differentiation in the sphere of consumption was the sole remnant of human inequality. From this assumption, two relatively simple conclusions could be drawn and – for the time being – relatively easily digested:

(i) that what remained from the detestable memories of class divisions was the harmless and justifiable differentiation of rewards and incentives which were open to constant readjustment because politically manipulated;

(ii) that by concealing the most obtrusive and blatant displays of unequal consumption social differentiation itself could be disposed of.

Given these considerations, it is difficult to say whether the notorious self-enforced isolation of the political elite, protected by one of the largest police bodies in the history of mankind, was a result of a neurotic Stalinist fear, or (at least in some measure) of an effort by the privileged to conceal their privileges. Whatever the reason, this was the epoch of the grey homogeneous crowd in the streets and of privilege hidden behind the 'yellow curtain'.

It was only when the new privileged group felt itself safely established and when the egalitarian fervour of the post-revolutionary honeymoon had subsided that privilege could and had to be revealed. This development was directed, if often unconsciously, towards the transformation of culturally discriminatory signs, which were previously derivatives of social position, into position-generating signs. In the previous period, the main division had been between those condemned to the common, dull and uniform market, and those entitled to enter the privileged ('yellow curtain') shops. A high income alone did not bring preferential treatment if not accompanied by an entrance permit to the privileged shops. Only a free market supplying differentiated (in quality and in price) goods could automatically solve the 'status congruence' problems which left the clumsy bureaucracy helpless and incompetent. This was precisely – so it appeared – the class essence of the October

Revolution of 1956, that is if the class character of revolutions is determined by the kind of interests which profit from them, and not by the social forces which made them. From 1956 two uninterrupted and parallel processes developed in Poland:

(a) The shift of more and more goods from the non-market sphere of bureaucratically-administered distribution to the sphere of less and less restricted marketing. Representative of the process was the buying of flats, the diminishing role of scholarships, drastic reduction in the number of holiday facilities offered at nominal rates, payment for medical services and medicines. This was accompanied by a pronounced shift from a 'welfare state' to a 'welfare individualism' type of reasoning.

(b) A widening of the differentiation in goods serving the same kind of needs, paralleled by the introduction of 'quality shops' intended for moneyed customers.

Thus practically and ideologically the new role of commodities and consumption as semiotic attributes of class-like social differentiation was acknowledged and sanctioned. The call for unrestricted free-market competition is always stimulated most vigorously by those whose preferential bargaining power is safety entrenched in non-marketable assets. The new trends would not find such enthusiastic support and encouragement from the privileged group were the latter not convinced of the stability of their privileged position. The vague hope that 'democratisation' of the consumer market would lead 'in the last instance' to the benefit of all, including the present-day underprivileged, should be seen as the rationalisation of guilty consciences, 'Market democracy', if not accompanied by a thorough democratisation of political and trade union representation and struggle, can only lead to the open expression and stabilisation of existing class divisions. In one respect of course it is socially creative, in unmasking the class structure of society and making class differences particularly provocative in the context of continuous lip-service to socialist equality. In this way it can mobilise the deprived and contribute effectively to their class maturity.

This process is already under way, and thus provides for the *second* problem every group in power must handle. It faces and will continue to face for many years to come the dilemma of two alternative solutions: either to continue with present policies and thereby strengthen social divisions and grievances at the risk of producing positive social unrest, or to apply some kind of 'protective' and 'welfare' policy and so risk alienating those profiting from and supporting (even reluctantly) the *status quo*. Another option which still remains open though hardly in practical terms is the solution chosen in 1937 by Stalin and 1968 by Mao in an attempt to solve their 'second generation' crisis. In essence, this solution consists in maintaining an unequal distribution of rewards between positions at the expense of the personal safety of the temporary incumbents of these positions, in the event of some 'cultural' or other revolutions or purges. Thus the basic structure of the system is preserved. But the personal (or rather family) bonds, which ascribe individuals to different rungs of the ladder, cannot petrify. When it was applied for the first time, the expedient of permanent purge may well have been intended to prevent the rigid systemic structure of power from generating an equally rigid class structure. If this was indeed its aim it was scarcely achieved (hence the fact that the Chinese version has been supplemented by an effort to eliminate the differences between manual and intellectual labour). Both solutions seem however unlikely in countries which cannot afford to foot the enormous bill of – even temporary – economic collapse.

At present the self-consciousness of the immature Polish working class (the question of immaturity will be dealt with later) is confined to resentment against 'dignitaries' and 'bosses' and mostly against particular dignitaries or bosses. The only apparent concession to the working class was precisely a promise to remove 'particular' dignitaries and 'particular' bosses; there was no acknowledgement beyond that of any distinctive general labour interest. This was a fair reflection of the state of working-class consciousness in Poland. It takes less time to create a class structure than for it to become apparent. But it will become increasingly difficult for any prospective ruling elite in Poland to satisfy working-class demands once they become articulated.

TRANSITIONAL STAGE OF A CLASSICAL CONFLICT

Even a superficial comparison of the Polish and Czechoslovak responses in 1968 to a nation-wide crisis in the system reveals two radically different patterns. In Poland, one sees an isolated revolt of radical students, supported by a group of intellectuals, arousing the hostility of white-collar workers and foundering in the apathy of a working-class apt to sympathise with governmental actions against 'pampered intellectuals' and 'troublemakers' (and on the other hand, the manifest inability of intellectuals to sympathise in any practically relevant way with, let alone appropriate, the genuine grievances of the workers). In Czechoslovakia, on the contrary, one saw a solid and cohesive front of intellectuals and workers, united well before the invasion by a common national programme expressing common interests; the Czechoslovak working class had realised what their Polish counterparts had failed to realise, that the demand for intellectual freedom represented more than a simple manifestation of the vested interests of a *Schöngeist* caste.

Most writers explain this contrast in terms of the existence and non-existence of pre-socialist democratic traditions in Czechoslovakia and Poland respectively. More sophisticated analyses rightly distinguish between the differing nature of industrialisation in the two countries. In Poland, rapid forced industrialisation producing all the hardships of the take-off period, characterised the early years of the socialist regime. In Czechoslovakia socialism was established in a society which already possessed a basic industrial network. What remains to be ascertained, however, is the way in which these historical discrepancies are relevant to the present situation, and the exact nature of the social forces or cultural institutions which incorporate, transmit, originate and preserve such differentiations.

According to a nation-wide survey conducted by Stanislaw Widerzpil, 56–65 per cent (depending on the branch of industry) of Polish workers in 1964 had recently left rural areas. Only 27 per cent had been gainfully employed before the second world war, and only 15 per cent were then workers. According to a study by Vera Rollova, in the same year 60 per cent of Czechoslovak workers were 'traditional proletarians'. According to official statistics, the total number of industrial workers in Poland increased in the period 1938–64 by 125 per cent. In Czechoslovakia, the corresponding increase was 35·6 per cent.

The sociological significance of these figures is unambiguous.

Fifteen per cent of a social group (in itself representing, through elimination, the least active, least politically-minded and socially-orientated sector of the pre-war class) could hardly provide an effective leaven for the political education of the remaining 85 per cent. It would tend, rather, to be overwhelmed by the latter, and would by its sheer numerical inferiority be incapable – even if it had the will – of transmitting its militant traditions to the majority. A more important factor, however, was the socio-cultural character of the new groups, whose ideology became that of the working class as a whole (but which in Czechoslovakia, on the contrary, was subsumed in the working-class tradition). They were still culturally (and in many cases too – because of the persistence of small-scale peasant farming – economically) peasants. The individualist and acquisitive values they brought from their village communities made them particularly susceptible to the attractions of urban consumer society and, in turn, to political quiescence.

The enormous rate of industrial expansion in Poland drained off those elements most likely to have formed an articulate and militant working-class elite (35 per cent of the Polish national income compared with 14 per cent of the Czechoslovak national income was ploughed back in investment). Here again we see the process of elimination.

There were of course valid reasons for the interest in consumer goods. The well-being of the Polish working class, relative to that of the Czechoslovaks, was insecure and remained to be consolidated (in the typical Polish working-class apartment one will invariably smell fresh varnish; but rarely in Czechoslovakia, where the working class reached the same level much earlier). The national *per capita* income in Czechoslovakia rose by roughly 20 per cent in the period 1955–65, whereas in Poland it more than doubled.

The standard of living of the Polish working class was too low for them not be interested in obtaining consumer goods; yet at the same time the rate of improvement was sufficiently rapid and marked for temporary hardships not to result in social protest. This factor should be noted in an analysis of the following table, for it reminds us how misleading the simplified assumption can be that a lower standard of living at any given moment is most likely to give rise to dissatisfaction and revolt.

TABLE 2

	Poland 1965	Czechoslovakia 1964
Consumption, per capita		
Meat (Kg)	49	59
Fat (Kg)	15	20
Bread	141	123
Potatoes (Kg)	215	119
Density of Accommodation		
Persons per room (1961)	1·7	1·3
Cinema-Viewers, per 1,000 persons	550	904
Indicators of Educational Expenditure		
Pupil/teacher ratio in secondary schools	22	15·5
Student/teacher ratio in colleges	11	8

(Note: figures relating directly to the situations of the two working classes are not available. It is very likely, however, that the differences on the working-class level are even more pronounced, as the differentiation of living standards and incomes is much less sharp in Czechoslovakia than in Poland.)

The position of the working class confronts the present or prospective Polish leadership with certain practical dilemmas. The actual weight of the working class in Polish politics bears no proportion to its scant ability to voice its own interests in an articulated form. The sensitivity of the Polish leadership towards the (normally overestimated) potential of working-class discontent stems not only from its ideological tradition, but also from the strategic position of the working class. As the most numerous and rapidly expanding class, the only one capable of paralysing the most vulnerable areas of the socio-economic system, it is the only group which could enforce its will on the system. The socialist revolution of 1945 was made in the name of an almost non-existent working class. Paradoxically, this revolution has now produced a social class which can challenge the claims made in its own name.

Until 1968 this class seemed however to be vitally, though perhaps temporarily, interested in tight governmental control and in impeding all managerial efforts to relax centralised administrative power.

Contrary to a widespread but totally misleading assumption that technological developments lead inevitably to articulated pressures towards a multi-party brand of political democracy, and that business leaders are by definition in the vanguard of this movement, a managerial stratum brought into being by and within the context of a centralised administration is as un-interested in political democracy as can be imagined. The managerial demands of administrative decentralisation are frequently but unjustifiably taken as demands for democracy. What is really at stake from the managers' point of view, how-ever, is a limited and purely economic reform, with as few as possible political implications. Economic reform is seen as giving them security and stability over and above their existing privileges, and as transforming them from a *privileged class* into a *class of privileged*, unremovable individuals safely entrenched in their enjoyable positions which safeguard continuity of their preferential access to goods. Mr Husak in his speech in the May 1969 plenary session of the Czech Central Committee brilliantly formulated the managers' viewpoint on an ideal political regime, when he promised on the one hand that 'there will be no return to old bureaucratic administrative methods of managing our economy', and on the other that a main aim of economic policy must be 'the restoration and the strengthening of the authority of the leadership at all levels of management from the federal and national bodies to the management of enterprises'. It is the managerial world view alone which en-sures that the two statements do not sound contradictory.

This kind of managerial limited reform leaves the working class, while remaining weak and helpless itself, confronted by a powerful adversary, whose strength rests on a purely economic basis. The only defensive weapon that labour could possibly possess would be, on the contrary, of a political nature. So long as it remains deprived of its own organs of power it must, within the present socio-political context, depend on the centralised power of the state to blunt the effects of a free competitive interplay of economic forces. The state in turn strengthens the 'economically irrational' elements within the system in an attempt to counter the possibility of a workers' revolt. It has been discovered by researchers that at Cegielski Works, fairly typical for the largest economic enterprises in Poland, 20 per cent of the staff on the pay roll lead a fictitious work existence. These people, who continue to receive their basic wage every week, would be unemployed as soon as a managerial-type reform took place, but would have no spokesman to voice their grievances and represent their interests. That is why they need either a stronger, centralised, political state dominating the management of the economy, or its total and thorough democratisation. Half measures are the worst solution from their point of view. This helps to understand the failure of 'workers' self-management' in the form given to it after the Polish October. Workers did not support the idea of working councils acting as a link in a chain of decentralising, managerial efforts to strengthen the managerial position, and not part of a thorough democratising process. In general – in the framework of the present political regime the unorganised and amorphous workers in Poland are more likely to support the state than the managers in the event of an open clash. Anyway, they apply to the central (mainly party) organs to voice their grievances against managers, not the other say round.

Thus we arrive at the *third* dilemma of the Polish political scene. It can best be expressed in terms of a choice between three alternative types of political models, represented in a schematic and rather crude and oversimplified way below:

MODEL 2

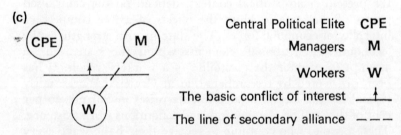

(a) *The present model* i.e. a centralised state satisfying the demands of some preferentially treated groups but at the same time giving the necessary minimum satisfaction to the demands

of the underprivileged. This is the least efficient system, although in the absence of a radical and democratic alternative
(and only then), that which is most acceptable to the working
class. By suppressing the free expression of contradictory
interests the system is vulnerable to sudden explosions of
tension, such as the Poznan riots, and thus seeks to control this
by initiating deliberately directed and traditional witch-hunts.

(b) *The model of limited and purely economic decentralisation.* This
would inevitably consist in an abandonment by the state of its
monopolistic control over the means of production to the
managerial class, which would assume the role of 'private
collective owners of the means of production'. The second but
most important aspect of this model is the maintenance of the
monopolistic political power of the state. The managerial class,
while freed from control from above, will nonetheless need to
depend on, and will therefore support the police powers of the
state in order to overcome dissent caused by the inequality of
distribution and lack of control over production.

The economic achievements of this model are likely in purely
input-output ratio to be better than those of the first model.
But even a qualitative change in the economic sphere alone is
hardly likely, as the basic reasons for inefficiency and waste-
fulness lie in the political and not the economic spheres. What
is most wasteful is the absence of channels of political communication and the consequent frustration of class interests
producing tensions which have to be channelled at considerable
cost. It is precisely this factor which is the least likely to be
eliminated in this model. The only saving of the system is
likely to be a reduction in friction between managers and
politicians.

(c) *The process of a radical socialist democratisation accompanied by
decentralisation.* This model does not postulate the 'separation of
economic and political powers', and in this sense it is not simply
an extension of the second model. It is, rather, the alternative
way out of the vicious circle of the first model. Preserving the
basic unity and indivisibility of the citizens' sovereignty, it puts
both the political and the economic aspects of political power
under the direct control and management of representative
institutions. The Yugoslav system appears (especially after
the March 1969 Party Congress) to be approaching this model.
This is the only model likely to gather more or less resolute

support from all classes and interest groups – although in the transitional period the workers are liable to suffer from un-limited managerial power.

Even in purely economic terms this third model has every chance to prove its superiority over the other two. In broader terms, it seems a system capable of containing the hitherto apparently incompatible principles of socialism and of political efficiency. What is worth noting particularly is that this third model, which apparently differs from the second model by the addition of one single factor, assumes in fact a completely different class character.

ILLUSORY AND ACTUAL CONFLICTS

The analysis of socialist and political developments in Eastern Europe in terms of the alleged conflict of interests between 'party bureaucracy, and 'managers' (treated usually not as institutionalised organisations, but as two distinct class-like interest groups) has become a time-honoured though rarely examined process. The traditional Western and 'Spencerian' distaste for political intervention in the business world has greatly contributed to this kind of mistaken analysis. If there are businessmen (and managers coupled with engineers are allegedly the businessmen of the East), they must treat their own role as basically non-political and therefore hold pro-fessional politicians in constant and deep disregard. If the analogy of Western capitalist experience proves anything, it proves how difficult it is to rid oneself of culturally determined prejudices.

It is extremely difficult to maintain that party bureaucrats (i.e. 'politicans') and managers (i.e. 'businessmen') are, in the framework of the Polish socio-political system (and that of most countries of Eastern Europe) really separated into two classes with different and conflicting interests. On the contrary, many intrinsic attributes of their respective social positions and roles testify to their basic sociological unity. Let us examine some of them.

(a) Both groups live in some way on the 'surplus value' produced by the working class, and so their relatively privileged situation depends on the subordination of the latter. As has been seen, this is largely achieved by political means. The 'professional politicians' are thus not so much rivals as the necessary allies of the managers. This identity of interests, decisive in the long run, does not exclude the institutionalised struggle for authority. But it insures that it is kept within secure and relatively restricted limits.

(b) What is more important, the very dividing line between 'politics' and 'economy' in the Eastern socialist system is very much less clear than it was once in the West. The dividing lines became blurred to the point where singling out any slightly satisfying definition of the difference between the two becomes a hopeless task. Were it not for the fact that the two bodies preserve their traditional labels we would be deprived of the ability to talk of them at all. When the economy is one of the many aspects of the state, and when political activity consists first of all in managing the economic processes of production, distribution and circulation, the distinction (comprehensible in another framework), becomes very vague indeed. It remains to be proved how and whether a more or less permanent clash of interests could possibly be built on such a fragile and brittle foundation.

(c) In view of the foregoing considerations we need not be astonished at the far-reaching institutional and personal union of these two theoretically separate bodies. Many a body, formally constituting an integral part of, say, the 'party apparatus', owes its existence exclusively to participation in industrial, or transport, or distribution management; but on the other hand, the apparently expert and 'non-political' bodies of professional managers take the most 'political' of all decisions taken in the state. The overlapping of personnel is even more striking: the same group of people on all possible levels of state administration can meet, with only minor adjustments, first in the capacity of a party body, then in the capacity of, say, an industrial board. There is plenty of difference from the legal point of view; from the sociological perspective the difference between the two situations is practically nil.

(d) The above implies a large rate of horizontal mobility between the two apparently distinct bureaucratic hierarchies. There are alternating periods in which the predominant trend is from one hierarchy to another; 'experienced party workers' are commissioned 'to strengthen' the economic mechanism, or else skilled 'managers' are 'mobilised' to bring the party into closer touch with industry, transport, agriculture etc. Even if the large-scale trends such as these are not apparent, individual mobility is always present. It would be difficult to find a top-level party or non-party activist (excluding possibly the older generation) whose career does not include both activities, and in these conditions it is extremely difficult for two distinct and antipathetic standpoints to develop.

Consequently, both the 'object' opposition of function and role which is a necessary condition of any conflict of interests, and the relative psycho-cultural isolation which constitutes the prerequisite of any conflict of ideologies are lacking in the case of 'party functionaries' as a whole juxtaposed to 'managers' as a whole. This does not mean, however, that within the privileged and influential sectors of East European society there are no important cleavages capable of producing both ideological and interest conflicts. They do exist, but cut across any conceivable 'party/managers' division.

The division which provides the most useful insight into conflicts within East European society is that between the 'specialists' and the 'non-specialists' (I have chosen these somewhat ambiguous and elusive terms for lack of any more suitable ones. And the threat of misunderstanding is genuine as in our usage, the term 'non-specialist', contrary to semantic intuition, is intended to be free of any evaluative overtones. Our 'non-specialist' is not necessarily a 'bad specialist', he simply owes his status to other factors than those measurable by purely 'specialistic' criteria.) To avoid misunderstanding let us define the concepts as applied in the present context.

Each functionally specified organisation has its own criteria of 'fitness', which, though not always applied in actual personnel policy, are determined by behavioural and personality prerequisites of given organisational roles and collective organisational goals. 'Specialists' are taken to be those who fulfil these requirements, 'non-specialists' we take to be those who do not. The latter owe their organisational position to some criteria which are alien to the functional prerequisites of the organisation itself. Their basic search for security cannot be satisfied by conformity with the principles of the organization in which they are employed unless they succeed in imposing criteria which they are certain of meeting – which is in fact what they try to do.

Now, in a post-revolutionary party whose role consists predominantly in economic management, there is not only a strong demand for specialists, but those who are needed are precisely those who have the same kind of skills as required in 'specialised' economic organisation. Seen within a systemic frame of reference this assumes some significance.

The Polish state, like most of those in Eastern Europe, is a totalitarian state and like all totalitarian states it cannot tolerate a situation in which an important proportion of influential people base their strength and influence on something other than the will of the state itself, especially if this 'something' cannot be easily manipulated. Thus the deepest functional contradiction of this state is that as the executive board of a giant economic enterprise, it creates conditions which as a totalitarian state it increasingly attempts to eradicate. By playing freely with the 'political criteria' of promotion, the state must make the self-confident 'specialist' constantly aware that he cannot rely on his skill alone.

Only the 'non-specialists' appear flawless when measured by the second set of criteria. They do not need to be reminded that obedience – 'loyalty' – is their cardinal virtue. This is why all brands of state administration – both 'economic' and 'political' – need 'non-specialist' no less than 'specialist' personnel, and preferably a not too excessively stable mixture of the two.

But behind the two abstract functional demands emerge two real social groups with ostensibly conflicting interests. The conflict can be seen where a caucus of local 'non-specialists' unites to counteract the undesirable influx of 'specialists' following the formulation of regional development plans; or when a long period of relatively 'peaceful' and 'normal' development leads to the temporary ascendancy of impersonal and ideologically indifferent 'specialists'; and the frightened state leaders do their utmost to justify a new ideological witchhunt; in this they can always be certain of the support of the 'non-specialists'. The functional contradiction between 'loyalty' and 'skill' finds its correlate in the notorious ambivalence and hesitancy of the official decalogue and the otherwise inexplicable alterations of the political history. The come-back of the 'non-specialist' constituted the essence of the Polish *coup d'état* of March 1968.

The conflict between the 'non-specialists' and the 'specialists', is played out simultaneously on the level of group behaviour, organisational building principles and bureaucratic rationales. It is not the conflict between 'politics' and economics; it is about how these two increasingly indistinguishable functions are to be carried out. Neither is it a conflict between party and government, although in duumvirate periods this may be exploited for tactical reasons.

One way or another, therefore, the 'non-specialists' – 'specialists' dilemma seems to provide a *fourth* conflictual dimension of political choice in Poland. The possible blends of the two categories does provide for a relative freedom of manoeuvre. But so long as the totalitarian character of the state persists, they constitute an inseparable feature of socio-political reality with which each faction of the political elite has to deal and can count on.

SOME REMARKS ON THE ANALYTICAL MODEL

We have enumerated above four basic social conflicts underlying the Polish (and perhaps not only the Polish) political scene. Apart from the question of whether this number could be increased (which it undoubtedly could) there is a methodological question to be solved; precisely what is the possible use of our knowledge about social conflicts if we are interested predominantly in analysing, understanding, and predicting the course of political struggle, defined as a confrontation between organised or loose groups of competing candidates for political power? In other words, what is the exact place of social conflict in the analytical model whose first aim is to 'decipher the code' of political events?

The single model consciously or unconsciously applied in most analyses which examine the political scene from a sociological perspective is a rather simple one, still haunted by the ghost of *homo economicus*. It is based mainly on Western experience and is roughly as shown in MODEL 3.

The applicability of the above model to the Western multi-party/parliamentary political scene remains to be proved, although this does not concern us here. Its shortcomings are revealed immediately, however, when it is imposed on an East European political system. What the model tacitly assumes is a measure of correspondence (indirectly endorsed by the use

MODEL 3

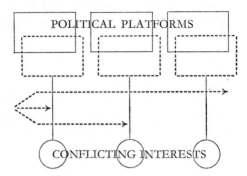

of the term 'distortion') between the content of political platforms and the content of group interests. But this is precisely
the assumption which makes the model unworkable and misleading. The real interdependence between the two poles of
the analytical axes is much subtler and more complicated. It
can be put, perhaps slightly too schematically in the following
way:

MODEL 4

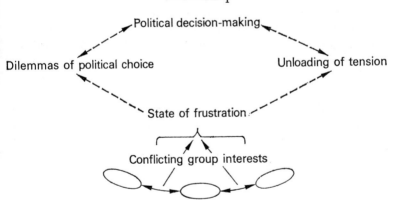

The main distinctive features of this alternative analytical
model are the following:

(a) It stresses not only the determined, but also the determining position of the focal point of political decisions. This is
always significant, and is of crucial importance in the context
of a centralised state. So far as the practical conclusions of this

are concerned, the model directs our attention towards the role played by 'subjective' factors as well as to the role of structural relationships within the political centre in the process of choice.

(b) What is more important, however, is that this model focuses attention on the fact that whatever the nature of the political decision-making centre, it acts within a double frame of reference: that of the 'objective' dimensions of manoeuvre, and that of the functional requirement of unloading accumulated frustration. Both originate from the same source, both are in their specific ways determined by the pattern of interest conflicts (although the first may in some circumstances be shaped also by other factors allocated outside the system under analysis), but each later develops an impressive measure of relative autonomy and produces its own logic. Because they are autonomous, they do not necessarily push in the same direction, and what seems to be perfectly rational when projected into the first frame of reference may appear inexplicable within the second. This is what makes prediction so difficult and unrewarding whenever the system under discussion is analysed. It is also the one factor which deters any thoughtful scholar from trying to trace political decisions to their social-conflictual roots. The real subject of political decisions is not so much representative of differentiated group interests as the 'unloading of tension' by one of the solutions possible in the existing dilemma.

Having accepted the alternative model, the present author has restricted himself to outlining the basic political dilemmas within which any kind of ruling group has to act in contemporary Polish society. It is not much, but it seems that there is little more the sociologist of politics is entitled to attempt. The remainder is for political struggle to decide.

Hugh Seton-Watson

On totalitarianism[*][†]

SERIOUS STUDY BY SOCIAL SCIENTISTS OF TOTALI-
tarianism has been surprisingly small: the field has been too
much left to the cliché-mongers of popular jounalism and professional politics. The work of Friedrich and Brzezinski, first
published in 1956, is one of the best available, and has justly
been praised by critics and recommended to students. This new
edition has been brought up to date by Friedrich alone, and
includes some references to recent developments in the Soviet
Union, China and Eastern Europe, and to recent secondary
literature. This is an opportunity to recommend it to readers of
this journal, and at the same time to raise some of the problems
involved in the analysis of totalitarian regimes.

The book is divided into seven parts, which examine in turn
the 'general characteristics of totalitarian dictatorship'; the
dictator and party; the ideology; propaganda and terror; the
economy; the 'islands of separateness' which partly escape the
pressures of the regime; and the effects of totalitarianism on
international policy. All the descriptive sections are well designed, and contain useful and relevant information soberly and
intelligently discussed. Especially good is the sector on the economy, in which the authors discuss with admirable realism the
controls exercised by Hitler over the German economy, noting
the differences between these and the Soviet 'socialist' system
but disposing of the silly clichés, still recited as a ritual incanta-
tion by so many of the self-styled 'Left' in the West, that Hitler
left capitalism essentially untouched. Incidentally, it is a pity
that an ingenious phrase proposed by the authors has not

* Vol. 2, No. 1, October 1966–January 1967.
† A review: Carl J. Friedrich and Zbigniew K. Brzezinski, *Totalitarian Dictatorship and Autocracy*, 2nd edition, revised by Carl J. Friedrich, Harvard University Press, 1965.

received wider use: they suggest (p. 239) that in the Third
Reich the economy was removed from the 'credit system'
characteristic of capitalism, and placed under the 'timet system'
based on intimidation of the whole business class by the Nazi
party leaders.

Less satisfactory, however, are the authors' attempts to
identify the essential features which separate totalitarian from
other forms of government. The six points, stated on p. 22 as a
summary of these essential features, are perhaps the part of the
book which has become most widely known and accepted in
the ten years since the first edition appeared: they are also, in
this reviewer's opinion, the weakest part of the book. Briefly,
the six points are ideology, mass party with a single leader,
police terror, control of mass communications, control of all
military weapons and central control and direction of the
economy. The conditions are formulated in a more exact and
sophisticated manner than this, and the reader is urged to read
them for himself. But the subtler points can be covered more
usefully in discussion than by reproducing a whole page of the
book in this review.

In my opinion, all these six points are *inescapable* features of a
totalitarian regime, but only two of them are *essential* features,
in the sense that they are not found in non-totalitarian regimes.
Moreover, there are other essential features which are not included in the six points. The whole task of presenting the essence
of totalitariansim needs to be thought out more carefully.

Police terror is not confined to totalitarian regimes. Many
governments of the past used this intrument. The phrase
'police state' was used in the 19th century. Modern democratic
governments possess 'secret' security police organisations. Even
the allocation to the security police of a territorial empire within
the bounds of the state – one of the best-known features of
Stalin's regime – is not specific to the totalitarian state: it was
to be found in the Russia of Ivan IV, in the form of the *oprichnina*.
This is not to say that police terror does not have some new
features in totalitarian states. In the authors' words, it is
'characteristically directed not only against demonstrable
"enemies" of the regime, but against more or less arbitrarily
selected classes of the population', and it 'systematically exploits
modern science, and more especially scientific psychology'. But
these new features derive not from the fact of a system of police

terror, but from two other factors – the development of modern science, and the views of the totalitarian rulers as to who constitute enemies. The police is a tool, and its use depends on the will of the ruler and on the means available. The same applies to the control or, in the authors' words, the 'technologically conditioned near-complete monopoly of the effective use' of armed force. Most governments of the last centuries have controlled armed force within their boundaries. In Western Europe this was one of the consequences of the replacement of the feudal political order by centralised monarchy and in many other parts of the world it dated from even earlier. Admittedly, the nature of modern weapons is different. Only a vast bureaucratic military machine can cope with a nuclear armoury. But this again is a result of modern science, and applies to non-totalitarian states as well. The same can be said of control of publications. This has been practised by states for centuries past. In earlier ages the means of communication were cruder, and affected fewer of the citizens, but despotic governments kept them firmly under control. The variety and quantity of modern mass media, and their impact on the population, are a result of science. Not all governments which control them are totalitarian: some are old-style dictatorships, and in times of crisis even democratic governments go very far in their control. To draw a distinction between such control and the 'near-complete monopoly' which the authors ascribe to totalitarian regimes would be very difficult. Here once more the essential factor is the will of the ruler, the will to control *all* media for some supposed higher purpose, rather than merely to suppress critical opinions. Finally, the direction of the economy is not specific to totalitarian regimes. It is true that few governments of the past did much in this direction: the reason was that, no doubt with some exceptions, neither the need nor the means were present. Modern economic and scientific development have made effective economic control possible, and modern social needs have created a demand for it. These facts have affected the governments of all economically developed societies, totalitarian or not. In the second world war the 'central control and direction of the entire economy' was not appreciably, if indeed at all, less in Churchill's Britain than in Hitler's Third Reich.

This leaves two of the authors' six points – ideology and the party. These are indeed specific to totalitarian regimes. The

official secular state ideology has no parallel in pre-modern
states, or in non-totalitarian modern states, whether democratic or traditionally dictatorial. The state party is different in
kind from political parties as they have been known in history.
At first sight the parallel with religions and churches is intellectually attractive, but it is only partly valid. The great religions
are oriented to another life. The final settlement of accounts
will not take place in this world. The final judge is not an earthly
ruler but Almighty God. Morality is based on absolute com-
mandments, independent of earthly rulers and derived from
divine revelation. Churches are concerned with spiritual things,
not with secular government. Admittedly there is a vast overlapping zone between the two. 'Render unto Caesar the things
that are Caesar's' has been difficult to interpret. Popes have
sought to dictate to emperors. But in no stable Christian state
has the church sought to direct and control from above the
whole apparatus of government. Exceptions to this statement
can almost all be regarded as short-lived revolutionary inter-
ludes. In Moslem states there was less clear division between the
secular and the religious, yet the function of the *ulema* and the
function of the ruler and his administration were different. Nor
did the Buddhist priesthood set itself up as a political super-elite
to control and direct government. This is what the totalitarian
party has done.

If the accounts are to be settled in another life, or if the soul
must be reborn until the extinction of its Karma, the power
the earthly ruler is limited. Of course there were earthly rulers
in past centuries who made enormous material and spiritual
claims on their subjects. The argument that Ivan IV and Philip
II would have become totalitarian rulers if only they had had
modern mass media and means of coercion at their disposal, is
plausible but not convincing. Both men accepted moral standards that were beyond their control, though in their lives they
may have violated these standards. The totalitarians reject not
only the other life but all absolute morality. Hitler declared,
Recht ist, was dem Volke nutzt, and then proceeded to express in
his person the interests of the *Volk*. After having Röhm shot, he
declared that for twenty-four hours German law had been
incarnated in himself. In Soviet doctrine, all morality derives
from Marxist-Leninism, for which the quality of exact science
is claimed. However, the essence of this science is incarnated in

the Central Committee of the Communist Party, which by its insurrection in Petrograd in 1917 made the Great October Socialist Revolution, thus inaugurating the last stage in the social evolution of the human race. That the insurrection had this apocalyptic quality was asserted by its maker, Lenin, and his successors have repeated it. Admittedly most members of the Central Committee have been unmasked as saboteurs or agents of foreign powers (certainly no ruling group in history has had so high a proportion of alleged traitors), but the 'line' of this treason-riddled party has invariably been scientifically correct. The infallible wisdom of the party was in fact incarnated in its all-wise leader, Stalin, until his death. Stalin's position above morality and law was basically similar to Hitler's.

These two men at least willed total power over their subjects. Both had the consuming passion for unanimity. Every one must praise them, including their tortured opponents. *Arbeit macht frei*, the concentration camp inscription stated. Slogans of praise for Stalin's genius, and of gratitude for the happy Soviet life, adorned the Soviet camps from the Arctic to the Central Asian steppes. Both men denied all autonomy to private life. At work and at play, in bed or in the lavatory, always the subject must think of the benevolent wisdom of the Leader. Both designated 'objective categories' to be exterminated, or merely to be deported from their homes to forced labour in distant lands and alien climates: Jews, gipsies, kulaks, Chechens and others. All this was new. Religious persecution, mass vengeance and hideous cruelty are very old, but liquidation of objective categories is a 20th-century phenomenon. Rulers and demagogues had ranted in the past about their enemies as 'vermin' to be destroyed. But Hitler and Stalin, two half-educated men without class or profession, learned their trade as rabble-rousers in the multi-racial hate-ridden cities of Vienna and Baku, and when their time came they signed the orders for the extermination of Jews or Russian peasants or Polish officers, and the orders were carried out by other faceless classless men at Auschwitz and Katyn and other establishments. This was new.

Most of these things are mentioned in this book and some are admirably discussed. But the priorities, it seems to me, have gone wrong. The basic problem is the will to total power. How this arose, little attempt has yet been made to discover. Our university history departments are full of learned specialists

busily training Ph.D. students to train other Ph.D. students to
turn out dissertations in more and more words about less and
less, couched in ever more learned gobbledygook. The expansion
of British universities, and the wisdom of Lords Robbins and
Franks, will no doubt notably accelerate the rate of growth.
But the study of the rise of totalitarian man, the product of
many decades of social, political, cultural and moral change in
various but mutually influenced societies and polities, is something from which the Ph.D. merchants prudently shy away.

It would be unreasonable to expect Mr Friedrich and Mr
Brzezinski to provide us with a history of social change and
morality. But the absence of a systematic discussion, in their
book of the moral dimension in totalitarianism is striking, and
is, I think, significant of the state of the social sciences in the
West.

Perhaps we can make another shot at summarising the essence
of totalitarianism, not as an alternative to the authors' inadequate six points, but as a point of departure, not for further
'research' (*parole fatale* which has done so much to wreck the
humanities ever since their spokesmen eagerly took it over from
the natural scientists), but for hard thinking and careful writing.
Perhaps there are three specific conditions: the concentration
of political, economic and spiritual power in the same hands;
the denial of any moral or spiritual authority independent of
the will of the ruler; and the denial of any autonomy to private
and personal life. To these must be added one non-specific
essential condition: the availability of the most modern means
of publicity, communication and coercion.

These conditions applied to the conscious policies of Stalin
and Hitler, and probably apply to that of Mao. During the last
years of Stalin's life they also applied, to a slightly lesser extent,
to those of the East European rulers, imposed by Soviet occupation. All did their best to impose on all their subjects a regime
based on these conditions. How far they succeeded is, however,
another question. It is clear from available evidence that the
family preserved its autonomy in the greater part of the Soviet
Union, though at the height of the 1937–9 purge in the great
cities reality came pretty close to an ideal picture of atomisation
of all social life by totalitarian power. In Germany the 'islands'
were better preserved. They included not only the family (which
was much less touched than in Russia), but also to some extent

the churches, the army and even bits of the legal and civil service apparatus. Only in the weeks following the unsuccessful revolt of July 1944 did the terror make effective inroads into them. Incidentally, the discussion of these 'islands' is among the best things in the Friedrich and Brzezinski book.

Any thoughtful reader of this book today will ask himself whether it refers only to a past epoch. This is a real question, but it should be considered without wishful thinking. In China, about which neither the authors nor this reviewer claim expertise, it still looks at first sight as if totalitarianism survives, in almost classical form, and this may also be true of the regimes in North Korea and North Vietnam. One would guess that, as under Stalin and Hitler, it is effective at the government level but only partly effective in the real life of the citizen. In the Soviet Union much has changed since Stalin and even since Khrushchev. There is no single Leader, the territorial police state within the state has been abolished, the powers of the police are sparingly used, and there is far more freedom of opinion, orally and in writing, outside the limits of politics in the normal sense. Thus the regime is beginning to look more like a traditional dictatorship. Nevertheless the ideology and the party, the legitimising myths and the rejection of any independent basis of morality, remain. The Soviet regime is still nearer to the totalitarian than to the traditional dictatorial model, and the machinery could quickly be set in motion if a decision were taken to 'retotalitarise'. Broadly the same is true of most East European communist regimes, though in all there has been a remarkable change of climate, far exceeding changes in Russia.

By contrast, Poland and Yugoslavia cannot be called totalitarian. The Polish communist leaders would like to have a totalitarian regime, but they have not even succeeded in creating the institutional framework. The spritual power is not united with the political as long as the Catholic Church remains a visibly strong and militant factor: the vast crowds at the recent celebrations of Poland's millennium proved this beyond doubt. The economic power is not united with the political as long as the peasants remain uncollectivised. In Yugoslavia the churches are not so strong as Polish Catholicism, but they have at least some freedom. The peasants are uncollectivised. But perhaps the most striking thing about Yugoslavia is the non-totalitarian

spirit that is to be found, side by side with undoubtedly totalitarian elements, within the political machine itself. This was
shown by the independent attitude of the judiciary in the
Mihajlov case, something unthinkable in any other communist-
ruled country.

Spain and Portugal, for all their flirtations with fascism in
the days of Hitler's ascendancy, cannot be regarded as totalitarian. They are traditional dictatorships, based on an alliance
of army, church and capitalists (but with dissident elements
within each of the three component groups). Nor can South
Africa be so regarded as long as the judiciary is independent
and the press has considerable freedom. Nevertheless there
appear to be trends towards the appearance of an official
White South African secular ideology which could become the
basis of a totalitarian regime in the future. Totalitarian trends
were also visible in Ghana under Nkrumah, and may already
prevail in Guinea under Sékou Touré. These two countries'
experience deserves study from the point of view of the possibility of imposing a totalitarian regime, through skilful use of
modern mass media, on an extremely unsophisticated people.
Egypt appears rather dictatorial than totalitarian. It must however be noted that there is a real danger that its combination of
dictatorial power, personality cult, nationalist hysteria and
imperialist ambitions (directed towards Arabia and tropical
Africa) may end up as totalitarianism.

The complete totalitarian hell has not yet been built on earth,
and if free men keep their wits and their courage never shall.
But the totalitarian model is worth study by political scientists,
because it refers to a type of government distinct both from
modern mass democracies and from old-style oligarchies of
either the liberal or the dictatorial brand. Governments approxi-
mating to this type have existed and still exist. Though much
has still to be learned about it, we must be grateful to Mr
Friedrich and Mr Brzezinski for the light which they have shed.

Carl J. Friedrich

In Defence of a Concept*†

IN THIS REVIEW I SHALL CONCENTRATE ON THE
issue of totalitarianism, because Ionescu seems to be troubled
by it. I am rather bewildered by the author's position on this
central issue. For on the one hand he ranges himself with those
who would apply the term 'totalitarian' only to the Stalin and
Hitler regimes which actually are rather extreme (and early)
forms. On the other hand, his entire treatment is cast in terms
which correspond to a realistic and functional concept such as
I myself favour. Ionescu tells us that 'it is impossible to call
contemporary Spain or Yugoslavia "totalitarian" *in the same
way* as Nazi Germany and Stalinist Russia' (p. 13 – emphasis
added). Who could possibly disagree with that proposition, or
who has ever done such a thing? He goes on to ask: 'Can one
say that the UAR, Pakistan, and Paraguay are "totalitarian"
like Albania, or East Germany, or China?' I should answer:
certainly not. Ionescu would lump them all together under the
heading of one-party regimes – a procedure which has just
recently been trenchantly analysed and criticised by Giovanni
Sartori in his report on 'Typologies of Party Systems – A
Critique' to the IPSA Congress at Brussels. In this he showed
that clear distinctions are needed between totalitarian and
authoritarian, between hegemonic and predominant one-party
orders or systems. There may yet be advantages to such lumping
together, as well as to distinguishing between different kinds of
one-party arrangements. For an understanding of totalitarianism surely the latter is more important. Be that as it may, I do
not see how one can hope to answer the questions just cited

---

* Vol. 3, No. 2, Spring 1968.

† A review: Ghiţa Ionescu, *The Politics of the European Communist States*, Weiden-
feld & Nicolson, London, 1967.

without having a reasonably well-defined concept of totalitarianism and of totalitarian regimes. Why then shy away from the well-established and meaningful term 'totalitarian regime' – unless it were done for the purpose of assuaging the feelings of representatives of these regimes themselves. In such cases I have suggested that we call totalitarian regimes 'perfect democracies' – in contrast to our imperfect ones – provided we agree on the syndrome of interrelated traits which give these regimes their distinctive character. This Ionescu seems quite prepared to do; in fact he analyses these European regimes in precisely those terms. And if he prefers the word apparat-states, I see no particular objection from a scholarly viewpoint, though surely it makes it harder to communicate with non-political scientists on the subject in hand.

I welcome Ionescu's study as a major contribution to the developing theory and knowledge of totalitarianism. For this is an ongoing task, seeing that these regimes are going to be with us for some time. The concept is often objected to on 'ideological' grounds, sometimes by people who dislike its pejorative connotations, at other times by those who on account of an ideological commitment to one or another of the totalist ideologies are angered by anyone pointing out the similarities between all these regimes. Like all major concepts of political discourse, totalitarianism has, of course, an ideological dimension. But the ideological or propagandist employment of a key concept for purposes of political persuasion and propaganda need not prevent the political scientist from using it, provided he is aware of such employment. Except for those who worry about such ideological use, misuse or abuse, it is now fairly generally agreed that the kinds of autocratic regimes that have sprung up in this century in the wake of movements of violent protest against traditional political orders are different from past autocracies. The term 'totalitarian dictatorship' has been so widely used for designating these regimes that it seems the better part of wisdom to continue its employment, if one wishes to communicate effectively about these regimes. Such a statement does not, of course, settle the question of what are the distinguishing features of such autocratic regimes. What seems to set them apart from other and older autocracies are six outstanding characteristics: (1) a totalist ideology, (2) a single party committed to this ideology and typically led by one man, the dic-

tator, (3) a highly developed secret police; and three kinds of
monopolistic control, namely (a) mass communications, (b)
operational weapons and (c) all organisations, including economic enterprises, thus involving a centrally planned economy.
This way of restating my earlier position (*Totalitarian Dictatorship and Autocracy*, with Z. Brzezinski, 1956, rev. ed. 1965) makes
allowances for some of the evolving theory and practice of
totalitarian dictatorship. For totalitarian regimes *are* evolving
(as is parliamentary democracy) and therefore call for reassess-
ment. Indeed, one might, if greater simplicity is desired, group
these six features into three: a totalist ideology, a party reinforced by a secret police, and monopoly control of the three
major forms of interpersonal confrontation in an industrial
mass society.[1]

Now it is to be noted that all these features are important
elements in the analysis of the apparat-state by the present
author. Ideology is discussed several times and with care, and
its vital importance in legitimising the communist regimes he
discusses, recognised. There are sage comments on the changing
content of communist ideology, but the content is not decisive
for determining its function, as long as it is realised that the
ideology is 'totalist', and that not *any* belief system, but only an
action-oriented programme constitutes an 'ideology' in its
specific functional sense. Ionescu does not speak of it as 'totalist',
but this term seems to me preferable to 'totalitarian'. What is
significant, however, is Ionescu's opinion that ideology is growing weaker, because 'revolutionary fervour is being replaced by
respect for efficiency and good administration'. He speaks in
this connection of a link of allegiance which he believes to be
growing weaker, as is also the legitimacy based upon it. It seems
to me that the facts suggest precisely the opposite: the growing
general consensus in all these regimes is replacing the revolutionary fervour (always only shared by a minority), the totalist
ideology is being ritualised or, as Max Weber would say,

---

[1] In addition, the great expansion of bureaucracy, indeed the 'total bureaucratisation' implicit also in the expression 'apparat states', should be mentioned
here. I made it an integral part of the discussion of totalitarian dictatorship (cf.
ch. 17). This aspect has recently been emphasised by e. g. Alfred G. Meyer, *The
Soviet Political System*, who believes thus to minimise the totalitarian nature of these
regimes; in point of fact, he reconfirms it. Ionescu minimises this dimension by
speaking of 'state administration', though the *apparatchiks* are *prima facie* bureaucrats.

routinised (*veralltaeglicht*), and the legitimacy of these regimes traditionalised, rather than weakened.

Curiously, Ionescu recognises this himself later on, when he discusses the concern of the leadership with ideological indoctrination (pp. 172–3). Mobilisation of the minds he rightly describes as one of the 'most important elements' in their operation. But let me turn next to the role of the party. Its central position is of course fully acknowledged. Indeed, a very interesting discussion (pp. 70–4) concerns the juxtaposition and contrastation of the army-apparat state and the party-apparat state. After citing Stalin, our author asserts that 'the integral discipline, the *esprit de corps*, the self-dedication and the main function of the party as an institution come originally from the army, as an institution'. I doubt whether this way of putting it can be historically or theoretically justified; for the characteristics mentioned here are found in all kinds of fighting groups, including, e.g. the Jesuit order and the Calvinists. The latter probably have, historically speaking, a pretty good claim to having helped to shape communist as well as capitalist ethics. The key point to note is that these regimes are described as 'party states' (pp. 76 ff.) which as in the case of China and Yugoslavia may in fact be army-party states, when actual sanguinary fighting has played a decisive role in their establishment.

Ionescu also discusses very interestingly the theory of Wiatr and others who have coined the term 'hegemonic party' for a communist party which associates with itself other parties, in contrast to the 'mono-party system' in which there is no competition for power. But is there really any division of power? Ionescu rightly points out that the Polish Catholic group *Znak* constitutes 'the only case of genuine organized dissent in the whole of Communist Europe' (p. 250), and that e.g. the noncommunist parties in the DDR are nothing but 'anachronisms' – no real competitors for power. There is of course factionalism within the communist parties, as there was within the fascist parties. How could it be otherwise, the laws of politics being what they are?

In short, Ionescu fully recognises and indeed stresses the second feature of totalitarian regimes, the central role of a single party. What about the secret police? He prefers to speak of it as 'security police', but in fact very ably describes the operations of the secret police as a crucial part of the governmental system of these regimes. He also quite definitely acknowledges the role of the terror, as I have done. Recalling Lenin's (and of course Stalin's) recognition of the need for terror in revolutionary regimes, Ionescu rightly points out that the bloody terror of the initial phase gradually is replaced by the 'subtler terror of social pressure' and that its instruments are 'education and indoctrination' (pp. 82–3). He also fully appreciates the dual role of the terror: against the opposition and against the apparat itself. He at length discusses the complex and ever-changing relations between the party and the police (pp. 104–13). He skilfully analyses the 'malformations' of the police, and yet recognises that in times of crisis the party remains vulnerable to the police and its instrumentalities of terror. He shows that there is a sort of oscillation between the two: '. . . it is difficult to distinguish between them and to know, at times, which is in command of the other . . .' (p. 106). When the party is in the ascendancy as 'the main apparat', 'one of the first symptoms will be the subordination of the political police' (ibid.). The data which he adduces in support of these propositions, drawn from the several communist regimes, serve as a matter of fact as valuable confirmation of the relevancy of the third characteristic feature of these regimes.

But what about the three major control monopolies? We find in Ionescu's study relatively little discussion of the monopoly of mass communication media, neither press nor broadcasting figuring in the index. This is understandable enough, since the relative smallness of the communist stakes he is analysing makes it very difficult if not impossible to maintain an effective monopoly. Hence he rightly emphasises that there is a quite definite awareness of the outside world and its posture in these countries and Ionescu contrasts this with the Soviet Union, and China. I am not equally sure about Hitler Germany which he adds. The wide distribution of *Neue Zuercher Zeitung*, e.g. would argue against this notion. Linguistically, these communist states would, in spite of their smallness, be more secluded than Germany ever was, were it not for Radio Free Europe which has broadcast in the native tongue for many years now (it would have deserved a brief analysis in this connection). The DDR is of course in a particularly vulnerable position, as far as the communications monopoly is concerned, and some of its harshest features are probably explainable on this score. In any case, the limitations on the monopoly of communication are probably the most important factor weakening the totalitarian character of all these regimes.

Leaving aside the monopoly of operational (mass destruction) weapons on which Ionescu has little to say, though it is crucial for the maintenance of these regimes (with the Soviet tanks always lurking in the background, after the deomonstrations in the DDR and Hungary), we finally come to the organisation monopoly, and the related problem of pluralism. The author is greatly concerned with this problem and discusses it at length (pp. 88–95, 273–8 and elsewhere). He in fact makes this problem perhaps the central issue of his analysis under the heading of 'plural checks'. His emphasis on these plural checks is we suspect the reason for his hesitations about the term totalitarian. Yet, my own and others' analysis of totalitarian regimes has always taken these pluralisms into account. I discussed some of them under the heading of 'islands of separateness' from which a degree of dissent and even opposition has time and again sprung in all totalitarian regimes. What is worthy of comment is that Ionescu does not fail to note that 'any society is to a certain degree pluralistic, and therefore cannot be monolithic' (p. 88). This true observation constitutes part of the critique of totalitarianism, but the question is one of degree. And here we find that with laudable attention to both Eastern and Western writings in the field Ionescu retains – correctly, I believe – the characteristically totalitarian notion that *only those groups* which the main apparat of the party is willing to permit can operate in such a regime. Within that area of political assent, these groups do of course develop an *esprit de corps*, and as I have just said, a life of their own. Because of that fact, they may indeed influence and check the official party line, but they may also be censured and in fact destroyed. No one who has watched recent goings-on in the cultural field in a number of these regimes in connection with the differences over the official line *vis-à-vis* the Arab–Israel conflict can have any illusions on this score. And where is the Polish author or professor who would or could organise a society for improving relations with America or Germany, no matter how convinced he might be that this would greatly benefit his country? Or could it be seriously maintained that an enterprising businessman could organise, except clandestinely and as a black market operation, any production or distribution unit, even if he proposed to do it not for profit, but 'in the public interest'? In fact, Ionescu offers some very acute critical observations on some recent attempts to over-emphasise the pluralism (e.g. p. 93). His discussion of planning (esp. at pp. 52–65) gives further evidence that he is fully aware of the total organisational control which is part of the syndrome, a near monopoly of all effective organisation devoid of almost all independent individual or group initiative.

All in all, as this brief commentary on the author's discussion has shown, the communist regimes analysed by Ionescu exhibit the key features of totalitarian systems, some more so, some less. Such differences in degree are typical of other 'systems', such as monarchical absolutism, democracy of the imperfect Western variety, or constitutionalism in its various forms. Ionescu has enriched our knowledge of these possible varieties, he has presented in a scholarly and convincing way the social forces and historical traditions which account for some of these differences, and he has greatly indebted every student of comparative totalitarianism. He thereby has proved the validity and utility of the concept of totalitarianism for characterising the novel autocratic systems which the 20th century has produced. They have been built in response to a Utopian totalist challenge by utilising the instrumentalities which advanced industrialism places at the disposal of contemporary rulers. Ionescu's book is a major contribution to the literature of comparative politics.

Phyllis Auty

The Origins of National Communism in Yugoslavia*†

THE YUGOSLAV COMMUNIST PARTY WAS FOUNDED IN 1919 only a year after the creation of the Yugoslav state. Like the new Yugoslav government, it had immediately to face what came to be known as the national question – the problem of the rights of different nationalities in a multi-nation state. This was the problem that destroyed the royalist state and split the Communist Party in the inter-war years. It was one of the major difficulties that Josip Broz-Tito had to deal with when he became General Secretary of the Yugoslav Communist Party in 1937. During the second world war national differences were exploited by the Germans for their occupational purposes; Tito became leader of a national resistance movement which embraced all national groups and was able to forge a unity that had not been present before. Yet the problem still existed in the post-war state; the federal solution that was proposed during the war was incorporated into all post-war constitutions, but it did not solve all the issues of the national question in peacetime.[1] With the development of industrial and economic revolution during the 1950s and 1960s it became apparent that economic and social aspects of the national question were as obdurate and difficult of solution as political problems had been. Solutions in modern terms are still being tried out in our own

[1] The Federal principle was accepted at both the Bihac (1942) and Jajce (1943) Anti-Fascist Councils during the war, and all pronouncements were addressed equally to all peoples. A rough balance between delegates from various parts of the country was maintained and this remained the general principle in election of people to both state and party office in the post-war years. In party offices mathematical equality was not strictly maintained between the nationalities, and minorities were rarely represented.

* Vol. 4, No. 2, Spring 1969.
† A review: Paul Shoup, *Communism and the Yugoslav National Question*. New York and London, 1968.

times. In addition, the national question has always had international aspects. The fact that the Macedonian people live in parts of Bulgaria and Greece, as well as in Yugoslavia, has formed a major problem in itself – and one that still today is unsolved, as is also the problem of the large Albanian minority which affects both internal affairs and relations with Albania.

All this is the interesting and complex subject of Dr Shoup's important book *Communism and the Yugoslav National Question*. This is the first detailed and substantial work on this subject to be published in the English language; it is both outstanding and scholarly and can be recommended to general readers as well as specialists in the subject. It is based on the many multilingual sources which provide the complicated material for our knowledge of this recurring theme in 20th-century political life.

Dr Shoup shows how the national question dominated the history of the Yugoslav Communist Party from its beginnings. It was the cause of feuds amongst its leaders and of the factionalism that was so often denounced in communist literature in the 1920s; it was the reason why Yugoslav communists were so often rebuked by the Comintern. In the final analysis it was also one of the reasons for the independent development of Yugoslav communism.

The choice between centralist and federal government which faced the Yugoslav state in 1919 was affected by the different historical traditions and political legacies of the Serbs, Croats, Slovenes – and the Macedonians who were not at that time considered as a separate nationality. The Serbs were the only group who had in modern times had their own state, developed their own political institutions and had their own army. They had also developed their own aggressive, imperialist nationalism incarnated in the person of Pašić who dominated the political scene in the immediate post-1918 years. There was no tradition of federalism in Serbian history, and Pašić saw the Serbs as liberators of the other South Slavs. 'It has always been the ideal of Serbia to free them from the Austrian yoke', he once told Wickham Steed, editor of *The Times*, 'only Serbia is qualified to do so'.[2] King Alexander Karadjordjevic, whose dynasty was accepted by other nationalities because there was no other immediate alternative, was of the same opinion. The

[2] Quoted in P. D. Ostović, *The Truth about Yugoslavia*, New York, 1952, pp. 88–9.

unstable conditions of the times also seemed to demand strong government, and it was natural that the king should think in terms of a strong centralist solution. This was incorporated in the Vidovdan constitution forced through parliament on 28 June 1921, and Pašić and the king hoped that the national problem had been solved.

The position of the Yugoslav Communist Party at this time had its own difficulties. It had been created by the union of social democratic parties from Serbia and the different South Slav parts of the Austro-Hungarian monarchy, but all had divergent ideas about the new state. Yet it was the only party with support from all national groups, and this was the main reason why it received strong support in the parliamentary election in December 1920 and became the third largest party in the first Yugoslav parliament.[3] Yet its potential unity and Yugoslavism – and its strength as an opposition party – was vitiated by its ideological opposition to the whole concept of the new state which was denounced as a capitalist creation of the treaty powers. The Yugoslav Communist Party was banned on 29/30 December 1920, it did not vote on the Vidovdan constitution, and it became illegal on 30 July 1921. It remained illegal for the whole interwar period. The disorders and violence which were the pretext for the ban were no more than a pretext, the underlying reason was that the party was seen as the most dangerous opponent to the king's great Serb solution to the nationalist question.[4]

Conditions of illegality destroyed the Yugoslav communists' revolutionary hopes which had seemed so bright in 1920; they

[3] 432 delegates attended the unification congress held in Belgrade from 20–23 April 1919. They represented social democratic parties from Serbia, Bosnia-Herzegovina, and the Vojvodina as well as a number of socialist and communist or pro-communist organisations and trade unions. All had strong regional associations, but the major dividing factors were ideological, between those who supported the Second International and those against it. See *Pregled Istorije Saveza Kommunista Jugoslavije*, Belgrade, 1963, pp. 38, 39.

[4] The Communist Party received 198,463 votes and had 59 deputies representing all regions of the country; its share of the poll was 12·4 per cent compared with 19·9 per cent for the Democrats, and 17·7 per cent for the Radicals – both Serbian parties, and 14·3 per cent for Radić's Croat Republican Peasant Party (HRSS). It is notable that in two wholly peasant areas, the communists had exceptionally strong support – 38 per cent of votes in Montenegro and a high proportion of votes in the region that is today Macedonia, at that time called S. Serbia. This strong peasant support for the Communist Party was repeated in the first election after the second world war.

also brought divisions in the leadership about attitudes to methods of opposition, and made it easier for the party to come under the close control of the Comintern. The outstanding personality in the Yugoslav Communist Party at this time was Sima Marković, a Serb, who also believed in centralist government, and thought that the party should compromise with the king's government in order to regain legalisation and be able to operate an effective opposition. There were many people in the party who opposed him – especially among the non-Serb nationalities, and debate on both issues was carried on throughout the 1920s. Marković and his supporters were characterised as the right-wing, their opponents as the left.[5] Dr Shoup shows how the Comintern was able to use these rivalries as a disruptive force against Yugoslavia which resulted in party resolutions calling for the separation of Croatia, Slovenia and Macedonia from Yugoslavia and the creation of independent republics. Marković stubbornly maintained his position and eventually took part in a dramatic debate in 1925 with Stalin at the Fifth Plenum of the Comintern. Stalin argued that the national question was part of the general conflict with imperialists and said that self-determination was a right which might ultimately lead to a Soviet type of federalism. He emphasized that the existing borders of Yugoslavia could under no circumstances be taken as 'a starting point and legal basis for the solution of the national question'.[6]

This denationalising policy led the Comintern to call for local revolts in all parts of Yugoslavia in 1928 when it was mistakenly judged that conditions were ripe for revolution. They were easily crushed. Josip Broz was one of the communists who answered the call and was gaoled for his efforts. The Yugoslav Communist Party was virtually broken as a result more of Comintern policy than of factionalism over the national question. Up to 1928 the Yugoslav Communist Party had been dominated by Marković and his Serbian supporters. With his defeat, and following the 1928 *débâcle*, the centre of party activity moved to Croatia. Croats became more important and federal views prevailed.

[5] Sima Marković was born in Belgrade in 1888 and became a teacher of mathematics. He had a varied career in the Yugoslav Communist Party moving from being Comrade 1 to Comrade 10 and eventually disappearing in Russia in Stalin's purge. He wrote a book in defence of his views – neither centrist nor federalist as he said – whilst serving a prison sentence in 1923.   [6] Shoup, p. 29.

The Comintern attitude to the national question was changed when the Russian leaders adopted the Popular Front policy in 1934. After the Seventh Comintern Congress (July 1935) the slogan of self-determination for Yugoslav nationalities was dropped from party policy and the Yugoslav Communist Party was able to identify itself with Yugoslavia as a national concept. It is interesting, however, as Dr Shoup shows, that Yugoslav communists 'continued to present themselves as champions of national groups opposed to Belgrade'. This resulted in new quarrels within the party over the rights of nationalities, with Croats and Slovenes afraid that their rights might be submerged in the all-Yugoslav policy of the Popular Front.

This period coincided with the rise to prominence in the Yugoslav Communist Party of Josip Broz. After he came out of gaol in 1934 he was immediately co-opted to the Central Committee of the party and began work in Vienna.[7] He was secretary of the Yugoslav delegation at the Seventh Comintern Congress and became the right-hand man of the party's General Secretary, Milan Gorkić, in putting into effect the new policies in Yugoslavia. Sent to work in the field Tito found local sentiment strong in Croatia and Slovenia. 'What guarantee have we Slovene comrades that when the legal state has been achieved, the interests of the Slovene people will not be harmed?' was a Slovene woman member's comment quoted in a report sent by Gorkić to the Comintern.[8]

When Gorkić was summoned to Moscow and disappeared in Stalin's purge, Tito, after some lapse of time, was confirmed in his position as Gorkić's successor, so that it was he who had to deal with local nationalism and mould the party along Yugoslav lines in the years immediately before the second world war, at a time when, as Dr Shoup says, 'the features of a truly Yugoslav party began to emerge'. And of all the political parties in Yugoslavia at this time, he adds, only the Yugoslav Communist Party was truly interested in defending national rights and 'reaching a genuinely just solution to the national question'.[9] The *Sporazum* or agreement made in 1939 between

[7] He attended meetings of the Yugloslav Central Committee in Vienna on 10, 11, 13, 16 and 18 August under the name of Tito – the first written record of the use of this name by Josip Broz. P. Damjanović, *Tito na celu Partije*, Belgrade, 1968, p. 23.

[8] Institute za Radnički Pokret, Belgrade, Archives KI 1937/12.

[9] Shoup, pp. 41–7.

Maček, leader of the Croat Peasant Party and the royalist government, again caused trouble with Croat comrades (including probably Andrija Hebrang) who thought the agreement might be better for Croatian nationalism than the all-Yugoslav policy of the Communist Party.

At the same time, the Nazi-Soviet Pact (23 August 1939) also threw the party into confusion, and encouraged some communists to feel that national solutions might be better than accepting a general party line that could be reversed without warning by the Soviet leaders. Besides difficulties with Croats and Slovenes, Tito also had to struggle with local disaffection in Dalmatia, and a strong challenge to his position as leader from some Serbs and Montenegrins led by Petar Miletić. Opposition from these groups was eventually overcome, but it is clear that although arguments had been couched in ideological terms, the root of the differences lay in national disputes.[10]

In these years, Tito, who was a Croat, was building up a leadership to unify the party along Yugoslav lines; the colleagues he chose were to stay with him throughout the war and for several – in some cases many – years after. They included Kardelj a Slovene, Ranković, a Serb, Djilas, a Montenegrin, Bakarić and Lola Ribar who were Croats; Macedonia proved more difficult to incorporate into a united Yugoslav leadership. It was not at first represented in the inner circle of leaders, though it was later to provide strong Tito supporters.[11] In 1940, a Macedonian, Šarlo Šatarov, was elected to the Yugoslav Central Committee on orders from the Comintern – not brought from Paris by Tito as is stated by Dr Shoup. Šatarov was strongly pro-Bulgarian and after the German invasion of

[10] The challenge to Tito's authority by Petar Miletić is mentioned in general terms in most histories of the Communist Party and was referred to by Tito in his speech to the Tenth Conference of the League of Communists, see *Večernje Novosti*, 18 April 1967. Miletić was leader of a revolt against Tito's authority amongst communist prisoners in Sremska Mitrovica gaol. After his release he was aided by the Comintern to escape to Moscow where he intrigued with Bulgarian members of the Comintern against Tito but was defeated only after Tito had appealed to Dimitrov for aid. Miletić disappeared, assumed to have been arrested and liquidated, but there were rumours that he had been seen in Moscow in 1945, and that he may have been one of those working against Tito in Moscow during the Cominform break.

[11] Macedonia's development was greatly advanced by internal and foreign aid after the Skopje earthquake of 1963, and this led to greater satisfaction, and paradoxically to demands for increased national independence.

Yugoslavia tried to move the Macedonian communists into the Bulgarian party.

Dr Shoup points out that the defeat of royalist Yugoslavia by the Germans in 1941 'marked the first stage in the development of a truly national and independent Yugoslav Communist Party'. A result of the chaos following German occupation was that the party had to act largely on an *ad hoc* basis, and after the Nazi invasion of Russia on 22 June 1941, it was left virtually to its own devices though contact was maintained with the Comintern.[12] Tito's preparations for war, his flair for organisation and charismatic leadership resulted in the creation of an all-Yugoslav partisan movement, though he met some strong – and at first effective – national opposition in Macedonia, some uncontrolled independent action in Montenegro, and in Slovenia, though under his orders, the partisan movement always employed considerable autonomy. In Croatia, partisan activity was slow to start because of strong local feeling which at first was inclined to support or remain passive towards the independent puppet state of Pavelić's Croatia. Even some communists failed to respond to the party's general call to resistance so that for a time party action in Zagreb was paralysed. The Comintern had its own employee in Zagreb, Ivan Kopinić-Valdes, who was in charge of the secret radio station which Tito had to use for communication with Moscow. There was a brief period in the summer of 1941 when Valdes and some Zagreb dissidents, on separate orders from Moscow, tried to take over the resistance movement in Croatia from Tito – an incident that has never been properly elucidated and which Dr Shoup himself mentions only briefly. Tito was able to re-establish his own authority and the Comintern did not again interfere directly in his leadership during the war.

In Serbia, resistance was polarised between Mihailović and his Četniks who represented strong Serbian nationalism and loyalty to the great-Serb policy that had characterised the royalist government, and Tito's partisans with their appeal for all Yugoslav national resistance led by the communists. Tito

[12] The secret Comintern radio installed in a house in Zagreb in 1940 was used by Tito for sending his almost daily reports until January 1942 after which he had his own radio station in the field and maintained direct contact with Moscow until the arrival of the Soviet Military Mission in February 1944. After this his communications were channelled *via* the mission radio.

met Mihailović twice and made repeated efforts to persuade him to agree to joint resistance, though neither leader trusted the other. Mihailović refused for ideological reasons and because he was already in touch with the royalist government in exile. A British liaison officer Captain (later Major) Hudson had already joined him by the time of his second meeting with Tito (Brajići 27 October 1941), and Mihailović was expecting British help.

In the end fighting between Četniks and partisans developed into a civil war that was fought parallel with the partisans' war against the occupiers. Though the national question was not solved in the partisan movement during the war, it was transcended by the over-riding necessity of first fighting the occupying forces and their allies.[13]

The concept of 'liberated' territories was also a brilliant piece of political strategy as well as practical war-time organisation. The National Liberation Committees – established in some places as early as the autumn of 1941 and numbering many thousands by 1945 – enabled Tito to lay the foundations for post-war power, and to impose his own solution of the national question long before the end of the war. The Second Anti-Fascist Council – AVNOJ – held at Jajce (29 November 1943) set up a provisional partisan government and laid down a blue print for a federal solution of the Yugoslav national problem under communist rule. In tracing these developments in his chapter, 'Nationalism and the Partisan Movement', Dr Shoup does not accept the official view of Professor Čulinović that a truly federal system was put into effect after the Jajce session. He states his belief that 'centralization of the government of the liberated areas really commenced in earnest at this time'. He believes that as the partisan movement gained international recognition and a dominant position in its agreement with the royalist government, its leaders appeared to move towards the view that the national question could be solved by a guarantee of equal federal rights for all nations in a reunited Yugoslavia and that this should be combined with strongly authoritarian communist government. He points out the late date at which

[13] For details of these negotiations see J. Marjanović, *Ustanak i Narodno-Oslobo-dilački Pokret u Srbiji*, 1941, pp. 127, 128, 354–74, and J. Marjanović, 'Prilozi Istoriji sukoba narodnooslobodilačkog pokreta i četnici Draže Mihailovića u Srbiji 1941 godine', in *Istorija XX Veka*, Zbornik Radova, I, 1959, pp. 191–201, 217–19.

republican organisations within the party actually achieved
autonomy–republic parties had been created in Slovenia and
Croatia before the war; Serbia had its own in 1945; in Montenegro and Bosnia-Herzegovina, they were not created until
1948–9 after the break with the Cominform; Macedonia had
achieved its autonomous party after much bitter negotiation
during the war, in 1944.

In this chapter on war-time developments, Dr Shoup also
writes on the national question in its international aspect,
especially in relation to Tito's ideas about Balkan federation.
Tito denied that he personally had ever any idea of federating
Yugoslavia to the Soviet Union, and all his actions seem to bear
this out. 'I did not have this idea. Perhaps Stalin did.' Tito said
in 1968, 'He mentioned such a possibility in his conversation
with Kardelj in 1948. Stalin said "What about waiting a little
with the federation with Bulgaria? Perhaps in the meantime the
USSR could join the Yugoslav federation?".' This conversation
took place when Yugoslav and Bulgarian leaders had been
summoned to Moscow to put an end to the schemes for Yugoslav-Bulgarian federation which had been discussed between
Tito and Dimitrov (and earlier between other representatives)
at Bled in the summer of 1947. Although Yugoslav-Bulgarian
federation was stopped by Stalin, it is doubtful – as Tito stated
later – if it could have been put into effect at that time in spite
of the friendship of Tito and Dimitrov.[14]

The question of Macedonia is the most involved national
problem in Yugoslav politics and Dr Shoup deals with it
throughout the book as well as in a special chapter on 'The
Macedonian Question'. Not everyone will agree with his conclusion that 'If the great powers had not finally intervened, the
Yugoslavs would have succeeded in enlarging Yugoslav
Macedonia at the expense of Bulgaria and Greece.' It is
doubtful if this could have been done without fighting which
Tito would not have wished to undertake. Dr Shoup quotes
the significant fact that when it came to the Cominform break
between Tito and Stalin in 1948, the Macedonians were strongly
united behind Tito and proved it by the very small numbers of
Communist Party members who were purged because of
Cominform sympathies.

14 Tito's interview with this reviewer, October 1968. See also M. Djilas, *Conversations with Stalin*, London, 1962, pp. 120–4, 155–68.

A chapter on 'Titoism and the National Question' analyses political changes that have taken place in Yugoslavia since the Cominform break, and the important influence they have had on national relations within the country. As a result of the campaign to decentralise the considerable powers exercised by the central government in the immediate post-war years, new powers and responsibilities were acquired by the republican governments. Dr Shoup believes that 'the republics soon gave up their economic responsibilities to the enterprises', but he does not emphasise the important economic powers exercised by the communes. And it is probable that the republics have actually retained economic powers almost as great as those previously held by the central government. It is also open to question whether it is correct, as Dr Shoup states, that 'Decentralization in the early stages of Titoism, was not linked with the concept of increased freedom for the republics, or greater rights for the nationalities'. It seems more likely that the reverse was the case. Reduction of state interference was meant to lead to more political activity in the republics. It had the practical aim of leading to greater efficiency during a period of rapid industrial expansion based on foreign aid. Decentralisation was meant to give greater powers to the nationalities, and thereby increase Yugoslav unity. In fact it seemed for a time to have sharpened national rivalries and conflict. This was specially true in the economic field in the 1960s, after economic development had demonstrated that the more underdeveloped republics were unable to lessen – and had in fact increased – the gap that divided their standard of living and productivity from those of the more advanced regions.

The author traces the attitude of leading Yugoslav communists to these changes. He notes that the right of self-determination was no longer mentioned in the 1953 and 1963 constitutions. He believes that decentralisation undermined the *élan* of the party leaders by allowing them to develop regional interests. He sees the issue of the struggle against Alexander Ranković as a gain for members of the party who supported greater regional powers against those who wished to develop a new form of the Yugoslav idea. Dr Shoup also believes that decentralisation led to increased powers for the Chamber of Nationalities and a form of 'polycentrism' among the nationalities with the republics 'bargaining among themselves almost as sovereign states'.[15] The author believes that the increase in republican powers show that 'a totally new solution to the national question was in the process of realization', and believes that this will lead to an upgrading also of the position of minorities.

His other suggestion, which as yet remains unproved, is that Ranković had been associated with a movement for abolishing all republics as a solution to the national question – and that this and the unitary powers that he had exercised through his security control had again raised the spectre of Serbian hegemony. That this spectre had been raised there can be no doubt; what Ranković's own part and ideas in it were has yet to be discovered.

Throughout the book Dr Shoup makes many references to the Yugoslav idea, and he probably exaggerates its acceptance as a concept, or its importance to the Yugoslav communist leaders including Tito himself. Dr Shoup believes that the Yugoslav idea was finally abandoned in the 1950s; thus he identifies centralist rule with Yugoslavism. At the same time he believes that the political differences in nationalism in present day Yugoslavia are less important than economic rivalry which he characterises as 'the single most important factor contributing to the rise in nationalism in Tito's era', adding his belief that nationalism will remain a problem 'as long as inequalities in levels of existence persist in Yugoslavia'.

The author sees Tito as the only all-Yugoslavian figure on the present political scene, though it might be commented that Tito's acceptance by all Yugoslavs as leader, symbol of freedom, national myth belonging to all nationalities does not make him a supporter of Yugoslavism. Dr Shoup rightly states that during the war Tito's propaganda never attempted to propagate the idea of Yugoslavism; nor has this been his policy in post-war years. In 1968, at any rate, he did not believe in Yugoslavism, and did not think it necessary to the stability of the Yugoslav state: 'It is such a distant prospect that it is hardly possible to consider it at present. We have five nationalities and six republics and all have different characters, different traditions. They have to be united. We do not see any difficulties in being a community of peoples in the sense of all contributing something to the common good. Yugoslavia is the state, but even

[15] Shoup, pp. 227ff.

in this state the nationalities must respect one another; any other solution would be artificial. Those who wish to call themselves Yugoslavs can do so.'[16]

The Yugoslavs are today experimenting with new solutions for the national question, and it may well be that this is one of those political problems that defies finite solution and demands continuous solutions. There are at present proposals for further constitutional innovations and extensive changes in the national structural organisation of the League of Communists. Dr Shoup's stimulating and informative book is necessary reading for all who wish to understand something of the involved background to present and future developments in the national problem in Yugoslav government and opposition.

[16] Interview with Tito, October 1968.

Leonard Schapiro

Totalitarianism in the Doghouse[*][†]

'TOTALITARIANISM', AS A POLITICAL TERM ENTERED THE
English language at the end of the 1920s, having been imported
from Italy. In Italy 'totalitario' seems to have started its career as
a popular term in politics – meaning either 'un-liberal', 'dictatorial', or 'manly', 'determined', 'traditionally Roman' –
according to one's point of view. Mussolini and Gentile (the
latter somewhat reluctantly) then turned it into a term of art
for the new corporative fascist state – 'lo Stato Totalitario'. In
English its usage between the wars was not very frequent, and
(on the evidence of *Webster*) usually restricted in the USA to
fascist Italy and national socialist Germany. But *The Times* (in
1929), Carlton Hayes, and G. H. Sabine (among others) are
on record as having used it as a term applicable to all three of
the major contemporary dictatorships – Italy, Germany and
the Soviet Union. It is, of course, the case, that the more
frequent and extensive use of the term belongs to the post-war
period. Statesmen, journalists and political scientists have all
made frequent use of 'totalitarian' in the past two decades to
describe the Soviet system and the other communist regimes
modelled upon it. We are even offered totalitarian 'parties',
'movements', 'processes', 'leaders', 'ideas', and (from de Gaulle)
'totalitarian crushing policies'. Thousands of books and articles
have been devoted to what has usually (until of late) been
treated as an entirely novel form of polity, with distinct and
recognisable features, and by implication in stark contrast to
the distinctive features of 'Western democratic' polities. But
more recently the whole term has fallen under a cloud of suspicion among a section of, mainly American, political scientists.

---

[*] Vol. 6, No. 1, Winter 1971.
[†] A review: Carl J. Friedrich, Michael Curtis and Benjamin R. Barber, *Totalitarianism in Perspective: Three Views*, Pall Mall Press, 1969.

Certainly the time was ripe for some kind of re-examination of the word. This therefore is a most valuable and welcome symposium, which grew out of a panel held at Chicago as part of the APSA convention of 1967. It originally included Herbert J. Spiro, who, as readers of his article on 'Totalitarianism' in the new *Encyclopaedia of the Social Sciences* will know, is one of the main contemporary advocates of the view that the term is a 'cold-war' product, is misleading and should be dropped. Spiro had to leave the panel before it had concluded its labours. But his view is fully represented by both Barber and Curtis; Friedrich, on the other hand, one of the pioneers in the study of 'totalitarian dictatorship', defends the continued survival of the term.

Before examining the cases as presented by the three authors, it is worth bearing three points in mind. First, historically, (as the few facts assembled above show) it is not true that the term is a 'cold-war' product, since it was in fact applied without distinction to nazis and communists long before the 'cold war' existed: this does not, of course, necessarily mean that the usage may not have become much more extensive and even inaccurate as the result of the mounting hostility of the liberal democratic powers to communist expansion after the war. Secondly, methodologically, it is useless to talk about 'totalitarianism' in the abstract: forty-five years is not very long for a political concept to acquire any accurate and distinct meaning outside the context of the concrete situations to which it has in fact been applied. So, whether we like it or not, the search for the meaning of 'totalitarianism' must begin with a comparative examination of fascist Italy, nazi Germany and Russia under Stalin, since it is to these three that the term has, in practice, been applied. It is from such an examination alone that the kind of answers that are being sought can be found: Is there a pattern common to all the three? If so, what other polities, past or present, can it be applied to? Is it a new pattern, or are its features merely a contemporary form of past political patterns? The third point to bear in mind is that the main impetus to the criticism which has been levelled at 'totalitarianism' comes from the changing nature of all the communist polities which has been observable since the death of Stalin, both in the Soviet Union and in the former 'satellites'. These changes raise further questions: is the term 'totalitarian' applicable to them now? If not, was it ever applicable? Or have these communist states been wrongly treated as *sui generis* when they should be, and should have been, regarded as merely types of polities – with some features in common with other polities (including the so-called liberal democracies), and with some which are different? I think these three points fairly summarise the starting point of the essays in this volume.

At the risk of oversimplifying the whole problem, the arguments against the validity of 'totalitarianism' as a concept fall into three categories. First, that it is a 'cold-war' term, and not a scientific term at all. The view on this subject of the radical left in the United States is typified by Herbert Marcuse. His criticism is based on the contention that the restrictive and authoritarian features which are said to characterise, say, the Soviet Union are little different from those which characterise states that are wrongly contrasted with the Soviet Union, such as the United States. The forms in the United States may be different – the several political parties, the variety of newspapers, the seeming freedom of expression, the apparent absence, or relative absence, of constraint. But this apparent liberty 'under the rule of a repressive whole' becomes 'a powerful instrument of domination. The range of choice open to the individual is not the decisive factor in determining the degree of human freedom, but *what* can be chosen and, what *is* chosen by the individual . . .' [1] This eccentric view (which must cause some cynical laughter among Czech or Russian intellectuals) is not supported by any of the authors of this symposium. What the Spiro-Barber view amounts to is that 'totalitarianism' was pressed into service, when the USA became hostile to the Soviet Union after the war, in order to provide a 'counter-ideology': the American way of life was thus clearly distinguished, for popular consumption, from the Soviet way of life, and a black and white contrast, so useful for propagandists, was made that much easier to depict. Now, there may be some truth in this, in the sense that increased study of communism led to the need for a generic term to describe what appeared to be a novel type of dictatorship. Certainly, the ugly new word offered a simple short-hand way of describing what appeared to be the contrast between a

[1] *One-Dimensional Man*, quoted by Barber on p. 50, fn. 101. Cf. Marcuse on 'repressive tolerance' in R. P. Wolff, Barrington Moore Jnr and Herbert Marcuse, *A Critique of Pure Tolerance*, London, 1969, pp. 95–137.

communist party-ruled state and a presidential, or parliamentary, multi-party state. The type of dictatorship may not be novel, and the short-hand term may be misleading: indeed the main purpose of this symposium is to discover whether or not this is so. But it seems to me totally irrelevant, when considering the validity and accuracy of the term, to concern ourselves with the reasons why journalists, politicians and political scientists found the term useful: its validity or otherwise still depends on facts.

Nor do I find it very convincing to read in Curtis's essay that the use of the term totalitarian, as applied to the Soviet Union, has had the deleterious effect of making US policy too simplistic in its implacable hostility to the Soviet Union as an 'inevitable enemy', and, 'the embodiment of evil'. Foreign policy is not formed quite as simply as that. There are now available nine new volumes of documents on US foreign policy in the year 1945 published by the US State Department within the last few years, from which the passage from naïve hope to disappointment and then on to hostility can, its seems, be traced quite independently of intoxication with words.[2]

Actually, Curtis has many wise and interesting things to say in his essay, 'Retreat from Totalitarianism'. He accepts the value of the term 'totalitarian' in enabling us to recognise in nazi Germany and in Stalin's Russia a form of dictatorship which had novel features, distinguishing it from the tyrannies and despotisms of the past: modern technology; and particularly insistence by the rulers on mass participation and enthusiasm, (a point often missed by writers on totalitarianism). In general his analysis and criticism of the concept as applied to the two great tyrannies of our age are shrewd and full of insights. His argument may be taken as typical of the second category of the fashionable assaults on totalitarianism as a valid term in politics. 'Useful though the term has been', the time has come, he says, for a new concept which will take account of the changes which have taken place in the communist countries since Stalin's death: moreover 'the concept of totalitarianism, if applied automatically to all the Communist countries, disregards not only the changing nature of the Soviet Union, but also the diversity of the different regimes in which changes have

[2] See Geoffrey Warner, 'The United States and the Origins of the Cold War', *International Affairs*, Volume 46, No. 3, p. 529.

occurred at varying rates'. In the light of all the changes, he contends, to cling to the term merely obscures the process of political comparison by erecting an artificial mental barrier between a communist polity and a non-communist one.

There is much validity in his argument – there is no doubt, for example, that many studies of Soviet politics have been vitiated by their failure to recognise that many of the problems discussed in them are not *sui generis*, but common to all polities. It is also true that many distinctive features of Stalin's era are gone – there is no Stalin, there is much less widespread physical terror, there is a dissent movement, there are signs of incipient group pressure, and so forth. Perhaps the most cogent evidence in favour of Curtis's thesis is that amassed by Peter Ludz in his monumental study of the ruling elite in Eastern Germany [3] (which Curtis, incidentally, does not cite). Ludz's findings, based on detailed analysis of the East German ruling elite, show a shift towards what he calls 'consultative authoritarianism'. This is exemplified in a younger and more technically minded party Central Committee, greater mobility within the party apparatus for the technicians and, so far as concerns ideology, in a kind of institutionalised revisionism which is moving in the direction of greater rationality in decision making.

Important as Ludz's study is for the whole question of totalitarianism, it does not seem to me to bear out the case which Curtis and others are trying to make for the abandonment of totalitarianism as a concept. In the first place the process observed by Ludz in Eastern Germany is not taking place to anything like the same extent in the Soviet Union. In spite of considerable increase in technical training among the middle party elite,[4] there is, as yet, not much sign of the emergence of the younger generation at the Central Committee level; and although there are signs of revisionism in some ideological spheres, it is far from 'institutionalised': indeed, it is characterised by its insecurity – as witness the recent rout of the editorial board of *Novyy Mir*, or the effective silencing of critical voices among the academic lawyers in recent years. In any case, these

---

[3] Peter Christian Ludz, *Parteielite im Wandel*, Cologne and Opladen, 1968.

[4] See on this whole question the important study by Jerry F. Hough, *The Soviet Prefects*, Cambridge, Mass., 1969. And see also a recent study, 'Representation of Career Types in the Soviet Political Leadership', by Frederic Fleron, in R. Barry Farrill (ed.), *Political Leadership in Eastern Europe and the Soviet Union*, Chicago, 1970, pp. 108–39.

changes noted by Ludz, Hough and Fleron, among others, are merely one side of the whole process of government – the 'output', or command side. There is no doubt that there have been big changes on this side, both in the Soviet Union and in the other communist states. But has this altered the essence of totalitarianism as studied under Stalin? This is far from certain, and Curtis seems to me to fail to make out a convincing case in his examples, some of which (the economic reforms, the policy of co-existence) have been rendered even less convincing within the three years which have elapsed since the Chicago panel met in 1967.

The essence of what has been called totalitarianism seems to me to be the persisting ability of the political elite (whether one man and his agents, as under Stalin, or a kind of committee as now) to get its own way – even though the leaders of this elite may change as the result of palace revolutions of the kind which occurred in October 1964. This ability depends on three factors, all of which are still present, in the Soviet Union and elsewhere in the communist world – with the exception of Yugoslavia: direct control over all key appointments, and indirect control over the livelihood of each and every citizen; control over the means of communication and information; and control over the courts.

Barber, whose analysis of the concept is the most thorough and penetrating of the three, would not, I think, accept the view which I have just expressed, because it is based on the premise that a polity should ultimately be analysed in terms of the relationship which exists between those who rule and those who are ruled. Barber's approach falls into the third category of arguments against the survival of 'totalitarianism' as a valid term. He rejects the ruler-ruled approach as out of date and irrelevant in modern conditions: 'Totalitarianism', he says, 'has a generally accepted meaning only in so far as we focus on the totalistic element in it, conceived in narrow statist terms; statism, in turn, makes sense only if we presuppose in the manner of traditional liberal theory a dualistic cleavage between abstract and private spheres.' This view is out of date, he contends. 'In the present century, it has been generally acknowledged that power can be a function not simply of a formally defined public realm but also of social and economic forces that stalk, but are not part of, the private realm and that individuals can be victimized by "private" monopolies beyond the pale of public regulation or control. Indeed, because the state is politically controllable and its activities are visible, its threats to personal liberty are, in some ways, less pernicious than those emanating from unrecognized influence-sources operating under assumed but totally unreal conditions of equality in a supposedly fragmented and pluralistic private sphere.'

Now, there may be some truth in all this – though the very language used ('stalking', 'influence-sources') smacks of the occupational disease of many American political scientists – the paranoid or conspiratorial view of government. No doubt the United Fruit Company or the Labor Unions can exercise a great deal of influence behind the scenes which affects the individual's liberty adversely in many ways; it is conceivable that their power can in some way be seen as analogous to that of the KGB or the Union of Soviet Writers – though I doubt it. If it is true that analysis of the US polity should be based on the relationship of the elite to the non-elite, then it is probably equally true of the Soviet Union. Indeed 'statism', which implies a rational, fixed legal order, is alien to Soviet political practice: what, indeed, is observable in practice *is* the relationship of the elite, the ruling *apparat* (party or government officials acting in consort) to the non-elite – those denied access to the real sources of power or even influence. And here the parallel between the Soviet Union and the United States breaks down on the question as to what the elite can do in each country, bearing in mind the familiar Soviet features – the absence of independent courts, control by the elite over publicity, the absence (or virtual absence) of pressure groups, and so forth. Moreover, it seems to me to be totally false, even granted Barber's argument that 'statism' has become irrelevant (i.e., the 'individual/state', or 'public/private' criterion of analysis) to argue from this that the 'elite/non-elite' or the 'ruler-ruled' yardstick of assessing government has also lost its relevance. For how is the distinctive nature of any polity to be determined in any way that makes sense except from the point of view of the individual citizen, or possibly group, in assuring his, or its, sphere of liberty of action? And it is here that comparison between the USA and, say, the Soviet Union breaks down. The US citizen has available to him competing choices of occupation, freedom of expression, the courts (which are not always ineffective) emigration, and latterly even the opportunity of violent protest with comparative impunity. None of these are available to the Soviet citizen. This is a plain and manifest difference of kind, not of degree – and no amount of argument will get round this fact. We must be grateful to Barber for his analysis of the 'Conceptual Foundations' of totalitarianism, which is among the best that I know. But his general conclusion that the concept has no right to exist seems to me, on his argument, at any rate, to be fallacious.

In his essay 'Evolving Theory and Practice' Friedrich, who is a pioneer in the study of this whole subject, ranges widely, with immense erudition, over the trends of the past decade or so. His conclusion, reached nearly twenty years ago, that totalitarianism is a distinct and unique form of political rule remains unshaken, changes in the communist states notwithstanding. But he expresses the view, 'not as a conclusion but as a final reflection' that totalitarian dictatorship 'like other political phenomena, is a relative rather than an absolute category', and that it is meaningful to speak of totalitarian features 'in terms of more or less', and of 'totalitarian trends'.

The effect on one reader, at any rate, of the two essays which argue the other point of view is: *eppur si muove*. You can strip the Soviet system, for example, of many features familiar under Stalin – mass terror, the dominant leader, grotesque ideological controls and the like – the result is certainly different, and yet it remains in its essence the same system. The ruling *apparat*, the arbitrariness, the unpredictability of the rulers and the ultimate powerlessness of the ruled still remain.

One last thought on an important aspect which is only indirectly touched on in these essays – though Friedrich and others (Barrington-Moore for example) have explored it elsewhere. Is totalitarianism really a new political phenomenon (apart from its greater technical capacities for oppression)? Or is it no more than one more form of the kind of tyrannous government which seems to have been the fate of man intermittently from earliest times? I believe it is new, and that it should therefore have a name to itself: elsewhere I have suggested that totalitarianism is 'the tyranny of despotism of the age of mass democracy', [5] and I think this view can be defended. In the first place, totalitarianism has a greater kinship with democracy

[5] Leonard Schapiro, 'The Concept of Totalitarianism', in *Survey*, No. 73, Autumn 1969, pp. 93–115.

than any previously known despotism. The legitimacy of totalitarianism is always in theory democratically based, and its
appeal is always shaped as a mass appeal. It is for this reason
that Carl Schmitt, the ideologist of national socialism, described
the nazi regime as the true derivative of 1789, as distinct from
the false derivative, liberalism. Sir Arnold Toynbee, in some
recent centenary meditations on Lenin,[6] suggests that the
triumph of bolshevism in Russia in November 1917 symbolised
two forces, both of which are forces with a strong mass appeal:
the repudiation of the modern Western middle-class way of life
and the revival of an intolerant and dogmatic religious faith.
He may well be right in this, but the mass appeal of bolshevism
delves much deeper into the dark recesses of the mob mind. It
draws response from the fear of freedom, the envy, the anti-
intellectualism, the chauvinism – in short from all the characteristic ambience of mass man (the 'anti-individual' whom
Michael Oakeshott has so skilfully dissected)[7] with his own mass
morality, his crude egalitarian and levelling aspirations and his
herd paranoia. It is this mass democratic character of totalitarianism which distinguishes this form of rule from anything
that has gone before; and moreover has placed it in its context
of a distinctive phase of the history of 20th-century Europe. In
the talk which I have referred to, Sir Arnold Toynbee, with
that bland and good natured prophecy of doom which so often
characterises him, suggests that Lenin's victory may have been
'a trial trip for a coming world dictatorship'. I *hope* he is wrong.

[6] Arnold Toynbee, 'A Centenary View of Lenin', *International Affairs*, Vol. 46,
No. 3, July 1970, pp. 490–500.
[7] Michael Oakeshott, 'The Masses in Representative Society', in Albert Hunold
(ed.), *Freedom and Slavery*, Dordrecht, 1961, pp. 151–70.

List of Contributors

PHYLLIS AUTY is Lecturer in the History of the Danubian Lands at the School of Slavonic and East European Studies, University of London.

ZYGMUNT BAUMAN is Professor of Sociology in the University of Leeds.

JULIAN BIRCH is Lecturer in Soviet Politics at the University of Sheffield.

A. H. BROWN is Lecturer in Soviet Institutions in the University of Oxford and Fellow of St Antony's College.

J. DJORDJEVIĆ is Professor of Political Science in Belgrade University and President of the Legal Council of the Yugoslav Federal Republic.

WINSTON M. FISK is Professor of Political Science in Claremont Men's College, California.

CARL J. FRIEDRICH is Eaton Professor of the Science of Government in Harvard University and Professor of the Science of Government in the University of Heidelberg.

DAVID HOLLOWAY is Lecturer in Politics at the University of Edinburgh.

DAVID E. POWELL is Assistant Professor in the Department of Government and Foreign Affairs and Director of the Center for Russian and Communist Studies at the University of Virginia.

LEONARD SCHAPIRO is Professor of Political Science with special reference to Russian studies in the University of London (London School of Economics and Political Science).

HUGH SETON-WATSON is Professor of Russian History in the University of London.

H. GORDON SKILLING is Professor and Director of the Centre for Russian and Eastern European Studies at the University of Toronto.

Index

Huntington, Samuel, 76 n, 77 n
Hus, Jan, 105, 108, 134
Husák, Gustav, 126, 126 n, 129 n, 130, 231
Hysko, M., 97

Idashkin, Yury, 210 n
ideology
  legitimacy and, 26–7
  monopolistic party and, 16–18, 22
  power struggles and, 5
Imperial Russian Government, 11
Indra, Alois, 125 n, 129, 129 n
Ingber, D., 179 n
interest and pressure groups
  as form of dissent, 7–8, 88–90
  in liberal states, 7
  in one-party states, 8–9, 24, 27
  intellectual, 96–8
  organised, 94–5
Ionescu, Ghiţa, 8, 11 n, 15 n, 20, 73 n, 77 n, 85 n, 89 n, 100, 100 n, 139 n, 150, 150 n, 217 n, 249–55
Israel, 9, 97, 117
Italian Communist Party, 70
Italian communist press, 198
Italy, fascist, 30
  totalitarianism in, 268–9, 271
Ivan IV, 26, 242, 244
Ivanov, N. D., 159 n

Jajce Anti-Fascist Council, 256, 263
Jakova, Tuk, 192, 194
Jaworskyj, Michael, 203 n
Jesuit Order, 252
Jews, Soviet, 9, 245
Jodl, Miroslav, 93n
Joravsky, D., 154 n, 155 n
Jotishcky, L., 179 n
Justizstaat, 139 n, 141
Juviler, P. H., 169 n

Kadar, Janos, 11, 83, 83 n, 95 n
Kadet Party, 34
KAN, 112, 130
Kapo, Hsyni, 188, 189 n, 190 n
Kapitsa, P., 177
Karadjordjevic, King Alexander, 257

Kardelj, E., 50–1, 53–7, 261
Kaser, Michael, 15, 29–30
Kasimati, Sabiha, 194
Kassof, A., 169 n
Katona, P., 179 n
Katyn, 245
Keech, W. R., 198 n
Keldysh, M. V., 164 n, 167, 169, 177
Kellezi, Abdyl, 25, 30, 184 n, 186 n, 188
KGB, 6, 216, 274
Khrushchev, N. S., 12, 30, 44 n, 46, 48, 59, 70, 122, 133, 160 n, 162, 166, 169, 180, 194, 195 n, 196–198, 202, 203 n, 204 n, 205, 247
Kindersley, Richard, 143
Kircheimer, Otto, 84
Kirov, S. M., 43–4
Kiselev, Ya., 212 n
Knightley, P., 191 n
Kolakowski, Leszek, 86, 98 n, 99 n
Kolleka, Spiro, 188
Kopinić-Valdes, Ivan, 262
Korenevsky, Yu., 214 n, 215 n
Korol, A. G., 169 n
Kosygin, A. N., 49, 165, 202
Kotarbinski, T., 98 n
Kozera, Edward S., 204 n
Kozlowski, J. P., 153 n
Kraminov, D., 204 n
Krasniqi, R., 194 n
Kremlinological approach, 217
Krestinsky, N. N., 40
Kriegel, František, 114, 130
Kronstadt rising, 36–7, 40–1, 44
Kruglov, A. A., 213 n
Krylenko, N. V., 203 n, 206
Ksenofontov, F., 203 n
Kulturni Život (Czechoslovakia), 97
Kuron, J., 86, 99 n

Labedz, Leopold, 205 n, 215 n
Lakatoš, M., 87 n
Lakoff, Sanford A., 152 n
Lantay, A., 87 n
Laštovička, Bohuslav, 114
Latsis, Mikhail, 203
law in communist countries, 147–8
League of Nations, 104